Common Presenting Issues in
Psychotherapeutic Practice

Common Presenting Issues in
Psychotherapeutic Practice

Barbara Douglas & **Pam James**

Los Angeles | London | New Delhi
Singapore | Washington DC

Los Angeles | London | New Delhi
Singapore | Washington DC

SAGE Publications Ltd
1 Oliver's Yard
55 City Road
London EC1Y 1SP

SAGE Publications Inc.
2455 Teller Road
Thousand Oaks, California 91320

SAGE Publications India Pvt Ltd
B 1/I 1 Mohan Cooperative Industrial Area
Mathura Road
New Delhi 110 044

SAGE Publications Asia-Pacific Pte Ltd
3 Church Street
#10-04 Samsung Hub
Singapore 049483

Editor: Kate Wharton
Editorial assistant: Laura Walmsley
Production editor: Rachel Burrows
Copyeditor: Audrey Scriven
Proofreader: Anna Gilding
Indexer: Silvia Benvenuto
Marketing manager: Tamara Navaratnam
Cover design: Shaun Mercier
Typeset by: C&M Digitals (P) Ltd, Chennai, India
Printed in Great Britain by Henry Ling Limited, at
The Dorset Press, Dorchester, DT1 1HD

MIX
Paper from
responsible sources
FSC™ C013985
www.fsc.org

Library of Congress Control Number: 2013940778

British Library Cataloguing in Publication data

A catalogue record for this book is available from
the British Library

ISBN 978-1-4462-0853-3
ISBN 978-1-4462-0854-0 (pbk)

To Tim and Andy with love
To Richard for his constant interest

Contents

About the Authors and Contributors

Authors

Dr Barbara Douglas is a Chartered and Registered Counselling Psychologist. She is Registrar for the British Psychological Society's Qualification in Counselling Psychology, Honorary Fellow of Exeter University, and has a private practice in Edinburgh. Barbara previously taught Counselling Psychology at the University of the West of England and prior to that was Director of the North West Centre for Eating Disorders. She is co-editor of the third edition of *The Sage Handbook of Counselling Psychology* and has a particular interest in the histories of both psychology and psychiatry. Barbara was honoured to receive the BPS Professional Practice Board's Practitioner of the Year Award in 2011 and is a former Chair of the Division of Counselling Psychology.

Professor Pam James is a Chartered and HCPC Registered Counselling Psychologist and a Registered Psychologist Specialising in Psychotherapy (Senior Practitioner). She has been Chair of the BPS Qualification in Counselling Psychology and twice Chair of the BPS Division of Counselling Psychology. She held lecturing and management posts at Liverpool John Moores University for over 25 years where she was awarded Professor of Counselling Psychology in 2000, and she also worked in NHS Adult Mental Health for 10 years. Currently she has a private practice in Southport. Her doctoral thesis was in learning and she remains interested in the learning process per se, including the process of change whilst in the therapeutic relationship.

Contributors

Dr Dee Danchev has professional qualifications in Social Work and Counselling, and is a Chartered and Registered Counselling Psychologist. During the past twenty years she has taught trainees and supervised post-graduate research at Keele University, City University and the University of Oxford. She is currently Pastoral Advisor at Nuffield College, Oxford, Chair of the Board of Assessors for the British Psychological Society's Qualification in Counselling Psychology, and has a private practice in Oxford.

Dr Hamilton Fairfax is a Chartered and Registered Counselling Psychologist, and Associate Fellow of the British Psychology Society, working in adult mental health. His interests include trauma, mindfulness, OCD, personality disorder, neuropsychology and the therapeutic process, and he has published in these areas. He is part of the Division of Counselling Psychology Practice Board, with a particular role in developing neuropsychological practice in counselling psychology. A major research and practice interest is Adaptation-based Process Therapy (APT), an approach developed with a colleague, and its application to complex client presentations.

Dr Roly Fletcher is a Senior Counselling Psychologist in NHS community mental health services and private practice in Surrey. Alongside providing individual and group therapies, he provides supervision and consultation. He is actively involved with the British Tinnitus Association, teaching on their tinnitus advisor training course, and has over 10 years' experience in supporting children with special needs and their families to partake in sporting contexts.

Nicola Gale is an HCPC Registered Psychologist and BPS Chartered Psychologist (Associate Fellow). She is Clinical Lead for the Staff Psychological & Welfare Service at University College London Hospitals NHS Foundation Trust, and Senior Lecturer on the professional doctorate in counselling psychology at City University London. Nicola has previously worked in organisational development and training, management consultancy and finance, and she is an experienced manager. She has worked in different industries and on international projects.

Amanda Hall is an HCPC Registered and BPS Chartered Counselling Psychologist and Associate Fellow. She has been chair of the Division of Counselling Psychology in Wales. Amanda has worked in the NHS for 20 years and is currently Consultant Psychologist and Applied Psychology Lead for Psychological Therapies and Eating Disorders in Abertawe Bro Morgannwg NHS Health Board in Wales. She is also an Honorary Lecturer and Psychology lead for the Graduate Entry to Medicine programme at Swansea University.

Claire John is an HCPC Registered and BPS Chartered Counselling Psychologist. She has worked for over 20 years in the NHS, currently with Avon and Wiltshire Mental Health Partnership. Her role centres on delivering treatment to people with a personality disorder. She is part of a dialectical behavioural therapy team, offering a full programme to community-based clients, and is also involved in developing skills-based training for multi-professional teams as part of a trust-wide group.

Dr Carole Lund qualified from Liverpool Medical School in 1982 and moved to Leeds in 1983 to train in psychiatry. She became a member of the Royal College of Psychiatrists in 1986 and obtained a Master's degree in clinical psychiatry from

Leeds University in 1989. She is employed by Mersey Care NHS Trust in Southport, working in general adult community psychiatry. She has also worked in low secure care and psychiatric rehabilitation. In 2009 she obtained a Diploma in Counselling.

Tony Parnell is a lecturer in Counselling Psychology at the University of Manchester. He is an HCPC Registered and BPS Chartered Counselling Psychologist and works in private practice in the north west of England. His practice has an emphasis on trauma and PTSD along with supervision. His research interests include PTSD and predisposition, trauma and attachment, the use of metaphor in therapy, and mindfulness and post-traumatic growth.

Dr Mary Reid is an HCPC Registered Clinical and Counselling Psychologist and Associate Fellow of the BPS. She has a special interest in psychological processes accompanying physical disorders, and the relationships between emotion, anxiety and health. Currently she is leader for a postgraduate programme in cognitive behavioural psychotherapy at the University of the West of Scotland, and works both in private practice and with the NHS.

Sheelagh Strawbridge is a Chartered Psychologist, Registered Counselling Psychologist, Registered Psychologist Specialising in Psychotherapy (Senior Practitioner), and Fellow of the British Association for Counselling and Psychotherapy. Her publications include *Exploring Self and Society* (with Rosamund Billington and Jenny Hockey: Macmillan, 1998), as well as book chapters and journal articles, and she is an editor (along with Ray Woolfe, Barbara Douglas and Windy Dryden) of *The Sage Handbook of Counselling Psychology* (3rd edition, Sage, 2009).

Ray Woolfe is a counselling psychologist and psychoanalytic psychotherapist. After a career as a university lecturer at the Open University and Keele University, he now works independently as a psychologist and psychotherapist based in Bristol.

Foreword

Psychotherapy contains a variety of what might be described as narrative accounts or ideologies of what the practice involves. The authors of this book suggest that psychological services are largely framed within what they describe as two competing world views. One is termed 'psychopathological' while the other they see as emphasising the intersubjective world of client and therapist and the joint construction of meaning.

The former narrative offers a vocabulary in which mental and emotional health is seen as essentially consisting of two discrete states: health or illness. It relies on a philosophy whose roots lie in positivism and natural science in which it is held that the only truth resides in scientific knowledge. In turn, this leads into an emphasis on the experimental method in which the notion of a cause-effect relationship is powerful. The outcome of such an epistemological position is that aspects of the human condition can be identified objectively and then labelled through diagnosis. This is based upon the identification of symptoms which are then linked to specific treatment protocols. This narrative achieves its fullest flowering in the form of diagnostic manuals, most notably the *International Classification of Diseases and Related Health Problems* (WHO) and the *Diagnostic and Statistical Manual of Mental Disorders* (APA). According to the latter, for example, a client will meet the criteria for borderline personality disorder if they evidence at least five out of nine criteria.

The other narrative places an emphasis on understanding the client's subjective experience. Therapist expertise is seen as located in empathic engagement rooted in a belief that there is no objectively observable truth. Formulation replaces diagnosis. Provisional hypotheses are preferred to the greater certainty which resides in the attribution of labels. The idea of 'being with' the other person, the 'I and Thou' as Martin Buber put it, is emphasised. Priority is given to human reality over abstract thinking. As Kierkegaard famously expressed it 'life is not a problem to be solved but a reality to be experienced'. The construction of theory is grounded in practice and not vice versa, and emotional wellbeing is conceived as a continuum rather than in terms of either health or illness. From this perspective, labels such as borderline personality disorder represent an attempt at imposing an objectivity on a social world which defies such analysis.

These two world views exist in what the authors refer to as a 'tension', and in a series of chapters based upon client presenting issues the reader is offered an opportunity to explore how these tensions translate into the practice of psychologists, psychotherapists and other mental health professionals. This is territory in which there is little exploration in other psychotherapy texts. The authors set out to establish how these tensions can be handled in clients' best interests. There are discussions about anxiety, depression, eating disorders, psychosis, trauma and PTSD, bi-polar condition and borderline personality disorder. Each chapter contains three parts. The first two, written by Douglas and James, examine the developmental history of the presenting condition with an account of the current dilemmas associated with the diagnosis. The third part is written by an invited contributor and focuses on practice and research.

However, as the authors acknowledge, it is almost a paradox that the labels themselves form the proposed chapter headings. This suggests that we cannot do without some attempt at categorisation. While there are clearly substantial differences between the two positions perhaps there may be some value and the possibility for integration in conceiving of them heuristically as ideal-types. In the real world this is messy and confusing, but if we acknowledge this we may find that it is perhaps neither as objective as the psychopathology model would suggest nor as open-ended as the subjectivist tradition might imply.

All helping relationships involve interaction between human beings leading to the establishment of a working alliance. A relatively directive and structured therapeutic method such as that found in behaviourist protocols still requires that the therapist must get to know the individual client sufficiently well in order to know what rewards he or she will find reinforcing. This demands an ability to be empathic and to enter into the subjective world of the other and seems to be a sine qua non of any helping relationship. On the other side of the coin, professionals could not communicate, particularly in the field of mental health where inter-professional communication is a key characteristic, without some common language, and this inevitably involves a certain amount of categorisation. We cannot simply refuse to talk about depression or borderline personality disorder for example because we disagree about their characteristics or aetiology or how to respond to them. Language inevitably codifies but without it we are lost.

The boundaries of professional practice are not static. There is now a huge diversity of different therapeutic practices. Views which would once have been widely seen as heretical such as the need for supervision are now regarded as essential. Personal therapy or personal development is also seen as desirable if not essential across a range of occupations. Ethical codes used to be based upon somewhat rigid sets of criteria but are now much more aspirational in character. In other words, the professional has become an active meaning maker in her or his own practice. In the final resort all professional practice is both a science and an art. The scientific aspect involves theories, methods and boundaries in which some labelling is almost inevitable. However, it also involves an artistic component consisting of an imaginative leap into the world of the other as well as into our own inner worlds. Both are necessary.

The authors are well placed to write this book and it offers a unique insight into a key aspect of professional practice in the fields of psychotherapy, psychiatry and psychology. Mental health is a domain in which there is rarely just one way of understanding an issue. The central thesis of the book is that symptoms can be seen as expressions of pathology or as expressions of underlying thoughts and feelings experienced in a personal context. However, the fact that the two exist in a state of tension warrants exploration and understanding in the interests of best practice in the service of the client. In the process, the book offers the potential for a more personally integrated approach by the practitioner, whatever their occupation.

Ray Woolfe

1

Introduction

Introduction

Locating client and therapist within the world of social and cultural contexts, psychotherapy takes as its focus the intra- and inter-subjective world of client and therapist and the meanings they attribute to experience as fundamental to the process of therapeutic change. By contrast, psychopathology examines the nature of the problem or diagnosis attributed to clients' experiences. It analyses how this problem evidences itself across people, in patterns often described as conditions, as for example depression, anorexia nervosa or borderline personality disorder. Current psychological services are largely framed by the latter psychopathological, or condition-focused, culture. Consequently, clients tend to be signposted towards, or excluded from, services based on whether they meet the criteria for a particular diagnosis or condition. The apparent tension between these two world views is regularly experienced by applied psychologists, psychotherapists and counsellors. Such experience reveals the profound importance of analysing how this tension manifests itself in work with clients, yet to date there has been little exploration of these tensions or how they translate into practice and might be addressed in the best interests of clients. The contemporary relevance of this book is therefore significant for practitioners in the development of their work with clients.

By examining the relationship between psychotherapeutic practice and the presenting issues experienced by clients this book aims to meet a fundamental need of trainees and qualified practitioners. Its central argument is that tensions between competing world views of humanistic and medical models characterise the learning, development and practice of many applied psychology trainees, psychotherapists and counsellors. Indeed, this may also be the experience of qualified practitioners, as they work towards finding an integration of their values with a developing understanding and knowledge of theory, practice and research evidence. It concludes that this tension must be addressed head-on in the interests of best practice.

The book is made up of nine chapters: this introduction defines the scope of the book and the nature of the topic and addresses its tensions and debates. Seven subsequent chapters then focus on a specifically labelled area of experienced psychological distress or difficulty that is regularly seen within services. It is almost a paradox that the labels themselves form the proposed chapter headings. These include anxiety, depression, trauma and post trauma stress, bipolar, psychosis, borderline personality and eating disorders. The ninth and final chapter draws together the book's themes.

Each chapter addresses a specific named workplace/context and interweaves the historical context, theory, research, casework and inherent tensions in the work with clients. The topics included have been chosen because they represent the more frequent presenting problems encountered by trainee therapists and practitioners in their work with clients. Areas of practice which are perceived as more specialised, for example working with clients with a diagnosis of antisocial personality disorder, are excluded for pragmatic reasons of book size and on the basis that these provide less developmental potential for the wider readership within applied psychology, psychotherapy and counselling. We would acknowledge however that similar themes to those addressed in the included sections are likely to be of relevance to these other areas of practice.

For the purposes of this book we have chosen to use the phrase 'psychotherapeutic practice' to encompass those therapeutic relationships with clients with whom a range of professions engage. This includes counselling psychologists, clinical psychologists and counsellors as well as psychotherapists. Note also that the term 'psychologist' may refer to either clinical or counselling psychologists who are working psychotherapeutically, and the term 'counsellor' will refer to those who have undergone counselling training (they are also sometimes referred to as 'therapists'). Finally, the term 'psychotherapist' may refer to those who are trained as such, but also that the term's use in practice can be assumed by counsellors and psychologists. The authors suggest that this difference in naming has its origins in the historical context of psychotherapy: for example, the British Psychological Society's formation of a register of psychologists specialising in psychotherapy aims to collate those psychologists who are working in this way across the applied psychologies. In recent years, the British Association of Counselling has extended its description to become the British Association of Counselling and Psychotherapy.

Part 1: Exploring the Historical Context of Psychotherapy (Barbara Douglas)

The contexts within which psychotherapy is practised are both time and place contextual. It would be naïve, for example, to consider that such 'founding fathers' of psychotherapy as Sigmund Freud, Carl Jung or Carl Rogers emerged independent of their historical contexts.

The early nineteenth-century Quaker development of Moral Therapy (Tuke, 2010 [1813]) could in many senses be considered the precursor of the practice of psychotherapy with the term 'moral' having a different meaning from our current understanding – one that held a broader sense of the psychological. The development of psychotherapy within the nineteenth century can be viewed as a drive to search for a more optimistic view of the human condition than that of the pervading and profound despair of social Darwinism with its concepts of tainted heredity and degeneration, propounded so influentially in England by Henry Maudsley and in France by Benedict Morel (Dowbiggin, 1985). Before Freud's major works appeared, discourses of European psychiatry and neurology were already evolving an embryonic language of dynamic psychiatry that included notions about hypnotism, hysteria and the power of the unconscious (Ellenberger, 1981).

With the work of Freud came the powerful theoretical development of psychoanalysis. While Freud's theories changed over time he has become known as the founder of a view of psychological problems that emphasises the evolving, developmental dynamic structures of the psyche. The early emergence of psychoanalysis was jealously contained within the medical profession but also influenced by social geography. The clearest example of this was the 1930s' interweaving of its various schools of thought that was brought about by the persecution of Jewish analysts in Europe and their migration to England and America. The Viennese, Berlin and London schools were forcibly brought together during the late 1920s and 30s, each having to engage (uncomfortably) with the conceptual and practice emphases of the others.

While the early emergence of psychoanalysis was contained within the medical profession, the wider growth of psychotherapy was subsequently – and profoundly – influenced by the growing discipline of psychology. By the 1930s this had rejected introspection in favour of the study of observable behaviour. The resulting emergent behaviourist tradition lent itself to a very different form of 'psychotherapy', one which emphasised behaviour change through various programmes of conditioning and modification. These first took root in practice through the development of training programmes for children, psychiatric patients, and those contemporaneously referred to as 'mental defectives'. Increasingly, however, frustrations emerged at the limitations imposed by such rigidity. As the twentieth century progressed the focus shifted increasingly towards a concern with meaning and subjective experience, with resulting psychological and psychotherapeutic challenges to the behaviourist movement.

The development of concepts such as learned helplessness (Seligman, 1975) furthered a need to consider the subjective world of the individual, and as such cognitive behaviour therapy (CBT), with its emphasis on the role of cognitions, arose out of behaviourism. More recently, with the shift towards a postmodern constructionist ethos (across disciplines), CBT is also shifting its approach, placing increased emphasis on the construction of meaning as the link between thought processes and emotion, and acknowledgement of the importance of the therapeutic alliance and the break-down of CBT concepts into devolved subsystems of thinking in psychotherapeutic practice (for example, in the current development of mindfulness as a practice for depression: see Kabat-Zinn et al., 2002).

In the mid-twentieth century a challenge came also from Carl Rogers and a developing humanistic ethos. While the conditions of empathy, congruence and acceptance were conceived within a positivist framework of psychological research and experimentation, they were fundamentally challenging the limita-tions of such an approach by emphasising the importance of hearing and under-standing the subjective experience of the individual. Towards the end of his life Rogers took this further, grappling with a concept of 'presence' in which the inner spirit of the therapist would touch that of the client (Kirschenbaum and Henderson, 1990).

There emerged therefore a broad movement towards a relational, shared mean-ing place within the therapeutic relationship that evolved as part of a narrative development in the theory of knowledge, both within psychology and across other disciplines within the social sciences and humanities. The more recent emergence of narrative therapy with its ideas of shared meanings, re-storying and co-creating understanding within psychotherapy further exemplifies this shift.

Historically the locations of psychotherapeutic practice have also changed. While there was previously little place for psychotherapy within the financially constrained and bureaucratic world of institutional psychiatry, in recent years statutory and voluntary services have increasingly embraced forms of psycho-therapy. Psychological services in these broad frameworks are all now con-sidered stakeholders in the development of psychotherapeutic practice. Thus while changing theoretical models of the person have influenced the develop-ment and practice of psychotherapy, so shifting contextual factors – including issues surrounding the classification of psychological distress, and the need to provide services for much larger numbers of people – have played their parts as well.

The classification of mental disorders took a powerful turn at the beginning of the twentieth century with the work of German psychiatrist Emil Kraepelin (2011 [1904]). Much of our current classification of mental disorders, for which psycho-logical therapies are being offered, is premised on Kraepelin's influential nosology of psychiatric illness. Underpinned by a medical model, this classificatory system stressed aetiology and disease process and was based upon Kraepelin's longitudinal research evidence for his proposed twin underlying axes of all mental illness i.e. manic depression and dementia praecox (Greene, 2007).

But while current versions of the *Diagnostic and Statistical Manual (DSM)* embrace a medical approach to the classification of psychological distress that reflects Kraepelin's work, early versions were influenced by psychoanalytic concepts of the unconscious and by the psychiatrist Adolf Meyer (1866–1950). Initially immersed in Kraepelinian psychiatry, Meyer later argued for – and led the development of – a more socially-based view of mental illness, in which individual experiences were described as reactions, or responses to, individual circumstances, rather than biologically-based disease entities. It was this framework of individual response, continuum of experience and behaviours as manifestations of unconscious conflict that underpinned the original *DSM-I* (APA, 1952) and its successor *DSM-II* (APA, 1968).

Only with the *DSM-III* (APA, 1980) and its subsequent revisions was there a paradigmatic shift towards a categorical, and debatably descriptive, classification of psychological distress reframed as disorder (sometimes referred to as the rise of the second biological psychiatry: see Shorter, 1997: 239).

Much psychological distress, framed by the *DSM* as disorder, now has an associated treatment of choice psychological therapy approaches, and so medical model frameworks have increasingly become the framework within which psychologists, psychotherapists, counsellors and psychological therapists are being required to work (and sometimes resulting in tensions that are further discussed in Part 2 below). It could be argued that the development of manualised and prescribed therapy, introduced as an attempt to provide a service to all at the point of need, threatens the retention of an individual emphasis. The ideals of cost effective therapy for all who may benefit from it are to be applauded, but these also raise tensions that echo the very same dilemma experienced by institutional psychiatry in late-nineteenth and early-twentieth century psychiatry, when burgeoning numbers of patients resulted in the standardisation – and ultimately dilution – of the earlier aims of moral therapy.

Charles Mercier, a leading psychiatrist of the late nineteenth century, expressed the hope that 'management of patients by the gross will give way to management of the individual' (Mercier, 2011 [1894]: viii). Has this occurred or are we sometimes in danger of regarding science as linearly progressive towards ever greater knowledge and improved practice? Joan Busfield (1986: 18) expresses the view that 'psychiatry's history is viewed as basically linear and progressive, albeit at times halting (or even occasionally regressive), in which science and progress are seen as synonymous'. Foucault (1988) in his work on madness reframed the study of psychiatry within a much more critical analysis of madness, psychiatry and mental illness – their meanings within, and relationships to, contemporaneous society. Part 1 of each chapter in this book examines the history of each of the presenting issues with this in mind, inviting the reader to consider the interrelationships between practice and historical, social and political contexts.

While the above is a bald outline of the historical contextual development of psychotherapy, it serves to demonstrate that time and context sit side by side with theorists and practitioners as co-creators of any model of psychotherapeutic endeavour. It is to a discussion of the nature of current dilemmas in the practice of psychotherapy that this chapter now turns.

Part 2: Exploring Dilemmas, Evidence and Practice (Pam James)

In each chapter, dilemmas are discussed arising from the tensions and differences in professional opinion that can occur in psychiatry, psychology and psychotherapy. Such dilemmas may be considered as places where there is more than one way of understanding an issue – where there are different views about the impact of situational and personal factors associated with mental health and the appropriate therapeutic response. The reader is asked to pause in this uncertain place, sometimes evaluating the evidence, sometimes appreciating that there is no one absolute truth.

Those compiling the National Institute for Health and Care Excellence (NICE) Guidelines will review and grade evidence supporting particular therapeutic approaches, and a hierarchy of types of evidence exists where randomised controlled trials will have priority. This has resulted in a lack of emphasis on information collected by qualitative methods which are seen as a less preferred way for finding out about clients' experience, whereas Corrie (2010) takes a more inclusive view as to what constitutes evidence, suggesting that a consideration of the widest appreciation of what is happening for the client (and therapist) at the therapeutic interface is acceptable, and that research is only one part of the enquiry process.

In the UK the field of mental health could be perceived as a stage on which there are many players. Currently these include psychiatrists, general practitioners, clinical and counselling psychologists, psychotherapists, counsellors, psychiatric social workers, psychological wellbeing practitioners, high intensity workers and mental health nurses. The people who make up this multi-professional group do not all share the same understanding and explanation of the concept of mental health. Indeed it is only in the last ten years that the field itself has been so described, preferring for many years the term 'mental illness'. Psychiatrists may also have a varying emphasis on a biological or psycho-social focus. They are licensed to prescribe medication – symptoms are seen as identifiable markers that provide a basis for categorisation and the treatment response. Over the years, iterations of the *DSM* have aimed to group the similar, giving a framework at the descriptive level, and providing a pathway though the complexity of human experiences. This is one area where dilemmas and tensions may arise resulting from the impact, effect and perception of the *DSM* by clients and non-psychiatrists.

Amongst psychologists and psychotherapists working at the boundary with psychiatrists, differences of opinion that are reflected in practice will occur related to the use of diagnosis. The emphasis on symptoms – their measurement, reduction and management, maintenance and perpetuation – is not consistent. A prescriptive approach matches type of therapy to presenting symptoms. It is proposed then that all those experiencing similar symptoms would receive similar therapy. A less prescriptive approach sees symptoms as expressions of underlying thought and feeling in context. Here, various therapies are applicable: the therapist would take an exploratory approach and seek to respond to the individual's subjective experience in context. This latter approach is reflected in a recent text edited by Milton (2012) which illustrates change in therapy based on casework that emphasises relational constructs rather than a diagnostic focus.

Inter-professional differences

In the Layard Report (2006) economic underpinning was described whereby evidence-based practice would address large-scale anxiety and depression. Consequently, the government introduced two newly described workers into the field of mental health, namely 'psychological wellbeing practitioners' and 'high intensity workers'. This movement – entitled Improving Access to Psychological Therapies – is now several years into its programme and accompanied by the investment of significant resources. High intensity workers have been trained to deliver cognitive behavioural therapy to work with anxiety and depression in adults and training is now underway to work with different client groups, namely children and young people, people with long-term conditions, and those with medically unexplained symptoms and severe and enduring problems. There has been a large increase in the investment for increased personnel whilst initially offering only one therapeutic path, namely cognitive behavioural therapy. More recently, Counselling for Depression (IAPT Programme, 2011) and three other modalities have been introduced. More clients have been able to access therapy; however, the introduction of this new resourced workforce has resulted in significant shifts in the previous workforce. In the National Health Service (NHS) Primary Care across England, there are now very few counsellors and psychotherapists remaining as they have been retrained as high intensity CBT therapists or have left the service to work in the voluntary or private sector. After the New Ways of Working for Applied Psychologists in Health and Social Care (BPS, 2007), psychologists migrated into secondary care, learning disabilities, and assessing clients who have presenting issues that have compounding factors, or more recently, into managing IAPT Services. Their therapeutic skills in the public sector have been found to be less in demand than the need to manage departments and promote psychological thinking in the multi-disciplinary arena. Their supervisory skills have been only employable when trained in the IAPT model. So where is the dilemma? It is at the level of available employment for the psychologist, counsellor and psychotherapist. It is the displacement of trained therapists working from a variety of therapeutic approaches from the public sector into the voluntary and private sector. Will these professionals be commissioned in the NHS under the Any Qualified Provider Scheme (DoH, 2012)? The answers to these questions will affect the availability of free (NHS) therapy and client choice, and the amount of acceptable evidence that supports therapeutic change will most probably be a further deciding factor.

The client's perspective

The client's perspective is multi-faceted: their predominant wish is to not experience uncomfortable symptoms. These range from anxiety to depression, fear and uncertainty, and sleeplessness, as well as many physical symptoms including unexplained pains in different parts of the body, often associated with the digestive tract. It is not surprising that clients often want to take medication as they are familiar with the concept of a pill to cure a symptom. The general practitioner prescribes anti-depressants and with the client's agreement places that individual on the waiting list for therapy, usually CBT. What is ameliorating the symptoms? Is it the medication or the therapy? A client/patient in secondary care may then ask: who is in charge of my case? If located in mental health teams this will often be the psychiatrist, who holds the power of prescription. This key role can in turn be contested in overt or covert discussions by psychologists who hold the power provided by a knowledge of theory and concepts of human behaviour.

All types of therapy require the active engagement of the client and this process often involves talking about issues that are emotionally painful. The dilemma here is that speaking about painful matters can often result in opening up an issue that has been set aside. It is precisely this setting aside of difficult issues that creates the hidden distress in the first place. The message of therapy is that the outcome is worth the journey – whether the result is described in terms of an increased understanding of their personality, a shift in their unhelpful thinking patterns, an increase in the use of techniques to manage stress, or an internalised caring relationship to support them through difficult times. The inherent dilemma is that the life experience does produce distress and this is an uncomfortable truth. Can we sometimes weather the storm and sit in emotional pain, or do we need to reach for pills that will blur our experience to make life more manageable? Our ongoing struggle with psychological distress has deep historical roots as explained in Part 1 of this chapter: for centuries protection from emotional pain has been sought, sometimes by using alcohol and other mood altering drugs. How much upset can be tolerated?

Holding the tensions created by dilemmas and seeking ways forward: the opportunity to think and build together

When there are contradictory viewpoints about understanding a client's mental health, either at the level of causal origin or treatment, this is not helpful and can be exploited. There is the potential here for splitting – one professional may hold more client information than another, and the parents (professionals) are arguing about the child (client).

A battle for professional dominance or control of the client's mental health can then ensue. For example, the psychiatrist can change medication sometimes saying to the client that they will need to be on these pills for the rest of their life. Meanwhile the psychologist can be working collaboratively with the client to increase their understanding of their behaviour so they can learn to manage independently.

Many versions of the above can occur thereby creating a number of dilemmas which will not be helpful for the client. However, just as in any interpersonal situation with appropriate communication between the professionals concerned, who are respectful of each other's contribution and consistently open with the client, a helpful situation can be created. Like any relationship milieu, these connections need to be maintained via meetings and conversations which are time consuming. The focus must rest on the client's improved situation and not become a battlefield for inter-professional warfare.

There are various examples of inter-professional working where therapist and client realise together that the client cannot manage their experience without the help of the psychiatrist's prescription and a team of community mental health nurses. When meetings amongst professionals can occur about a client's case, then the stage can be set for something productive to occur. One of the hopeful aspects of such a relationship is that there is the opportunity for something to be created that is more than each person's individual contribution. Professionals are charged with holding the tensions of difference and yet must still work in clients' best interests.

In search of this productive meeting place, the chapter now turns to consider aspects of psychopathology as expressed by an NHS psychiatrist in conversation with the authors. Diagnosis, medication, care and cure make up the focus of the discussion and these concepts thread through subsequent chapters. It must be acknowledged here that this conversation could have been different if the psychiatrist had held views at other points along the continuum of a possible emphasis on biological and psycho-social factors. However, in the authors' views it is through the medium of shared inter-professional thinking and discussion that clients will benefit from enhanced practice. The psychiatrist was asked previously agreed questions, and these are highlighted in the larger type below.

Part 3: The Authors' Conversation with an NHS Psychiatrist Follows (Carole Lund)

Psychiatrists have different foci in their practice. Would you say that you have a particular emphasis? And is that as a result of your training and experience?

I would say that I like to think that I have a fairly flexible approach personally. In the general field of psychiatry, yes there are some psychiatrists who you would say were definitely more biological, and some who are more psychological. I would certainly consider biological aspects of people's presentation, but also try to look at where they are at psychologically, and also in terms of what stage of life they are at and their social situation. Issues are perhaps to do with housing, finances, or the criminal justice system, or immigration. I would like to feel that I have a fairly broad approach that could be adaptable depending on the person's presentation. In essence that does to some extent come from training and experience. I set out to work in as many different fields of psychiatry as I could, to get the widest training possible and I qualified in an age when training was slightly longer. Seeing different fields of expertise is helpful in enabling you then to be able to take a wider view of the problems that are presented to you.

Questions about diagnosis and formulation

How central is the concept of diagnosis to your work?

Coming from a framework of psychiatry one is very much trained to make a diagnosis, and I think there are pros and cons to that. It is useful to have a framework to enable you to get your head around the patient's presenting problems and how you might help them. I would like to think that I made a diagnosis at a time when I felt comfortable doing so, and I wouldn't necessarily see a person for the first time and feel that I could make a diagnosis. There are risks of jumping in to making a diagnosis too soon without a thorough assessment and thoroughly thinking out what you are actually doing, because I think there is a risk of labelling somebody, and that then becomes set in concrete and follows them around. I think it is not to be taken lightly.

I am also curious about formulation and where and how that sits in terms of your work or work with colleagues. Does it feature at all?

I think both are important really. Part of my job is to come to a diagnosis. The diagnosis is not necessarily the be-all and end-all, the formulation is also important. In our training we have to make formulations of people's presentations, and we still talk about formulations of their presenting problems.

So within your psychiatric training the concept of formulation is also present?

Yes, I mean I was talking more about formulation in the sense of looking at the psychological, social, developmental, and biological, rather than from a theoretical model.

Well I suppose in psychology, we might think of it as being model driven, for example as a psychodynamic or CBT formulation.

Where I trained, the psychotherapy experience we had as junior doctors was more psychodynamically orientated, whereas I think that has been superseded now by more CBT formulations.

I would say that on the whole, I am generally surprised at how accepting most people are of their diagnosis. I think sometimes how you actually explain what you think the diagnosis is and how you come to it may influence how people accept your explanation.

It seems that you are saying that the interaction around the explanation is nearly as important as the diagnosis?

Yes, maybe some diagnoses are seen as undesirable or negative. However, if you can explain to somebody what that actually means in a sensitive way, then you can explain most things to most people if you are prepared to do it in a well thought out fashion and considerately. I've generally found when you do explain, that most people say 'gosh that is me'. I've actually read paragraphs out of the *International Classification of Diseases* (ICD) to people and they said 'that is me to a tee'; then I think they are quite relieved that they are not the only person feeling this way and there is help available.

Certain diagnoses are more fashionable. For example, people now come saying 'I've got bipolar disorder'. They will come with material from the internet; it is a mixed blessing. It can be helpful for some people to realise there are other people who self-harm, that they are not alone and relief is available. Equally, there can be unhelpful sites, telling people how to kill or harm themselves.

What is your view of co-morbidity?

People don't always present with clear-cut diagnoses and often have multi-factorial problems. I see more and more people who have multi-layered problems, co-morbidities and physical illness, psychological illness, psychiatric, drug and alcohol problems all together. Different aspects of the problem form interlocking circles that all fit together. I think it helps to have a framework. Whether you then digress from the framework as you get more knowledgeable and experienced, or you look at different approaches or whatever, it helps to have some kind of framework for what you are doing, so in that sense I think it is useful.

Questions about working with other professionals

What is your view on a referral for psychological work?

I do refer people for psychological work. I would refer more people for psychology than other consultants in my position. I suppose I do feel that psychology has a lot to offer. It is very difficult to put people's problems simply and say 'your problem needs a pill' or 'your problem needs psychology'. So I would say that probably my referral rate for psychology is quite high. I think we desperately need more psychology, not only because of the complexity of the cases but also because of the complexity of the psychological work and the time constraints. Even if I feel I can do some quite basic work myself, I don't always have the capacity to really do that in practice.

It seems like many years ago psychiatrists carried out psychodynamic therapy and now there are all these psychological therapists around. Is there an element that psychiatry would like to reclaim some of that?

Well, yes, I would actually agree with you. I'm not setting myself up as any kind of expert in psychological therapy, but I think there was more capacity at one time to have longer appointments to take on certain individual patients for more psychological work. Now I think the demands on time almost pigeon-hole you into being a prescribing doctor, as opposed to somebody who has wider skills, and that can be one of the most frustrating elements of this job.

If we had more multi-disciplinary working, and more time and less demands, then I think more of this kind of work could be done. I think it is useful and valuable to see different people's perspectives on patients' presenting problems.

Sometimes it can become quite isolating sitting in an out-patients clinic, seeing 10 to 12 people in a morning. It can be stimulating and refreshing to have others' perspectives and to formulate people's problems slightly differently. The important thing is flexibility: I think it only works well if people are not too dogmatic in their views.

I tend to feel there are different roads from A to B, and so long as you get from A to B, some roads will suit some people better than others, and some roads may get there more quickly than others. If there are people who are so entrenched in their own model or their own perspective that they are not prepared to be a little bit flexible it can be difficult. If somebody says 'I am not going to see anybody who is on medication' I think that sometimes that can be quite difficult. I might really feel that somebody actually really needs that medication.

The pressure to discharge is increasingly becoming an issue. It sometimes leads to tensions as to when people are exactly ready to be discharged. The community team may discharge, but then patients come back to the out-patients' clinic.

Is it a modern-day equivalent of the revolving door?

Well I suppose it is really. I think it pervades most of medicine now, the idea that if you go and make an appointment to see your GP, you go with one problem. One appointment equals one problem and you get so many minutes, then you have to go and make another appointment to talk about another problem. You come with this particular issue and we give you six sessions of this, and then you wait six months and if that is not enough you come back and have six sessions of that.

Does that over-emphasise the problem?

It is difficult because we go into areas of funding, and how that is developing and what you will get paid for, what your illness is and how soon you should get better. It's a bit like going into hospital for a gall-bladder operation. Most people are ready to go home in five days, so the budget is for that and if you stay longer, gosh! That's coming into psychiatry too: if you come with depression you should have six sessions of the psychiatrist's time, two different anti-depressants, and so many sessions of CBT, and you should be better by then. I am not sure with people it is always as easy as that, really.

Questions about the use of medication

Medication is the province of the psychiatrist. Do you think that psychologists should know about medication and its possible effects?

I don't think psychologists need a huge in-depth knowledge of medication, but it must be helpful to have some idea of what people are talking about, an idea that this could be something to do with medication, or maybe they need to ask somebody who knows about medication. I think a basic knowledge would be helpful.

I am not sure that psychologists want to actually be dealing with other people's medication and side effects, or physical investigations. Where does it begin and end? It is helpful though to have an understanding of what patients say, for example, 'I'm on such a drug'.

I don't think we can all be experts in every field, can we? There is a risk of making everybody a generic worker so that you actually de-skill people in the fields in which they really need the expertise. I would prefer to work with a psychologist who was really good at doing psychology, than somebody who was prescribing medication.

In your view, do some patients think that medication will cure them?

The basic answer is yes. Some people do come along with the expectation that you will give them a pill and that would be the answer to all their problems and everything would go away with the pill. I do have to spend time explaining to people that it is not as simple as that, that it is not a magic cure, a magic pill, which it is not going to take all the ills away. It will help, it will help control some of the symptoms, but it is not the whole story, it is not black and white. Comparing in the sense maybe to asthma and diabetes, medication controls the illness, it does not always cure it as such. You can get rid of the respiratory distress or the high blood sugar in the first instance. Without the medication, your symptoms would come back.

In therapy sessions the medication can form quite a focal point.

Some people do focus very much on the medication and not on other issues, rather than talk maybe about what they could do to help themselves, or maybe where some of the problems come from and how they could address some of the difficulties either psychologically or practically. Sometimes to focus on the pill is less threatening. Many people feel that you can give them an answer, whether it is a pill or a few magic words.

Is there a different understanding about medication amongst members of the Community Mental Health Team (CMHT)?

I think it is complicated really. Certainly in terms of the social workers, the Community Psychiatric Nurses (CPNs), the occupational therapists, some of them (particularly the nurses) obviously have a good understanding of medication, side effects and use of medication, and in fact they are advising on and delivering medication. It can be very helpful to have people doing that role who understand medication, and I think sometimes problems do arise, maybe with some colleagues from other disciplines who don't really understand medication and haven't a huge interest in understanding it. Medication management is quite a big part of the CMHT's role. Sometimes questions are referred back to me, whereas someone with a little more knowledge of medication could answer without necessarily needing me.

The way you are describing it, it's like medication becomes one part of a complex story. Moving on then, what do you find is the most challenging patient presenting issue?

I am not sure how I would answer that in terms of patient presenting issues, I think the most challenging issues to do with patients are availability and access to community resources, timing, the availability of a psychology intervention; more political and funding issues. The biggest challenges to me personally are to do with the politics of service provision rather than the patient's presenting issues.

Someone might fall between two services: for example, borderline, wouldn't be accepted onto an IAPT service, or secondary care wasn't prepared to see them either. Almost the politics of practice?

This can be the case.

Questions about care or cure

What expectancies of getting better do you have for the patient? Do you hold a model of symptom management or recovery and relapse?

This is difficult isn't it, what is getting better? I really believe that everybody who we see can be helped in the right kind of way, and that with the right kind of help and support from the system, people can improve. People can not only improve in terms of their health, they can also improve in terms of where they are in their life, in terms of what they are doing, the path that they are taking, the decisions they are making. I do think that people can improve, they can make positive changes. It is this issue of cure. Although we can be positive, we have to accept there are some people who have long-term disabilities related to their mental health. To expect that everybody will get cured or better or recover completely is not realistic, and in a sense this can do people rather a disservice. Long-term illnesses like schizophrenia have long-term consequences, and I think sometimes that people can be done a disservice by not recognising that really.

For some people, it is unrealistic to think they will be able to return to full-time paid employment, or that they will be able to become self-sufficient in all aspects of caring for themselves. I sometimes worry that people who are disabled by their illnesses are not going to get the recognition or the help that they need to make the best of their lives, as if we are somehow putting an expectation on them that they will get better and somehow that if they don't get better it is some kind of failure almost either of them or of the system.

It sounds as if you're saying let's take the emphasis off getting better or cure, let's look at how help means more comfortable living.

If somebody is obviously presenting and complaining of hearing voices, then that is what they want to address. However, they may be living in totally unhygienic, squalid conditions. Getting better for them might mean getting rid of the voices, but maybe getting better for you is an element of improved social living conditions and care. I think that sometimes it is important to listen to somebody's opinion of getting better. Sometimes there are other dimensions of getting better, aren't there, that maybe the professional sees but the patient doesn't?

So it is not just the meaning to the patient, it is the meaning in a more professional overview?

I suppose, yes, without necessarily wanting to inflict your standards and perceptions on somebody else, but making sure they are not living in conditions which are totally unsanitary or putting themselves at risk.

So what might trigger a relapse?

Increased stress, non-compliance with medication, drug and alcohol issues, adverse life events, a lack of social support. Stress is a big trigger. They often all go together too: if you are more stressed maybe you drink more, maybe you don't take your tablets. Physical ill-health with chronic pain and disability can have a knock-on effect.

To what extent do you think that knowledge of those things you have just said, how can these be preventative, is there some psycho-educational aspect?

I think certainly: talking to people about the importance of not misusing drugs, keeping their alcohol use in check, making sure that they eat nutritionally balanced meals, take exercise, rest, don't take on too many commitments. Also looking out for early warning signs such as not coping as well as usual, and then getting help sooner rather than later, rather than leaving it until there is a crisis.

Questions about guidelines and protocols

So, turning now to the NICE Guidelines ...

They can be a double-edged sword, helpful, and also issues can arise. For example, my own personal view would be that the pendulum has swung maybe a little too far in terms of CBT, so that this is seen as the therapy for everything. I do really think that other therapies, interpersonal therapy, brief psychodynamic therapy, can be useful for people, and it is a shame that choice is almost being narrowed down to just CBT.

So there is a certain tension there?

We have touched upon what we said about patients and their relatives researching on the internet, coming in with articles and information. Some people come along saying that they have read that they should be having this and can you provide it? Is this or that available, can everybody have CBT, can everybody have this particular medication? There is publicity from drug companies too, saying for example that this medication you only have once a month, so can we have that? And why isn't your particular Trust giving it? Increasingly there are these kinds of issues.

I don't think it is altogether a bad thing if people challenge you about what you are doing, and what you are providing, and what the service is providing. It can be quite a good thing, because it can actually make you think about what you are doing, go and look at the research, and go and look at some of the ideas that maybe you have not heard of before, consider again what is in the NICE Guidelines. It actually can be more satisfying to have a discussion about the pros and cons of this and that approach, this and that medication. It's not necessarily a bad thing, but it is time consuming.

In a relationship can you build a little collaboration?

If people participate a little more in the decision, they can take better ownership.

In terms of making changes for the benefit of patients this is a humanitarian approach. I suppose I can become concerned about us becoming too assessment, tick box, packages of care orientated that we miss out on the basic humanity of dealing with distressed people. We are not just dealing with a commodity that can be shunted from A to B, and given C, and sent off into D. We are dealing with real people with real lives, and real families and real distress. While I think, as I have said, some frameworks and guidelines can be helpful, sometimes staff can become frustrated with the demands that are placed on them. There is a risk of losing an element of caring and that should be what actually informs the decisions you make. I don't think it is just in psychiatry, maybe even more in the general hospital.

Some of the protocols can get in the way?

I think they can almost become the focus. We must have all this paperwork filled in, and such angst goes into that, rather than really going into the bread and but-ter of what the service is about, which is about treating ill people, not filling in swathes of paperwork. It is important to keep coming back to the person, not to lose the focus.

In conclusion

Our conversation ended at this point, aware that a number of professions are located in a working context that brings its own perspectives on the politics of care. Wehowsky (2000) is perhaps primarily concerned with the debates around the use and misuse of diagnosis, however he does recognise the association with the resource that can be generated by appropriate diagnosis. At times in the conversation there were parallels between psychology, psychotherapy and psy-chiatry in the pressures coming from time constraints and resourcing, differing theoretical models, and protocols of practice.

In each of the preceding parts, there are references made to the politics of care and how this can overlay what was described in the dialogue as a humanitarian approach. It is from this point that the chapters that follow now turn to consider seven presenting issues that people experience and bring to psychotherapy in a range of contexts, and establish the history, dilemmas, practice and research relevant to each. The practice and research sections (Part 3) of each chapter have been written by seven different practitioners in order that the reader is exposed to a range of contexts and models in which therapy takes place. The ways in which these influence, and are reflected in, the nature of the therapeu-tic endeavour are something that as practitioners we often overlook within the immediacy of the therapy room. We hope this is something that the reader may wish to consider.

REFLECTION BOX

1 Do you think that Mercier's statement about nineteenth-century psychiatry has any relevance for current psychological therapies' provision?
2 How does the cultural and organisational context in which you and your client work together impact on, and reflect, your values and therapeutic relationship?
3 In your working experience, what terminology is used to describe those who work therapeutically with clients/patients? Do you think that the naming of professionals is a concern for clients?
4 What kinds of dilemmas have arisen in your multi-professional working context?
5 What do you understand by the terms 'diagnosis' and 'formulation' and their uses?
6 What perspective do you have on the use of medication in your practice with clients?

2

Exploring Anxiety

Introduction

Conceptualisations of anxiety include the historical, philosophical, cultural, medical and psychological. Historical religious notions for example considered anxiety as a healthy response to the fear of God (Burton, 2001 [1621]) while existential theories consider anxiety as inherent in human freedom, with the potential to facilitate our actions towards self realisation (May, 1996). Gendered constructs of what we term 'anxiety' have been variously framed around, for example, war cowardice in men (Shephard, 2002) or as a symptom of the hysterical woman with the latter's purported link to the uterus (Appignanesi, 2008). Psychological models of anxiety (e.g., Dugas et al., 1998; Leahy, 2010) look at processes involved in the development and reduction of debilitating experiences of anxiety, making collaborative sense of this through a formulation of the experience and therapeutic process. So conceptual frameworks of what we may term 'anxiety' are products of culturally specific explanatory systems. In contemporary western society there is a tendency to prioritise a medical model of anxiety in which groups of symptoms and experiences represent specific anxiety disorders. This chapter firstly explores the historical development of this emphasis; secondly examines some of the dilemmas of working with clients experiencing anxiety; and finally examines, and illustrates, through example, work with clients experiencing what is sometimes termed 'general anxiety disorder'.

Part 1: Exploring the Historical Context (Barbara Douglas)

A review of the concept of anxiety indicates that until the nineteenth century the diverse experiences and symptoms that are now clustered together under this term were not grouped together at all. Instead, objective symptoms such as palpitations, dizziness or sweating, and subjective experiences, such as a sense of dread or fear, were incorporated into the conditions that they were considered to be part of (for example, heart problems or inner ear conditions). Only during the nineteenth century did these various diverse symptoms and experiences come to be woven together into the notion of anxiety. However, as Berrios suggested:

> Irrespective of the name these states travelled under (i.e. the history of the words) or how they were explained (the history of the concepts) behaviours recognisable as 'anxiety related' are found described in the literature of the ages. (1996: 265)

This of course begs the question of what underlay the transmutation of diverse experiences and symptoms into a construct of anxiety disorders.

Pre anxiety

Although dissimilar in their cultural interpretation and meaning, *experiences* of what we might refer to as anxiety have been written about from earliest times. For example, the Ancient Greek and Roman understanding of men's fear of battle was conceptualised as characteriological cowardice, a view that persisted until after the First World War. The Greeks also coined the term 'agoraphobia', literally meaning fear of the marketplace, and the notion of hysteria (wandering uterus) was a concept that over the centuries has been held up as a source of many and varied physical and emotional conditions in women.

While bedrocked in a continuing Greek cultural influence, medieval and early modern cultures increasingly incorporated metaphysical, religious and superstitious understandings of fear. Fear of God for example was culturally valued and still apparent in Thomas Burgess' (1839, in Lane, 2007) view that anxiety was designed by God in order that reactions such as blushing would serve as a check on the individual and as a sign to others that the individual was violating sacred rules: 'The soul might have sovereign power of displaying in the cheeks the various internal emotions of the moral feelings' (Lane, 2007: 29). Experiences of fear were similarly held within the powerful notion of witchcraft, of which historian Diane Purkiss (cited in Brown, 2005: 50) stated that 'the witch acts as a carrier for the fears, desires and fantasies of women and men ...'.

The developing scientific zeitgeist of the Enlightenment in the seventeenth and eighteenth centuries saw earlier Greek and Roman inroads into the study of the human body re-emerge in anatomical dissection. Discovery of a bodily system of nerves paved the conceptual path for emerging notions of 'nervous disorders', although these were not psychologically framed as we think of the concept. Rather, nervous disorders were considered physical ailments that travelled through the nervous system causing illnesses in their wake, depending on the locus of travel. Nervous, Berrios argued, meant 'organic, not localised and related directly to the nerves and brain' (1999: 84). Within this understanding noted Edinburgh physician William Cullen (1769) coined the term 'neurosis' to describe a depleted nervous system which then resulted in a multitude of conditions, depending on where that depletion took place.

These earlier conceptualisations of nervousness, along with physical investigations of the body, resulted in an embryonic conflation of disparate experiences and symptoms into a single construct, of which one early proponent was the French physician Auguste Morel (1866, in Berrios, 1999). Morel introduced the view that both subjective and somatic symptoms constituted an anxiety which, together with obsessional behaviours, resulted from a disorder of the automatic nervous system.

Despite academic psychiatry's research into nervousness and its biology, institutional psychiatry of the nineteenth and early twentieth centuries on the whole considered worry as a potential *cause* of insanity rather than a condition, as is illustrated in Figure 2.1 below.

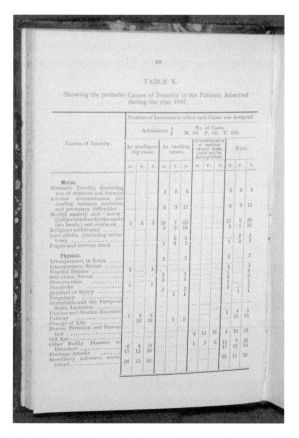

Figure 2.1   Probable Causes of Insanity Cornwall County Asylum 1907

Anxiety and its classification

The nineteenth century saw developments in biological classificatory systems, most notably those of Linnaeus and Darwin. Reflecting this emphasis there emerged attempts at classifications of psychological distress within psychiatry and an emergent concept of anxiety was no exception. Detailed attempts to categorise forms of anxiety included that of Carl Westphal (1872), who reintroduced the ancient classical term of 'agoraphobia', and Pierre Janet (1903), who coined the terms 'social phobia' and 'psychasthenia' (Lane, 2007). The late nineteenth century also saw the burgeoning notions of hysteria and neurasthenia, with George Miller Beard (1869) introducing the term 'neurasthenia' to describe weakness of the nerves (Shorter, 1997). The reader may spend a considerable (and interesting) amount of time engaging with these notions with their overlaps and differences, but suffice it to say that it was largely in reaction to confusing and overlapping theories of neurasthenia and hysteria that Freud (1894) proposed the term 'anxiety neurosis' to designate a separate developmental condition as a condition in its own right.

Thus it was with Freud that the concept of anxiety evolved fully into the conscious awareness of the medical and psychological worlds of western societies. By the 1920s anxiety was no longer simply a symptom, it had become an explanation.

Anxiety management

Conceptual shifts do not occur in a social vacuum and psychiatry willingly embraced neuroses, including anxiety neurosis, as a means to further its shaky professional status within the medical field. But this was also directly related to attempts to encourage people to seek early help, something that was highly problematic in the existing stigmatised and closed psychiatric institutions. Hence the early to mid-twentieth century saw the development of outpatient clinics and admissions wards where certification was no longer an admission requirement. This created the foundations for the validation of a psychiatric and psychological engagement with anxiety management, as well as a burgeoning role for the developing pharmaceutical industry (Tone, 2005).

W.H. Auden (1948) dubbed the political and social cold war period the 'Age of Anxiety', a view reflected in the launch and social uptake in the 1950s and 60s of the anti-anxiety drugs miltown, librium and valium. The reader interested in a critical analysis of the ongoing relationship between psychiatry and the pharmacology industry might look to the work of David Healy (2004).

More recent conceptualisations of anxiety have focused on a medical model that considers particular symptoms as evidence of specific sub-groups of experiences, separately classified under an umbrella anxiety cluster. *The Diagnostic and Statistical Manual of Mental Disorders IV-TR* (APA, 2000), for example, included 12 discrete sub-categories and this led to the hotly debated development of specific psychological therapies to manage these.

Conclusion

Within a medical model, the publication of the fifth iteration of the *DSM* (APA, 2013a) demonstrates that a move away from an integration of symptoms as an anxiety cluster appears to be apace, returning anxiety to separate destinations (trauma and obsessive compulsive disorder, for example, have been relocated). This is but one example from the above historical outline which indicates that as practitioners we might helpfully loosen our adherence to conceptualisations of psychological distress within specific frameworks, be these within descriptive psychiatry or specific psychotherapeutic theoretical models. History informs us that these are all culturally situated. Part 2 now examines how the varying current conceptualisations are played out in some of the tensions and dilemmas that may be experienced by psychotherapists working with clients who are experiencing anxiety.

Part 2: Exploring Dilemmas in Practice (Pam James)

What does anxiety mean and to whom? The dilemma of underlying models

There are different ways of trying to understand the nature of anxiety. Two clear routes are to consider a state that has a description of being a disorder or alternatively think about anxiety as a natural response to a situation or perceived situation. Various psychometric scales attempt to measure anxiety, acknowledging that there is both a person-based measure (trait anxiety scales) and a state-based measure (state anxiety scales) which attempt to reflect a response to a particular situation. These two measurements have an inter-relationship and for a particular person it can be helpful to know both. It is necessary to know the context in which a person reports that anxiety is being experienced (i.e., a more or less continuous feeling, or a feeling that occurs in response to what most people would describe as anxiety provoking). If there is a dilemma here, it is clarifying the person's response in context, taking into account their particular experiences.

Zvolensky et al. (2007) write that it was possible to determine an individual's anxiety sensitivity score, thus giving a trait-like quality to this description. People described as such are found to be more likely to become anxious in appropriate contexts. Social developmental factors also seem to play a part. Costa and Weems (2005) consider how maternal anxiety is mediated by maternal anxious attachment beliefs to bring about child anxiety. These two illustrative references suggest that anxiety has a person-based component which may or may not have come about by intermediary learnt factors. This is perhaps the seed of the dilemma – has the person a predisposition to be anxious and/or has this way of perceiving the world acquired a learnt connection?

Nevertheless, the medical model adopted by psychiatry leans in the direction of symptom categorisation. Bögels et al's (2010) study on co-morbidity categorises different symptoms of anxiety into a number of named groups, all of which are located under a heading of anxiety disorder. One of the main purposes of such a classification is to allow practitioners to communicate with each other about a person's collection of symptoms and possibly recommend subsequent treatment.

Experienced anxious feelings are associated with a wide range of symptoms, including palpitations, increased perspiration, stomach upsets and racing thoughts. These physical symptoms in themselves can frighten the person who experiences them and then produce further symptoms in an upward spiral of distress. In the midst of their anxiety can the person experiencing such thoughts and feelings access enough thinking space to work out what is going on in their bodies and minds? The meaning a person gives to these thoughts and feelings is often the task of therapy. Casework would suggest that until some talked-through explanation occurs with an appropriate professional, the person can wonder if they are 'going mad' and possibly losing touch with reality. In extremely anxious states, a person can perceive the world as speeding up, or not looking the same.

Psychiatric explanations that go first to descriptive labelling and naming can have a variety of effects. For some people, these can confirm their fear that a disorder is present. For others, it can give some comfort that other people have experienced a similar state. Subsequent prescribed medication aims to reduce or remove the anxiety symptoms. Psychological explanations are based on trying to understand the person's experience and their related belief systems. This involves learning about the context of the anxiety, its possible cause and associated factors, and its cessation or informed tolerance. Consequently, from the client's perspective, the beginnings of a dilemma emerge. These centre on a choice between controlling the symptoms of anxiety by taking medication, or working psychologically to contain these. In practice, a mix of medication and psychological therapy may occur simultaneously. For this latter group of clients, any improvements in their anxious symptoms may be as a result of either, as illustrated in work by Schutters et al. (2011).

Consequences of symptom identification and diagnosis: the dilemma of ideographic and nomothetic approaches when working therapeutically

A dilemma can present when a person reports anxiety in the consulting room of a GP or psychiatrist and the response is tranquillising medication, a labelled diagnosis *and* a referral to a therapist. On the one hand, some may be relieved that medication has reduced their anxiety and the symptoms have temporarily lessened. Alternatively, others may resent the reliance on medication, whilst still others might be puzzled as to why they are experiencing the symptoms at all. A further complication may be the side-effects of the tranquillising medication, as explained in the British National Formulary (BNF, 2005: 179). Client-reported General Practitioner (GP) responses to their anxiety include medication for symptom reduction concurrent or preliminary to referrals to therapy for psycho-social exploration. When there is a case-related dialogue (with client consent) between GP and therapist this can serve to increase the coherence in a client's progress, although this is recognised as time intensive.

Therapists may respond in different ways to clients' material as theoretical trainings propose various therapeutic paths. There is a possible dilemma for the therapist because while the NICE Guidelines (2011a) recommend CBT as the theoretical base for casework other evidence-based therapies are available also. Person-centred and psychodynamic approaches take the client's story as their initial thread and focus on their contextual narrative. Clients may use metaphors to describe their feelings: for example, anxiety as a train that keeps running round a continuous circuit, and the beginning of containment was when the client conceptualised a 'station' where thought occurred and permission was given to halt. Another client might describe anxiety as a horse that has bolted from the stable and is running amok. Again, containment began when the client was given the reins and she began to regain control.

Therapists trained in CBT models will proceed to a more prescriptive response that seeks clients' belief systems and an emphasis on their thinking processes. Although the NICE Guidelines propose therapies linked to CBT in a 'nomothetic response to all', there are clients for whom this method is unhelpful. This poses a possible dilemma for the therapist as they can see the NICE Guideline preferences, yet have experience in their casework that individual client issues often have hidden and salient aspects that cannot be immediately expressed or helped by CBT.

Symptom definition does not necessarily trigger a diagnosis. NHS primary care systems frequently use psycho-education and symptom management as delivered by a psychological wellbeing practitioner (PWP). If these two steps are successful, then a diagnosis and subsequent labelling may not occur. It is only when symptoms persist that Step 3 can be approached with the resulting sessions with a high intensity worker using cognitive behaviour therapy. The current system of treatment in the NHS has become increasingly detailed, whereby diagnostic descriptions (e.g., generalised anxiety disorder) have become linked with particular CBT ways of working. Cape et al. (2011) describe a more holistic appreciation of the contextual understanding of anxiety whereby the therapist is able to adopt a pan-theoretical perspective. Understanding anxiety from a person-centred perspective as discussed by Stephen et al. (2011) concerns working with a person's self-concept which is experienced as incongruent with their ideal self.

Consequences of a diagnosis or symptom recognition: the dilemma of which therapeutic response to adopt, use of medication and the concept of risk

The descriptions of anxiety as outlined in the most recent iteration of the *DSM* are varied and complex. Trying to group types of anxiety suggests that all are concerned with threats to the safety of the self. This could be physical safety in terms of accident or injury or destruction of the self, or wounding or insult or embarrassment to the psychological self which involves self-perception. Again a dilemma emerges, as it is impossible to ensure that no physical or psychological harm will occur. People are always living at some level of acceptable risk of harm. Yoder (1981) distinguishes between neurotic and ontological anxiety. Coping mechanisms involve a variety of defences – some will appear necessary, and some irrational.

One of the choices that clients may perhaps have to make is whether to accept the prescribed medication or wait until the psycho-education and symptom management becomes available due to waiting times. The extent of that dilemma will depend on how severe the anxiety is. Someone who experiences extreme symptoms of anxiety will usually wish to take medication to alleviate those symptoms. Casework suggests that medication is a transient alleviation with benzodiazepine medications having an addictive quality (see the BNF, 2005: 178).

Anxiety can occur in conjunction with other described states. For example, a person who experiences anxiety over a period of time may become self-critical about how they feel. This in turn leads to depressed feelings: a more complex situation has now occurred. A person may be so anxious that they cannot go out and as a result is in the house for long periods of time and becomes socially withdrawn and depressed. Hence the concept of a risk of self-harm and even suicide becomes a possibility, as does paranoia and psychotic thinking that can be precipitated by fear and extreme anxiety. This can present as a dilemma for the therapist following a more manualised treatment regarding which should be treated – the anxiety or depression? The holistic therapist possibly experiences less of a dilemma as the contextualised pan-theoretical position can place the client's experience meaningfully.

More persistent anxiety that is not alleviated by CBT may need therapy from another model. Cashdan (1988) argues that if a *symptom* is viewed as an unexplained, unexpressed or unconscious *feeling* as appreciated by psychodynamic therapy then the following example shows how the case might proceed. Consider the client who experiences the symptoms of anxiety when he is away from home and out of the country. After several CBT treatments his anxiety has persisted. In a psychodynamically-orientated therapy, whilst discussing his absence from home, it emerges that this triggers his acute fears of abandonment: he recalls an aggressive and critical father. His reactions to his father could not be expressed during childhood for fear of upsetting his mother (or father). His realisation and working through of the feelings towards his parents, both in childhood and currently, give him some sense of understanding. This in turn allows him to be more confident in coping with his anxious feelings, which themselves became less frequent.

Consequences of therapy: the dilemma of care or cure

Smail's (1997) book, *Illusion and Reality*, discusses the meaning of anxiety throughout, and one of his debated themes concerns to what extent therapy can be helpful. The concept of on-going care may be a probable outcome for people who present with persistent anxiety that seems to be resistant to any form of therapy. What remains then is the management of such using relaxing techniques and the least possible medication. The apparent burden of cure is removed from both therapist and client who may be continuously expecting that the anxiety might diminish and even disappear. This can be contrasted with less severe forms of anxiety which can be managed, understood, contained, and sometimes totally alleviated by using an appropriate therapy. Part 3 below both discusses and illustrates the use of particular therapeutic approaches with clients experiencing what is currently termed 'general anxiety disorder'.

Part 3: Exploring Research and Practice with Clients Experiencing Generalised Anxiety (Mary Reid)

Introduction

Generalised anxiety disorder (GAD) is a diagnosis including different sets of distressing and disabling experiences. The prevalence of GAD has been estimated at between 2 and 4.7 per cent of the population, with slightly more females diagnosed than males (Alonso and Lepine, 2007). This part will present a brief review of the diagnostic criteria and process-based theories of this particular category of anxiety disorder, and the therapeutic approaches applied to two cases. These will offer evidence that an effective approach requires a more individually tailored case formulation to guide therapy.

The diagnostic conceptualisation of GAD has changed over the years. Today, major systems of diagnosis – *DSM-5* (APA, 2013a), *DSM-IV-TR* (APA, 2000), and *ICD-10* (WHO, 2005) – recognise GAD as a specific disorder rather than a residual category of non-specific but pervasive anxiety experiences. The *ICD-10* definition requires an endorsement of symptoms indicating *chronic sympathetic arousal*, or free-floating anxiety with more than one target. Co-occurring panic/agoraphobia, social phobia or obsessive-compulsive disorder takes precedence over a diagnosis of GAD in this system. In contrast, a *DSM-IV-TR*-based diagnosis also depends on the *presence of excessive worry* that is difficult to control and causes significant distress, typically interfering with daily functioning. The worrisome thoughts need to be far out of proportion to their actual likelihood *or* the impact of the event or object of worry. Three additional symptoms need to be present for a diagnosis, including manifestations of chronic arousal or mood symptoms (e.g., restlessness/feeling keyed up, easily fatigued, difficulty concentrating, irritability, muscle tension, aches, disturbed sleep). This list may also offer potential criteria for other anxiety disorders, except for *ongoing muscular tension* that appears to be GAD-specific.

Depending on which system is used, it is possible that GAD may or may not be diagnosed for the same person. Physical symptoms caused by a relatively high state of chronic neurophysiological arousal may cause individuals to access primary care services often (e.g., chronic headaches, gastrointestinal upsets, back pain, disturbed sleep). A proportion will end up having costly hospital investigations, as well as suffering reduced work capacity and wellbeing (Hoffman et al., 2008). Importantly, the symptoms of GAD are associated with equally severe degrees of social disability as those in chronic somatic diseases (Maier et al., 2000).

Reviews of treatment reveal modest impacts with CBT therapy, however symptom reduction and improvements to wellbeing have been found. A recent Cochrane review (Hunot et al., 2010) showed that where GAD was the primary diagnosis in 23 UK and USA studies, clients assigned to CBT were more likely to achieve a clinical response with a greater reduction in worry and depressive symptoms than patients assigned to treatment as usual or waiting list control. The most effective treatment required 12 to 15 sessions. Between 31 and 78 per cent of the clients in these studies also met the criteria for other anxiety or mood disorders.

However, reviews of the effectiveness of psychotherapy for GAD have been limited by small sample sizes, the use of different outcome measures in individual studies, and a primary focus on symptom reduction. These results, along with the variations in maladaptive processes underlying their symptoms, support the need for individual formulation focusing on the unique pattern of processes underlying an individual's anxiety and its chronicity.

Consider the following two clients.[1] Both women were in middle life, and were diagnosed as meeting the criteria for GAD based on *DSM-IV-TR*. Both had attended hospital-based clinics for continued difficulty with pain and fatigue related to chronic fibromyalgia. Each was referred to a psychotherapy clinic after attending a chronic pain group, which was helpful in managing activity levels, but limited in helping each manage frustration and fatigue.

Fiona had enjoyed her life as an administrative clerk, mother, and sportswoman prior to her illness. She arrived with visible signs of anxiety, perched on the edge of her seat, wrapped up in a world of worries. She recognised that her pain symptoms,

---

[1]Both cases are in part based on actual clients seen by the author and pseudonyms are used.

although present every day, became worse if she became fretful and unable initially to detach from them long enough to engage fully with me. She depended on anxiolytic drugs to keep her anxiety 'under control' and was ashamed of her reliance. Worry themes quickly emerged: *Would her family come to some harm? Was her partner's affection trustworthy? What would happen if she could not perform her schedule of tasks the next day? What if her pain increased, and her ability to function decreased?* Upon exploration, most involved future events that had a low probability or a relatively low cost if they did occur. Fiona saw most situations as having uncertain outcomes and felt threatened. She recognised her anxiety as a lifelong trait; it was *part* of her, and initially did not believe it was alterable.

In contrast, Janet's self presentation was calm and thoughtful, her reactions measured. She was a successful professional in the world of business, a confident staff manager. Yet she continually battled against her own fears of failure, fearing a state where she would stop functioning altogether. Underneath her controlled persona she was continually fretting, often about how she would cope with yet another work- or family-related demand. Her self-expectations for occupational accomplishments and social engagement remained high and rooted in her past performance, pushing her to maintain a schedule that would exhaust a very fit person. Janet suppressed her bodily awareness of apprehension and discomfort until her anxiety rose too high. Overactivity in work, travel and managing others' relationships represented ways to distract herself from experiencing a lack of control over the outcomes of events around and within her.

Theoretical models of GAD

Several models describing GAD functioning have been developed over the past fifteen years, explaining how anxiety, arousal, tension and worry may become self-perpetuating cycles that are difficult to break. They share a grounding as cognitive-behavioural approaches, although four combine at least some aspects of experiential (e.g., emotion-focused) or interpersonal approaches. Each has stimulated at least some empirical support for its constructs. More extensive descriptions of these models can be found elsewhere (Roemer et al., 2006; Behar et al., 2009).

Early ideas about problematic processes underlying GAD included the recognition that repetitive fears about future events might evoke alternating responses of hypervigilance and cognitive strategies to avoid thinking about them. Initially, potential threats might provoke hypervigilance, stimulating emotional arousal until it too became aversive, when avoidance of both sensations and associated mental representations might occur (Krohne, 1993). Borkovec's *Avoidance Model of Worry* (AMW) first highlighted worry as a primary strategy helping people to *avoid* other distressing internal experiences by focusing on repetitive and unpleasant verbal thoughts (e.g., *The weather is bad; my son may have an accident! What if I don't get this job?*). Worry was believed to *inhibit* distressing mental imagery, resulting emotions and somatic arousal. Indeed, focused attention on verbalised thoughts had been shown to block imagery processes, at least in some individuals, and sustained attention on verbal thinking does dampen arousal (Thayer et al., 1996). A subsequent version of this model incorporated past interpersonal trauma and insecure attachment as factors contributing to GAD development, with ongoing difficulties in interpersonal inter-actions maintaining symptoms (Sibrava and Borkovec, 2006).

Dugas' *Intolerance of Uncertainty Model* (IoUM) highlighted intolerance of uncer-tainty as a key feature in GAD. IoU is defined as a low threshold for tolerating the unknown outcome of events and the predisposition to react negatively to perceived uncertainty (Dugas et al., 1998). High IoU leaves individuals feeling generally appre-hensive and finding more potential sources of danger in the environment. This model also gave a role to positive beliefs about the *function* of worrying (e.g. *'worrying will help me avoid disappointment* or *help me cope better; it keeps bad things from happen-ing'*), a relatively impoverished problem orientation, and *cognitive avoidance*, namely the use of strategies aimed at curtailing distressing thoughts or threatening images (e.g. distraction, and suppressive strategies).

In contrast, Wells' *Metacognitive Model* (MCM) shifted the emphasis onto the *extent* to which individuals engage in worrying. *Negative* beliefs about worry cre-ated problematic responses (e.g. *'worry is harmful and uncontrollable'*; Wells, 1995). Consequently these activated even more anxiety and ineffective efforts to stop wor-rying, leading to experiences of loss of control over one's own state of arousal.

The *Emotional Dysregulation Model* (EDM) also focused on helping clients manage adverse emotional and sensory experiences, as they created cognitive and behavioural avoidance (Mennin et al., 2004). It offered the view that worry is only *one* avoidance strategy employed for this purpose: an active suppression of feeling and distraction are also common. Indeed, perceptions of anxiety may become blocked at sub-threshold levels, leaving a person unable to access sensory/affective signals and thus unable to understand their purpose. Evidence supports the idea that a more general difficulty in understanding emotional experience is common in GAD (Mennin et al., 2007). Thus worry may not be a prominent feature, and yet a person may still function without adequate awareness of their chronic anxious arousal.

The *Acceptance-based Model* of GAD (ABM) added to these ideas by describ-ing individuals' tendency to cognitively *fuse* with these initial aversive, internal experiences (i.e. they lack the ability to separate an experiencing self from these experiences), and therefore have little sense that they can control them, often feeling guilty that others will criticise them (Roemer and Orsillo, 2002) and they become anxious at the onset of similar experiences. Attempting to alter the form or frequency of negative internal events even when doing so leads to unhelpful avoidance behaviour that has been described by Hayes et al. (1996) as *experiential avoidance*.

These models offer overlapping but multiple directions for therapeutic work. A clinician may be tempted to select one model (i.e. one that fits best within his belief system) and approach all clients diagnosed with GAD accordingly. This adherence, however, may offer a too-comfortable lens, and begin to unconsciously limit the clinician's exploration of the processes underlying a client's distress, possibly reducing the effectiveness of their chosen approach. In the case of Fiona and Janet, it was essential for both clients and clinician to become co-investigators of the processes underlying their anxiety, and the functions served by their responses to it, and select therapeutic interventions that derived from each of their personal formulations.

Fiona

Positive beliefs about worry and intolerance of uncertainty

Fiona believed her continual worrying helped her cope with potential threats by avoiding sudden shocks. She feared a lack of preparation would find her unable to cope with the overwhelming anxiety that followed. Further exploration helped us both understand the source of this idea: a strong but vague idea that it would lead to an endless descent, from which recovery would not be possible. Consequently, it was initially very difficult for her to attempt limiting her worry time via distraction or by focusing on more rational estimations of worse case scenarios. However she could challenge her worry beliefs by engaging in ongoing costs-benefits analyses (i.e. the benefits and drawbacks resulting from worrying), recognising that her worrying did take a toll on herself and others.

Establishing a capable self and useful interdependencies with others

Fiona became more aware of *worry themes* by record keeping. They revealed she viewed herself as unworthy of approval, and unable to cope with events without someone she could rely on. Her fear of a negative evaluation was high, corresponding with her belief that her acceptance and desirability were dependent on her capacity for serving others. Once she was able to recognise that my interest was genuine, and reflected a lack of disapproval, she became more willing to approach and challenge her responses to perceived threats. Articulating our responses to each other permitted an early challenge of her strongest negative self-belief.

We agreed that focusing on her concerns about the motivation of others' relationships with her and her predictions of their responses to her would initially take centre stage in our behavioural experiments. This also shifted the focus from her worry about pain and fatigue within a more medical framework, to the most vital thoughts – and consequently worries – that exhausted her psychological and physical energy. Fiona began to think about what she wanted from relationships, and increased her list of personal rights in relation to them. Agreeing she needed to learn new skills for self-assertion, she experimented with new behaviours in role-plays, including setting limits on her availability and requesting assistance with complex tasks from different people. Slowly we increased her exposure to *in vivo* experiments. What would happen if she said no when someone asked her to help, and resumed her plans for that day? What if she made demands on others and stopped thinking about the repercussions? The results of these experiments surprised her: clearly people valued her far more than she expected, and she became willing to revise some unhelpful beliefs.

Increasing problem awareness and resolution skills and re-engaging with her body unfettered by anxiety

We also worked on increasing her problem identification skills, to equip her with choices for thinking and behaviour when anxiety did arise. As she began to identify potentially resolvable problems more precisely (e.g. *'Does this twinge in my arm mean more pain is coming? I am not sure I have enough energy to do everything I planned today'*), Fiona could begin to separate more and less likely adverse scenarios, and her belief in her self-efficacy improved.

Deepening her awareness of bodily needs

As the periods in which she became more relaxed increased, she began to realise that some pain was caused by chronically high levels of muscular tension. She found relief in regular massage, later engaging in mindfulness practice, recognising that relaxation was mental as well as physical. She took time to recognise the signals her body sent her regarding its need for activity or rest. Her anxiety about her health and the wellbeing of her family began to subside as she became more confident about her ability to cope with even difficult situations. Finally, we developed a collaborative plan to reduce her reliance on anxiolytic medication: her own stepped plan permitted new opportunities to challenge negative self-judgements.

Janet

Deep sensory discomfort and self-criticism

When increasing activity was not a possible response to preoccupation to increases in somatic anxiety, Janet felt panicky and self-loathing. Exploring these sensations and thoughts led to a fear of an increasing and permanent disability.

However, attempting relaxation or a sustained inward focus was uncomfortable, eliciting a fear of being overwhelmed.

Positive and negative worry beliefs

Janet believed that worrying was a motivator: it helped her identify problems early and improved her ability to find solutions. However, she could easily distinguish between realistic and unrealistic concerns (i.e. low probability events or events over which she had no control) and agreed that for the latter worrying did not help. Worry records showed unrealistic concerns were more prevalent. She also identified a fear that worrying might escalate and lead to a state of collapse: she moved between task focus and worry throughout her day. Varying the amount of time she was permitted to worry and scheduling specific worry time helped her to realise her control over worrying. She began to decouple her associations between worry, anxiety sensations and harm.

Increasing exposure to avoided sensations and challenging negative self-beliefs

Janet's therapy gradually increased her exposure to and identification of internal sensations, and introduced new interpretations for these, thus depotentiating their threat. Next, we worked on evaluating the cost of her high self-expectations. She realised they impaired her wellbeing, but she loved the buzz of successful task completion and being seen as special for accomplishing more than others. A critical attitude began to surface: having difficulty coping with life demands was a *weakness*, and deserving of scorn. We devised successively larger experiments with new behaviours that set limits on the amount of activity she would undertake, and checked their impact on others' responses towards her. Further experiments helped her learn that others were not as critical as she was, nor did they appreciate her less. In the final part of her therapy she worked on developing a previously absent, internalised source of compassion, and setting up a dialogue between anxious, angry and compassionate voices within herself. Janet realised how deeply she had internalised early experiences of social responses to her productivity. By the end of her therapy, she felt more aware of smaller increases in arousal that signalled an increase in stress and her worry periods had reduced.

Both clients' gains were reflected in their outcomes as measured by several psychometric scales, as well as their spontaneous reflections. These cases demonstrate that exploring a client's history of symptoms and co-existing features and discovering deeper beliefs that may be initially inaccessible can improve the quality of outcomes (Butler et al., 2008). Working with Fiona was influenced most by the IoU, AMW and ABM models. Janet's therapy incorporated principles and interventions from the MCM, AMW and EDM models. For each, guided discovery of anxiety experiences constellated a unique formulation that suggested intervention choices.

Challenges for the therapist

Further challenges exist for a psychotherapist working with these clients, including working with avoidance. Individuals with chronically high states of anxiety seek immediate relief, giving rise to avoidance via cognition and behaviour in the first place. Clients may avoid exposure interventions as they may increase contact with internal and external situations thereby increasing anxiety and discomfort. Asking clients to tolerate increased anxiety without access to relief is counter-intuitive, so this challenge needs to be made explicit and agreed. Exposure is necessary to assist an identification of factors giving rise to worry behaviour, and to reduce the fear of anxiety itself. Clients may fear they will scream, flee, hide, or faint, thus risking social ridicule as well as intense distress. The importance of building a trustworthy and accepting therapeutic relationship in order to engage in these interventions and potentially witness extreme fear is paramount, and may be underestimated.

Therapists will need to manage their own responses to clients continually bringing experiences of pressure and fear into the room. They may be reluctant to pursue exposure or limit a client's recourse to safety behaviours, uncertain about their own responses. It may be valuable for therapist and client to discuss how each will respond to perceptions of internal distress, and agree to 'invest in discomfort' in the short term to gain relief in the longer term (Leahy, 2010). As Janet's example demonstrated, learning to tolerate distressing emotions may well be an important goal.

Another challenge is the depressive affect or low self-esteem often found in individuals with GAD. Where either also exists, there may be a poverty of good self-representations, along with unhelpful memories and prominent expectations of rejection. Where multiple negative beliefs about the self and world exist, each may need attention to prevent a relapse after improvement and for self-efficacy to occur (Butler et al., 2008).

Therapists should recognise that clients are also likely to present several cognitions underlying anxiety. Initial improvements related to working with only one or two may be temporary. Both Fiona and Janet required 15 sessions over six months before lasting improvements were achieved. Merely treating worry or focusing on a single maladaptive belief with traditional cognitive techniques may not go far enough. Interestingly, Mathews and MacLeod (2005) have pointed out that the role played by beliefs about worrying may reflect retrospective justifications for worrying rather than prove instrumental in *creating* this unconscious strategy. Fiona did not describe herself as a worrier: she interpreted her multiple cognitions associated with anxious arousal as problem-focusing. However, our exploration showed that these were often circular – not leading to constructive solutions, nor necessarily offering her insight.

Deeper layers of belief or experiential memories may benefit from exploration. Anxiety experiences may stimulate a wider association of negative memories for chronically anxious individuals (Butler and Mathews, 1987). Therapy may need to include past interpretations of interpersonal traumas or teach skills by which clients may learn to defend themselves. An existential approach may help people to learn to tolerate uncertainty and the fear of truly annihilating experiences (i.e. death) or find a basis for tolerating distress. Thus interventions that derive from more than one psychotherapeutic orientation may be useful, and must derive from the case formulation.

Others have argued that GAD processes are basic to dysfunctional anxiety in general and so researching them will have implications for all other anxiety disorders (Craske and Hazlett-Stevens, 2002; Roemer et al., 2002). There is certainly a need for further research and case examples to understand these processes and how they lead to either health or dysfunction.

Chapter Summary

Historically, and currently, there are a range of conceptualisations of anxiety. This chapter has explored some of these frameworks and how they may be manifested in the practice of psychotherapy. Historical, cultural, psychiatric and psychological models have been touched upon across the three chapter parts, being drawn together in the final part by the notion that while a range of interventions may be helpful these should draw from the collaborative formulation process for each individual in which both therapist and client share and develop their understanding of the client's process in the service of their finding a more comfortable way of living.

REFLECTION BOX

1 Fear has variously been seen as the *cause* or *condition* of human distress. What do you think?
2 How have people described their *experiences* of anxiety to you?
3 How have you worked with clients to include their thoughts and feelings about their medication (if prescribed)?
4 In your casework, to what extent does anxiety seem to be a natural response to life events?
5 Describe some evidence that the psychological processes giving rise to similar features of GAD may be different from client to client?
6 How might a therapist work successfully with a client's avoidance of situations provoking anxiety, and manage their own discomfort in working with highly anxious clients?

3

Exploring Depression

Introduction

Experiences of depression are widespread, bringing misery, ill health and death. Such experiences are often reported in medicalised terminology with terms such as 'disease', 'disability', 'morbidity' and 'disorder' part of the language that frames current understandings. Depression has been described by the World Health Organisation as the leading cause of disability in the developed world (Mulder, 2008). Figures suggest that in a specific week more than 2 per cent of adults in Britain were experiencing a depressive episode and an additional 7.7 per cent a mixed depressive and anxiety disorder (Dowrick, 2004). European figures also suggest widespread distress with a rate of 8.6 per cent (with wide variations), from which it is argued that the lifetime rate of major depression is between 10 and 20 per cent (Dowrick, 2004).

So the experiences, however framed, are of major social concern and will be the described experience of many of the clients seen by psychotherapists. This chapter seeks to explore experience(s) of depression through an examination of its history; some dilemmas in working with clients who experience depression; and the specific therapeutic practice of working with depressed clients in a student counselling service.

Part 1: Exploring the Historical Context (Barbara Douglas)

The term 'depression' appears to have a long history. Attempts to understand the experience and delineate its borders have, throughout time, perplexed clinicians and philosophers. And even today can we confidently say that we have a better understanding of what we would term 'depression'? Perhaps not. Historically, there are multiple discourses of sadness, and cultural understandings have been framed by a variety of underpinning notions, including the concepts of melancholy, melancholia and depression. As Richards (2002: 24) states 'naming endows the named with discrete status, raises it to consciousness, changes how it is experienced and managed – changes, in short, its entire psychological character'. How we understand and respond to depression today is in its own way as culturally and historically situated as were humoral understandings of melancholy by the ancient Greeks.

Ancient classical period

Humoral medicine of the ancient classical period framed ideologies of wellbeing within a concept of balance, both *between* nature and the body and *within* the body. In this conceptualisation, the world was composed of four elements – earth, air, water and fire – and the forces of nature emerged as the consequence of different balances of these elements. The body was similarly composed of matching elements – blood, phlegm, bile and black bile. Thus the external and internal worlds complemented one another and good health depended on a balance of the humors. Intervention, with the aim of rebalancing, was the remit of the physician, and this could be achieved by diet, rest, exercise and bloodletting, or purging the digestive system.

Ancient classical attempts to understand and alleviate melancholy were firmly located within such humoral frameworks. Aristotle (384–322BC), for example, said of its causation that 'If black bile be cold beyond due measure it produces groundless despondency', while a later description by Roman humoral physician Galen (129AD-c.200AD) held that melancholy was caused by an accumulation in the brain of the melancholic humor black bile (Horwitz and Wakefield, 2007: 57).

Medieval and Renaissance periods

Humoral medicine was the mainstay of medical understanding in general, and of melancholia specifically, within western cultures until the nineteenth century. Increasingly Christian and astrological constructs were incorporated and the priest physician was integrated with understandings of illness and pain as representations of the suffering of Christ. Notions of religious sorrow framed the human experience of 'normal' sadness, delineating it from one of melancholy. Timothie Bright (1551–1615), for example, argued that misery, rather than melancholy, should be considered as 'the heavy hand of God upon the afflicted conscience' (Berrios, 1996: 293). So according to Sullivan (2010), religious thinking injected a more positive view of sadness, as being a means to coming closer to God.

Yet experiences beyond ordinary misery were also of social concern. Burton (2001 [1621]: 174), in his classic study of melancholy, acknowledged continued confusion around causation and delineation, stating of melancholy that 'when the matter is diverse and confused, how should it otherwise be but that the species should be diverse and confused'. Interestingly, given the predominantly religious cultural backdrop of the period, Burton also put forward a developmental perspective for the causation of melancholy that would not be unfamiliar to many psychotherapists today. He argued: 'The first ill accident that can likely befall him in this kind is a bad nurse, by whose means alone he may be tainted with this malady from his cradle' (ibid.: 330–331). That events of infancy can have lasting emotional consequences for the person evidently featured in Burton's thinking about melancholy.

Early psychiatry

The term 'psychiaterie' was first used by a German physician, Johann Reil (1759–1813, cited in Porter, 2002), and mental illness within a psychiatric framework evolved from around the beginning of the nineteenth century. At that point, Porter suggests (2002: 153), 'in all the advanced nations, psychiatry gained a public face (if little prestige and much distrust)'. Berrios (1996), however, also suggests that the evolving psychiatric understanding of melancholia was not as we might understand depression, that is, as a mood disorder, with symptoms of persistent unhappiness, low energy and a lack of motivation. These latter symptoms, he argued, would likely have been considered within an economic rather than a psychiatric framework, and if they resulted in incapacity, would have been more likely to result in admission to the workhouse than the asylum. By contrast, nineteenth-century melancholia was largely understood in terms of obsessions, delusions and hypochondriasis rather than mood. This is powerfully reflected in the voices of those contemporaneously admitted to asylums with melancholia. Edward O wrote that 'I am too dead now to ever die or in other words not enough life left in the body to enable death to take possession of it', and likewise Isobel H wrote, 'although so hideous and diseased it makes my carcass more sensitive than ever. My inside is absolutely rotten and I am one mass of stinking, putrid diseased flesh' (Exeter City Lunatic Asylum, Devon Records Office).

Twentieth-century frameworks

So medieval religious notions helped our ancestors understand sadness and delineate it from melancholy while nineteenth-century melancholia was delineated from everyday misery within a legal and economic framework. This brings us to the separation of melancholia from grief in the early twentieth century understood in psychoanalytic terms (Freud, 1917). Freud developed and reformulated his dynamic theories of the psyche over the years between 1895 and 1939. His early work was based firmly in neurology: hysteria, for example, was fundamentally an expression of physiological problems that could be treated by hypnosis or later by cathartic expression. His subsequent development of the concept of the unconscious and psychoanalysis as a treatment for the neuroses was based on his understanding of developmental sexual energies as underlying human psychological functioning. While the surface symptoms of melancholia were similar to those of grief, Freud considered the difference to lie in the underlying psychic make up. Grief represented conscious sadness at external loss while melancholia was a manifestation of unconscious conflicts resulting from childhood developmental processes. The former was considered irretrievable while the latter was retrievable. This delineation was important in considering whether analysis could or should be undertaken with a particular individual.

Freud's theories on melancholia were only one small part of his vastly influential thinking, but in a broader cultural context were part of the power of psychoanalysis to offer psychiatry a renewed vigour and optimism that had dramatically waned since the earlier introduction of moral therapy. It also acted to introduce a psychological-mindedness to psychiatry (Shorter, 1997).

Social and legal processes in the 1930s also influenced understandings of depression towards those with which we may be more familiar. The introduction of voluntary patient status within state mental hospital provision paved the way for a predominantly medical perspective on clusters of experiences that more broadly incorporated affective states. Thus the notion of sadness was increasingly incorporated within psychiatric diagnosis.

Dynamic theories evolved, continuing to influence notions of misery and sitting alongside Adolf Meyer's (1866–1950) influential development of a bio-psychosocially based view of mental illness. In the latter individual experiences could be understood as reactions or responses to individual circumstances of a social, biological and psychological origin (Horwitz and Wakefield, 2007). Analytical and biopsychosocial conceptualisations of depression underpinned the original *Diagnostic and Statistical Manual (DSM)* (APA, 1952) and its successor *DSM-II* (APA, 1968). The latter, for example, says of depressive neurosis (300.40) that:

> This disorder is manifested by an excessive reaction of depression due to an internal conflict or to an identifiable event such as the loss of a love object or cherished possession. It is to be distinguished from Involutional melancholia (q.v.) and Manic-depressive illness (q.v.). Reactive depressions or Depressive reactions are to be classified here.

The emphasis then was on an individual response, continuum of experience and/or behaviours as manifestations of unconscious conflict.

Descriptive psychiatry framework

Concerns were being raised, however, about the myriad different underpinning causal explanations for mental illness and how these were impacting on research – were researchers actually discussing the same experiences? This research-driven agenda resulted in the paradigmatic shift of *DSM-III* (APA, 1980) towards one of categorical classification of mental disorders: its emphasis was on description rather than causation, with all the latter's apparent confusions. Importantly though this shift, along with *DSM-IV-TR*'s (APA, 2000) subsequent subsuming of major depressive disorder within a category of 'mood disorders', has had other suggested consequences: namely, that the current epidemic of depression is due not so much to an increase in disorder but to the re-conceptualisation and conflation of two concepts – sadness and melancholia – into the notion of depression. The former was previously defined in relation to social circumstances, and the latter as a disorder arising from within. In decontextualising the criteria this distinction was lost with the resulting increase in experiences classified as disorder and hence a perceived rise in incidence (Horwitz and Wakefield, 2007). This, suggests Pilgrim (2007: 536), resulted in an exploitation of depression by the 'not so hidden hand of the drug companies', whose earlier exploitation of anxiety had run its course when the benzodiazepines were found to have undesirable consequences.

Conclusion

Are we edging scientifically ever closer to a more accurate understanding and description of the experiences of depression? Or should we consider any understanding, including our own, to be culturally located and tempered? Implicit in acknowledging the changing frameworks of understanding human experience, distress and difference is that the stance of expert becomes tenuous. The latter suggests that, while therapeutic practice is importantly guided by research evidence, within the therapy room the practitioner needs to be attentively listening to, and attempting to accurately attune to, the particular meanings of clients' subjective and social experiences.

Mulder (2008: 243) makes the useful point that while depression may well be in part a cultural construction, it is also something that causes serious distress. The argument is therefore less about *comparing* constructions and more about 'which model best serves suffering individuals and their society'. Part 2 now considers some issues for practitioners in working within, or alongside, current models of depression.

Part 2: Exploring Dilemmas in Practice (Pam James)

What does depression mean and to whom? The dilemma
of underlying models

The word 'depression' has different meaning for different people. Those work-ing in the professions associated with psychiatry frame depression in the medical model, represented by the connection between symptom, diagnosis and subsequent treatment. Those working in the psychotherapeutic professions also recognise the importance of symptom recognition, where there is a range of emphasis on a result-ing diagnosis. Cognitive approaches emphasise negative thoughts arising from core beliefs. Other therapeutic approaches seek an exploration of underlying feelings located in context. The quest for the meaning of depression becomes blurred between the meaning for the professional and the meaning for the person experiencing the clutch of associated thoughts and emotions. The resulting dilemma is many-faceted, as from the clients' perspective there are different explanations regarding the way in which various professionals will respond to them. There is no unified understand-ing of either the meaning and nature of depression, or the professional response to it. Pilgrim and Bentall (1999) write from the perspective of critical realism and discuss related debates about psychopathology. This chapter stresses the implications for the psychotherapeutic practitioner and consequently also the client.

Consider the case of a person in his fifties who presented at his GP with a descrip-tion of a loss of interest in life, including his job, family and friends. Suicide had been attempted, and anti-depressants, in-patient care and Electro-Convulsive Therapy (ECT) had been used. Therapy had initially been refused, but when eventually it was tentatively accepted, a story gradually emerged of shame and embarrassment, so great to him that he preferred to accept a medical diagnosis and its subsequent treatment, rather than allow his very personal and private perceptions of his life events to be known.

Consider the case of another person, again in her fifties, who has times in her life when she knows that she is 'slipping down her life, spiralling towards despair'. It seems as though neither medication nor therapy can hold her away from the edge of suicide. Yet gradually over time in therapy she is able to articulate her fear of abandonment and isolation. These are her depressed feelings. When she starts to realise the awfulness of this, held in the therapist's existential framework, only then can she make a reconnec-tion and find meaning in her despair. There are a number of references to support this viewpoint, but see especially Tillich (1961).

Professionals associated with psychiatry refer to the diagnostic criteria in the most current iteration of the *DSM* to see the descriptors and the range of severity. The creation of this classification system represents a need to make order from a vast array of human thought, behaviour and feelings. However, in the creation of categories, the reality of human response to perceived difficulty, trauma and learnt irrationality becomes lost in psychopathology and its associated use of medication. In the use of anti-depressants, the medical approach aims to reduce the discomfort of exposure to the emotional pain and flat despair associated with depression. One client commented that 'since I have been taking anti-depressants, my destructive thoughts have stopped whirling round, but I can't feel anything at all. I am emotionally numb'. Working psychotherapeutically may be possible in such circumstances – part of the therapy becomes the dilemma of when to reduce the anti-depressants and begin to tolerate the range of human emotions.

The dilemma of underlying models occurs between psychiatry, psychology and psychotherapy; however, differences may occur *within* professions. For example, psychologists and psychotherapists differ concerning approaches to symptom assessment: some therapists will use psychometric tests, such as the Patient Health Questionnaire (PHQ-9) or Beck's Depression Inventory (BDI), others will not attempt to measure symptoms. Some will listen intently to the subjective experience of the depressed person, others will be more directive. All will use evidence-based therapeutic models derived from cognitive, humanistic or psychodynamic approaches. However, their understanding of depression and ways of responding to it will be different. The National Institute for Health and Care Excellence (NICE) Guidelines (2009c) indicate the preferred subsequent treatment which designates anti-depressants and/or cognitive therapy.

Cognitive models currently predominate, proposing that depression is the result of core beliefs that are biased towards low self-worth. Subsequent treatment focuses on appraising the underlying beliefs and challenging any negative thinking. Humanistic and psychodynamic models stress different views of the clients' experience and different therapeutic ways of working. If the psychotherapeutic response is symptom-focused, then symptom reduction will predominate. If a therapeutic intervention focuses on a person's expressed experience and how this has made them think and feel, then understanding, insight and cognitive change will be an integral part of a wider client narrative held in context.

Consequences of symptom identification and diagnosis: the dilemma of ideographic and nomothetic when working therapeutically

In following the pathway of symptoms, diagnosis (or non-diagnosis) to treatment or therapeutic response, unless sufficient time is taken to listen to the contextual narrative of the person experiencing depression, then the opportunity for meaning and explanation will be lost. Psychology is poised at the interface of the ideographic and the nomothetic: the former concerns the individual person's description of their experience, the latter with where particular psychometric scores fit in the range of measurement.

The NICE Guidelines have set out how to respond to particular client scores which represents an apparent simplification. The dilemma of which therapeutic model to use or whether the client should be taking anti-depressants or not has been 'solved'. The introduction of the Stepped Care model and low and high intensity IAPT workers using CBT could be seen as a further simplification of the complexity of clients' differences by responding using one therapeutic model to address the symptoms of depression: Hall and Marzillier (2009) offer their opinion on a more varied response. Interestingly, McPherson et al. (2009) write that there is no firm evidence base for CBT IAPT. What may be lost in this process are the particular experiences of those clients who are *not* helped by challenging negative thinking patterns.

The dilemma of clients' understanding of an explanation of their depression

Clients will express different beliefs about their depressed feelings, for example: 'it's my serotonin levels'; 'I always see the glass half empty'; 'I must be a bad person if I feel like this'; 'I'll need to take pills for the rest of my life'; 'I must have CBT'. For a therapist working with depressed clients, clients' beliefs about the nature of depression can be one of the associated dilemmas: clients who believe that serotonin levels are causal to depression will be less likely to engage in therapy; therapists can find themselves charged with answering client questions about depression. A dilemma can also occur when a client tells a therapist that they have been told by a member of the medical profession that their depression is a result of their body chemistry and they will need anti-depressants for a long time ahead. Some of the 'myths' of anti-depressant medication are discussed by Kirsch (2009) in his debates about the effectiveness of placebos.

Casework outlines that the explanations from professionals affect how clients perceive their experience. Clients who are told that their depressed feelings are due to brain biochemistry over which they have no control have a cautious and confused view of therapy. A dilemma can then emerge if the therapist holds a psychological understanding of depression, whilst the psychiatrist prefers a biological explanation. Any middle ground can appear blurred where the perspective given to the client is that medication will suppress difficult thoughts and feelings so that they will be able to carry on with everyday life, including working. A talking therapy may also be seen as an adjunct and can often not be available due to long waiting lists.

The primary focus here is clients' safe and ethical pathway through their depression and inter-professional issues resulting from the different underlying models are surely of secondary importance. However, casework informs us that these various explanations of depression do affect clients, and can assume a primary importance in therapy. There are only a few studies that have systematically collected clients' views of depression. One such paper, by Clarke and van Amerom (2008), looked at the differences between male and female self-reports, taken from internet blogs.

Consequences of a diagnosis or symptom recognition: the dilemma of which therapeutic response to adopt, use of medication and the concept of risk

Therapeutic approaches that listen to the client narrative heed the warnings that can be indicated by clients' intentions to self-harm and commit suicide, according to Reeves (2007). This narrative may contain descriptions about feeling suicidal which can be also represented in psychometric tests that assess risk. Risk is always a key consideration, because of the duty of care to preserve life, extreme depression can result in suicide and attempted suicide, and a masked depression can be difficult to detect. Once a client begins to enter the region of very depressed thoughts and feelings then the labyrinth of risk to life unfolds. Therapists holding psychological models and explanations of depression at this point will reach for the general practitioner and/or psychiatrist. They will ask them to prescribe medication hoping to suppress thoughts and feelings and hold the client away from suicide. However, the therapeutic relationship may not be sufficient to hold the client sufficiently at this time. There is no dilemma at this point, as the client's safety is paramount – a multi-professional liaison must occur. When this crisis passes, the dilemma may again present regarding the reduction of medication and the re-introduction of therapy which may have been briefly suspended. This then becomes more of a balancing act between the client's safety, therapeutic opportunity, and differing professional viewpoints.

Consequences of therapy: the dilemma of care or cure

For clients who take the therapeutic path, they may hold their own expectancies of outcome. Will I feel less depressed after therapy? Will I still need some medication? The answers to those questions are not uniform, as they will depend on the context of the client's narrative, the client's perception of their depression, the length of time they have felt depressed, how depressed they are, their expectations from therapy, and the theoretical model used.

A cure in the sense of never again feeling depressed may not be achieved in therapy, only the increased knowledge that care will be needed to maintain the person in a non-depressed state. To realise that care of the personality is necessary is not apparently acceptable in western culture, which has an expectancy of happiness and an apparent resistance to tolerating the misery of ordinary unhappiness. Shaw and Taplin's (2007) sociological critique of the expectations of happiness has cast some light in this respect. At this point it is to the therapeutic process in therapy that the chapter turns, with an examination of work with clients experiencing depression within a student counselling service.

Part 3: Exploring Research and Practice in a Non-Medical Setting with Clients Experiencing Depression (Dee Danchev)

Introduction

For the past twenty years I have worked as a counsellor and counselling psychologist in university settings. For the most part this has involved working with the whole university community – students, academics, and university staff. Although there may be access to university medical services it is not a medical setting, and this is helpful for several reasons. Firstly, there is the opportunity to intervene early at the very low end of the depression scale. The fact that no issue is too small to come and talk about is emphasised and there is no waiting list. This is not a luxury enjoyed by all educational settings but most practitioners would agree that early intervention is ideal (Lexis et al., 2011). Secondly, nothing is recorded on medical records. For people who anticipate high profile careers this is often a significant factor, as a fear of labelling and stigmatisation can prevent them from seeking help (Hayward and Bright, 1997). Thirdly, people are often trying counselling as a first approach before consulting their GP and being prescribed medication. While medication can be useful in cases of severe depression, and occasionally life-saving, if the level of risk is not high then counselling is a preferable first option. Counselling enables people to learn about the causes of their depression, how it can be resolved, and how to take action to prevent it from arising in the future. Medication, at worst, will leave an individual in the same state that they were in before medication, and if they do feel better they have only learned that medication is a solution for their depression. A dual approach of medication and counselling is often recommended but my experience is that the medicated state can work against any deep exploration of feelings and circumstances. Fourthly, in this setting people almost always refer themselves and are motivated to work in counselling.

An obvious drawback of a non-medical setting is that you do not have the security of a medical team around you, but this can be mitigated by establishing links with the local primary and secondary care teams so that consultation can occur readily if needed. Any discussion about individual clients, of course, can only occur with their express permission. (The exception to this would be a high risk of immediate harm to the client or others.) As people often present without having seen a medical practitioner, it is necessary to be alert to, and to refer appropriately, any more serious mental health problems or physical conditions – such as thyroid imbalances or anaemia – which could underlie depression. Equally there is only the need to medicalise the things that fall within the remit of the medical world. Whilst there are undoubtedly some physical conditions that have strong links with low mood states and some medications do improve the subjective experience of mood, I find it difficult to think of depression as a wholly medical disorder. Its causal factors are not exclusively located in the individual and research has shown that social and economic conditions and life experience have a significant impact on mood (Brown and Harris, 1978; Wilkinson and Pickett, 2009; Boyle, 2011). In a university setting the causal relationship between social conditions and depression can be seen most clearly when, due to financial pressures, students have to take on extra jobs involving long hours and night work. Interestingly the individuals affected will often present with feelings of individual failure rather than realising that their financial situation was the major factor.

It is also apparent that anyone can be affected by depression. Although individual resilience may be protective to some extent (Dowrick et al., 2008) given sufficiently negative circumstances anyone can become depressed. I see depression not as diagnosis but as a symptom that indicates a deeper underlying problem. Depressions always have causes. Often these are multifaceted – thing gets layered upon thing until the weight of depressing events results in a persistent low mood – and the person affected may not be aware of the constellation of causal factors. Most people will experience a low mood from time to time but generally there is a natural recovery: we feel low for a while and then as life moves on we spring back. With depression that persists our natural recovery is impeded. It is usually possible to function in the face of difficult circumstances if there is at least one area of solid ground, a firm anchor point. This may be work, home, family, a relationship or some other entity that gives life meaning. When several anchoring points are removed, or a major life event or series of events occurs, then we can start to feel crushed by life.

In an educational setting depression often presents as an inability to work, with increasing isolation from peer groups, feelings of inertia and hopelessness, and a loss of hope for the future. The frequent opening statement 'I haven't done any work for weeks' is usually followed by 'I'm so lazy'. The concept of laziness is freighted with static negative attribution: 'I can't work and I am at fault because I can't work'. The person's inability to motivate themselves has become a 'personality trait' and prevents natural recovery.

My theoretical orientation

As a counselling psychologist I take a pluralistic approach to depression. I am trained in both humanist/existential approaches and CBT. CBT is very useful at times. Sometimes I use a pure form but more often it is incorporated within a humanist framework (Elkins, 2009). My counselling psychology philosophy and approach to depression is underpinned by the humanistic philosophy that given optimal conditions human beings will flourish (Rogers, 1951). The main focus in my work is the establishment and maintenance of the therapeutic relationship as I am mindful of its strong links with successful outcome (Horvath and Symonds, 1991; Clarkson, 2003). Rogers' core conditions of empathy, congruence and unconditional positive regard are key to this process (Rogers, 1951). Achieving a profound empathic understanding of the depths of a depression can be a daunting task but is necessary to convey understanding and a sense of standing alongside the person. Congruence underpins trust – I strive to build an authentic relationship that combines a high level of support with appropriate challenge. Unconditional positive regard is not only important in the restoration of self-esteem, it is also key when working in a setting where a multiplicity of differences may be present, as universities include people from a wide range of countries, cultures and religions. Being aware of your own cultural 'peculiarity' and also being prepared to meet others at 'the crossroads of otherness' (Kristeva, 1999) underpin non-judgemental relating. The core conditions when effectively applied provide clients with the experience of an optimal relationship and a safe therapeutic space where they can explore their feelings in depth.

Research evidence demonstrates the efficacy of the humanistic therapies with depression (Elliott et al., 2004) and studies have shown the humanistic approaches 'to be no more or no less effective than any other approach' (McLeod, 2003: 153). I continue to work in this way because my practice experience confirms its usefulness in working with depression and, in particular, with the severer forms of depression that seem to be resistant to CBT.

Working with depression

How, then, do I work with depression within this humanistic framework? My work is usually short term, with 12 sessions or less being the norm. I assess thoroughly, but in a client-centred style, gathering a comprehensive understanding of the person and their history without taking a 'checklist' approach. Any suicidal intentions are carefully unpacked and if necessary urgent action is taken. Therapeutic progress can be disrupted by the rhythms of the academic year so these are thought through in the early sessions and the timing of assignments, exams and vacations noted.

There are three main strands to my work. These are described in a linear way but may well be covered in therapy in a spiral or non-linear fashion.

1 What has triggered this depression?

Here the task is to assume the position of co-researcher or co-investigator and embark on a journey of detection with the person to discover the precipitating factor(s). Sometimes these are multifactorial, extremely difficult to untangle, and will involve a complex mixture of elements such as life events, interpersonal relations, work- and time-related stressors, existential issues relating to meaninglessness, loss and fear, and wider social pressures. Often depression will be intertwined with anxiety and the origins of both will have to be identified. The aim in this phase is to facilitate expression: in enabling the person to talk about their situation they are becoming active and beginning to move away from their depressed state.

2 What is sustaining this depression?

Usually existing alongside the more apparent causes of depression will be deeper factors that are impeding natural recovery and sustaining the depression. These factors can be intra-personal, inter-personal, or due to wider institutional or societal policies and practices. If the sustaining factor(s) are not uncovered the therapist can find themselves going round in circles as each of the 'surface' causes are dealt with but the low mood persists.

3 Moving through the depression

This strand of therapeutic work involves facilitating a change in mood. An important aspect of this process is the instillation of hope (Yalom, 1998) and this is possibly the therapist's most delicate task. Initially it encompasses being a trustworthy point of anchorage for the person and holding hope for them when they feel completely hopeless. It is difficult to articulate the next phase but it consists of conveying the belief that they have the resources to recover and involves the provision of an authentic affirmation of their strengths and their capacity to heal themselves. Ideally this is done in an apparently seamless manner. An over-effusive affirmation will often be met with disbelief: a more successful strategy is a gradual drawing of attention to movements in the direction of health as they occur. Didactic approaches undermine the person's self-belief and the aim is to strengthen their sense of agency and develop their internal locus of control. Psycho-education can be helpful, and is well received when it is approached tentatively and in a way that builds on the person's own frame of reference. The therapist provides the framework for the person to make their own conceptual leap: Vygotsky (1987) describes this type of action as 'scaffolding'. It is a matter of reconnecting the person with their existing abilities and helping them to recognise that they are bringing themselves to health.

Boardman et al. (2010) identify a third factor in the process of recovery towards mental health. As well as hope and agency, they underline the need for opportunity. It is here that the individual comes into relation to the social world. It is also the point at which individual therapists can contribute to the prevention of depression by engaging with the wider political context, by underlining the need for increased opportunity for young people and drawing attention to policies and practices that may be causal or sustaining factors in depression.

There are of course practical ways of improving mood and these should be addressed. Exercise, strengthening social networks, and mindfulness practice all have strong research bases for mitigating against, and helping to alleviate, depression (House et al., 1988; North et al., 1990; Segal et al., 2002). Immobility and isolation can be features of academic life – sitting at a computer for hours on end alone in a room may form a large part of a student's day, and this is especially true for research students. Exercise improves mood, and encouraging people to review their social networks and improve interpersonal communication can also have a marked effect. Mindfulness practice is gaining an impressive body of research evidence for its usefulness in relieving depression: it enables people to focus their attention more effectively, and by becoming more expert on the nature of their wandering mind, aids insight, self-understanding and concentration. Above all it encourages a more compassionate relationship to the self and others.

Deep depressions

At times deep prolonged depressions will occur and the person may not have a clear idea about the causation. They have sunk in mood to the bottom of an existential pit and can see no possibility of release. Engaging with a profoundly low mood is one of the greatest therapeutic challenges: the central task is establishing the therapeutic relationship but in this regard it is like throwing a lifeline to a drowning man. The person may not have the strength to grasp it as deep depressions are often characterised by a shutting down and withdrawal. Speech can be slowed and functioning greatly reduced. The therapist has to search for a chink of light. A glimmer of something – it may be rage, it may be humour, it may be grief – has to be located, and the energy of that emotion utilised. Here the humanistic therapies show their worth. Focusing on experiential work can unlock emotions and the stuckness of deep depression. Therapist intuition, the avoidance of flight into structure, and the use of therapeutic creativity are important features of the work. There is sometimes a feeling of going 'off piste' and it can feel risky: faith in the process is essential. It is of course vital not to exacerbate any suicidal intentions which can be present alongside deep depression and these must always be carefully considered.

A mature, divorced post-graduate student in his mid-fifties presented in a deeply depressed state. For the past year he had been feeling very low and was experiencing panic attacks. He had refused the anxiety medication offered and his doctor had suggested counselling as an alternative. He was not enthusiastic about this but it seemed the only alternative possible and so reluctantly he gave it a try. He found he could not work and felt hopeless. He had had no previous depressions and no major life events apart from a reasonably amicable divorce and a cancer scare seven years ago that had proved unfounded. His father had been dead for ten years and his mother had had a fatal stroke at the age of 82 eighteen months previously. He felt that his childhood had been secure and happy and he could not identify any significant causes for his current state.

We explored the panic attacks. They occurred 'out of the blue' while walking into the bank, strolling along the high street, and twice in his shared university office. He said he felt terrible during these attacks, that he would feel like he was drowning and burst into tears. The feelings were very bleak but the description of these attacks did not fit classic panic attack symptoms. His general mood was very low but he did not feel suicidal. We spent five sessions exploring his history, the circumstances of the attacks, his current situation, his social support network, his view of the future and all the other usual avenues, including the loss of his parents and the marriage breakdown. None of these explorations gave rise to any useful understanding. We floundered around and I too felt increasingly hopeless. The low feelings and tearful, apparently random episodes were still happening.

During the sixth session we were focusing on his feelings and he described a moment of calm that had happened a few days previously. He was looking at a picture that he had over his desk at work. It was a Monet poster from a museum that he and his ex-wife had visited on a holiday in Provence. The holiday had been blissful and his face brightened up as he thought about that time and described the holiday: 'But it's not just that' he said 'the picture is wonderful'. I felt that something different was happening and asked him to bring the picture with him next time. A week later he placed it on the floor and we sat side by side opposite the picture – it was beautiful. Emerging from our reverie we started to talk about it. What was it that he liked about it? Was it the subject, the way it was painted with free flowing brushstrokes, the quality of the paint evoking both spontaneity and intentionality? Or was it the colours – the greens, purples and blues? We looked at it close up and from the other side of the room: 'I love everything about it' he said, 'but above all it's that blue, it's the incredible blue. It seems to get inside me, it seeps into me'. Out of nowhere I said 'it's air-blue'. He asked me what I meant as the blue in the painting represented water. I said that the intensity of the colour had brought to mind a line from a poem by Thomas Hardy that described a gown as 'air-blue'. He seemed to enjoy the session and left the room in a lighter mood. It felt significant and had certainly deepened our therapeutic relationship. But the next few sessions continued in the previous vein. I made a link between the blue of the painting and his remark that the tearfulness came 'out of the blue' but essentially we were no further forward. At the start of the eighth session he thrust a photograph at me and trying to explain burst into tears. The small colour photograph showed a group of people posing for a wedding photo. An elderly woman was wearing a blue suit – that blue. He explained that this was his mother and the blue suit had been bought for the wedding and then had been worn thereafter at family celebrations. He now understood that his low feelings were linked to the loss of his mother whom he loved and deeply missed. This breakthrough in understanding enabled us to acknowledge and work on his grief. Over the next couple of months he reported in therapy that his low mood was resolving, there was evidence that he was re-engaged with his work, and he showed signs of a growing capacity to enjoy life again by reviving his social interests and relationships.

This case underlines the importance of attending to the intuitive. What comes from apparently nowhere can be astonishingly percipient. If I had been even more in tune with my intuitions we could have saved several sessions. A few weeks after we had completed therapy I reached for the volume of poetry containing the Hardy poem. Looking through the titles I remembered it was called 'The Voice'. I turned to the page and read the opening line: 'Woman much missed how you call to me, call to me'.

As well as individual causes I have also underlined the impact that the institution and social environment can have on mood. In an educational setting it is vital to be proactive. Welcome and orientation events for students and staff can enable the formation of social networks and provide a point of anchorage, especially for international students and staff. Institutional interventions, such as the provision of workshops on enhancing wellbeing, establishing peer counselling schemes and student mentoring systems, can contribute to the prevention of depression. Therapists can also provide staff with information and offer consultation to help them identify students with depression, refer appropriately, and support students during recovery. Sometimes the institution will have procedures or individual management practices that will contribute to the onset of depression. It is important that where necessary the counselling psychologist draws attention to any practices that may be detrimental to mental health.

Self-care for the practitioner

For the practitioner working with depression is demanding, and it is worth bearing in mind Nietzsche's (1990: 102) remark that '… when you gaze long into an abyss the abyss also gazes into you'. When working with depression, and in particular with deep depression, good supervision and self-care are essential. It is not enough to embark on self-care when we realise we are feeling exhausted and low ourselves: we have to be proactive and review our self-care regularly in order to be capable of sustaining effective practice.

Conclusion

In this section I have attempted to highlight the value of working with depression from a humanistic standpoint. The evidence from my practice experience has underlined its usefulness and led me to understand that the most sensitive therapeutic instrument that therapists possess is themselves. The emphasis on structured interventions – familiar to those of us who also work with CBT – can detach us from the wisdom of our feelings and intuition. These are immense therapeutic assets and we should strive to remain in touch with them.

Chapter Summary

This chapter has demonstrated the inextricable link between individual and context in relation to experiences of depression. Part 1 evidenced that historically the explanations used to frame such experiences are culturally contextualised; Part 2 indicated how the explanations used by a range of professionals to account for depression may influence how clients make sense of their experiences and the avenues they explore to overcome it; and Part 3 illustrated how within a university counselling service an account of depression was co-created within the therapeutic relationship of client and therapist, thereby enabling the client to find a more comfortable way of living. The reflection box below invites the reader to explore some of these relationships further.

REFLECTION BOX

1 Psychologist Graham Richards suggested of psychological experience that naming 'changes its entire psychological character'. What do you think of this statement with reference to experiences of depression?
2 What is your understanding of a biopsychosocial perspective on mental health?
3 Consider some of your own casework with a person described as depressed. What kinds of perceptions have your clients had about their state of 'depression'?
4 What kinds of associated presenting issues have you encountered with clients described as depressed?
5 Should depression be regarded as a medical disorder?
6 How might you develop a therapeutic relationship with a depressed person?

4

Exploring Trauma and Post Traumatic Stress

Introduction

The word 'trauma' conjures up powerful images of deep physical, psychological and societal injuries. Returning from active military service with multiple injuries following vehicle incidents, involvement in or witnessing major disasters, and suffering long-term abuse as a child are just a few examples. Individuals who have experienced or witnessed powerfully threatening events may be physically and/or emotionally wounded, with their previous assumptions about the predictability and safety of their world shattered.

American evidence suggests a lifetime prevalence of Post Traumatic Stress Disorder (PTSD) for 8 per cent of the population (NICE, 2005). The *Diagnostic and Statistical Manual of Mental Disorders-5* (APA, 2013a) proposes four distinct diagnostic clusters: re-experiencing, avoidance, negative cognitions and mood, and arousal. The trigger for PTSD is considered to be exposure to actual or threatened death, serious injury or sexual violation.

Individuals experiencing post traumatic stress may be referred to, and be seen in, a number of different contexts including, for example, the NHS, private health insurance companies, private practice via case management companies working for the insurance industry, or specialist military trauma services. While the language used in the above description is framed within a medical model, it would be a misnomer to see this as purely a guide to therapeutic intervention. As will become evident, such a model is contextualised within current social, legal, political and military contexts that have seen pressures on diagnostic categorisation include treatment access and insurance purposes.

Part 1: Exploring the Historical Context (Barbara Douglas)

PTSD is a recent term, one that has emerged from current contexts, however historical evidence of experiences that are currently so grouped is recounted in both military and non-military contexts.

Pre-twentieth-century military experiences

Exploring military arenas Steve Bentley (2005: 1) cites the Greek historian Herodotus writing on the Battle of Marathon in 490BC, where an Athenian soldier – witnessing at close hand the death of another soldier – went permanently blind although he was 'wounded in no part of his body'. Further military experiences also historically cited as evidence of a post traumatic response include seventeenth-century Swiss military discussions of the term 'nostalgia', the Spanish use of *estar roto* (to be broken), and a condition named 'soldiers' heart' during the American Civil War. In 1871 Jacob Da Costa published a paper describing several hundred cases of 'soldiers' heart' in which the men suffered from palpitations, heart pain, and digestive and respiratory problems. The condition became known as Da Costa's syndrome (Shephard, 2002).

Pre-twentieth-century civilian experiences

The personal consequences of civilian traumatic events have also been considered using the diaries of a number of famous people. In 1666 the Great Fire of London destroyed most of the city and Samuel Pepys recounted its personal consequences, noting in 1667 that 'it is strange to think how to this very day I cannot sleep a night without great terrors of fire; and this very night I could not sleep till almost two in the morning through thoughts of fire' (Pepys, 2003: 734).

Interest in the psychological consequences of what we term 'trauma' developed rapidly in the second half of the nineteenth century following the construction of the railways and the emergent systems of litigation that resulted from the disasters which occurred. To illustrate, Matus (2010: 410) cites the experiences of author Charles Dickens who, in 1865, when travelling to London, was involved in a train derailment in which many people were killed. Afterward he described times of overwhelming terror and his children reported that on trains he gripped his seat and appeared to be in a trance. He subsequently wrote 'I am not quite right within, but believe it to be an effect of the railway shaking'.

The term 'railway spine' became common parlance, its causes widely debated. These were considered to be of either organic causation (for example, by the English surgeon Erichsen, 1867) or a form of hysteria (for example, by the French neurologist Charcot, 1877). Evolving terms included 'Erichsen's disease', 'nervous shock', 'local hysteria', 'traumatic neurosis' and 'fright neurosis' (Shorter, 2005).

Shell shock

In 1914 British psychiatry's outlook remained one of tainted family heredity, with the increasing numbers of people detained in the asylums regarded as an indication of the degeneration of the nation and empire. The eugenics movement impacted on ideologies and treatment of the feebleminded, and perceptions of an increased incidence of hysteria and neurasthenia – largely considered to be conditions of women – were seen as further evidence of a weak-minded and degenerating population. However, as early as December 1914 there was evidence that 7 to10 per cent of all officers and 3 to 4 per cent of all men involved in trench warfare were experiencing mental breakdowns (Shephard, 2002). Such stark evidence could no longer support hereditarian beliefs in the degenerate and hysterical woman.

New ways of integrating breakdown into medical thinking were thus required and these first found voice in psychologist Charles Meyer's conceptually groundbreaking, if contentious, definition of the term 'shell shock'. Psychological damage, Meyer suggested, resulted from organic brain lesions caused by the new heavy and noisy artillery. Resulting treatments included both physical and psychodynamic psychiatric approaches in the forms of faradisation or psychoanalysis for men and officers, by Lewis Yealland and William Rivers respectively (Stone, 1985).

The term 'shell shock' was officially discredited in the *Report of the War Office Committee of Enquiry into 'Shell Shock'* (2004 [1922]). The numbers of ex-service patients detained in mental hospitals had increased from 2,506 in 1919 to 6,435 in 1922, and burgeoning war pensions were crippling the government. Hence broader terms such as 'neurosis' or 'war neurosis' for war-related psychological effects were favoured, as these could – along with other agendas – limit pension costs by acknowledging additional causative factors such as individual character and prior pathology (Barham, 2004).

World War Two

Determined that lessons should be learnt to ensure fewer psychological casualties in the future, by the Second World War the military emphasis was firmly on both training and screening, both of which had been woefully inadequate in World War One. Reflecting the positivist position of contemporaneous psychology, and drawing particularly from industrial psychology, personality and intelligence tests formed the majority of the screening process. There is a suggestion that there was some success in reducing the numbers of men discharged for psychiatric reasons and fewer war pensions being paid, although as Shephard (2002) points out, difficulties in obtaining accurate statistics and the meaning of what is available make these unreliable indicators.

Of those who were repatriated to Britain with psychiatric problems many were sent to the Northfield Hospital in Birmingham, requisitioned by the military in 1942. Here, analytic military psychiatrists – including Bion, Foulkes and Main amongst others –were developing the notion of the group as a powerful therapeutic agent. Treatment focused on the level of the community rather than the individual.

This was based on the premise that, just as in war where the individual was part of a unit, so within the hospital he was part of a community and would be exposed to group influence, facilitated by the psychiatrists (Shephard, 2002). These emerging group experiments, now famously termed the Northfield Experiments, also had a much broader and powerful impact on psychiatric thinking, becoming the foundations for the development of therapeutic communities.

The Vietnam War

Here it is useful to turn to the USA as the development of the term 'PTSD' largely evolved from the different politics and public perceptions of World War Two and the Vietnam War. The Veterans Administration (VA), established in 1930 to look after the needs of USA military veterans, increased its role and functions substantially following World War Two when American ground forces alone suffered 504,000 psychological casualties (Shephard, 2002). Public perception of these veterans as valued contributors defending the world against an evil supported such an expansion of facilities. Subsequent Vietnam veterans, however, were regarded less favourably: atrocities committed by American soldiers were being heavily publicised. As a result its veterans returned to a very different reception, were less than welcomed into the VA and received little help. A great deal of campaigning by their advocate group, Vietnam Veterans Against the War, then took place, supported by New York psychiatrist Chaim Shatan (1972). With a long-term interest in trauma, and as a supporter of the Vietnam veterans' needs, Shatan published a highly influential article in the *New York Times* on Post-Vietnam Syndrome that resulted in the establishment of outreach clinics.

Coinciding with developments in military, psychiatric and psychological fields, wider psychiatric classificatory systems were being fundamentally revised from a predominantly psychodynamically influenced framework to a descriptive system which grouped symptom clusters regardless of causation and theory. In relation to experiences of trauma the original *DSM* terminology of 'gross stress reaction' (1952) had given way to the more amorphous grouping of 'adjustment reaction to adult life' in *DSM-II* (1968), a move that was considered highly unsatisfactory. As a result of the epistemological shift and the campaigning touched on above, *DSM-III* (1980) introduced the term 'post traumatic stress disorder'. The main feature distinguishing this diagnosis from other classifications was that it recognised the sole criteria as external factors, although this has subsequently been the source of much further debate.

Post Traumatic Stress Disorder

With a defined terminology the field of trauma dramatically took off with the establishment of the International Society for Traumatic Stress Studies and publication of the *Journal of Traumatic Stress* (1985), as well as military recognition of the term 'PTSD' (1986). Burgeoning research turned to defining traumatic situations, understanding why individuals were variably vulnerable, examining the role of individual meaning making, establishing neural correlates of post traumatic stress, and translating these findings into therapeutic practice. Current theories of post traumatic stress emphasise neuropsychological explanations, in particular different forms of information processing and their translation into memories. There is the suggestion that we process and remember traumatic events via different pathways in the brain. The speed of a traumatic event, it is argued, means that it bypasses cognitive memory processes and is processed by an emotional brain pathway involving the evolutionary primitive limbic system and the amygdala. The subsequent ability to process this memory in context may then be cognitively unavailable to the individual, resulting in their repeatedly reliving the emotional and sensory content of the event.

Conclusion

This brief historical overview highlights how people past and present have tried to understand traumatic experiences. It is precisely the *experiences* that they highlight however and not the diagnostic category of PTSD. As this section has demonstrated this term is a recent construct and remains much debated (Brewin, 2003). It is a diagnostic term which more broadly evidences the power of psychiatric diagnosis to impact on and change social, legal and political cultures, including that of psychotherapy. Language not only reflects culture but also changes it.

This chapter now moves on to examine some of the current issues in working therapeutically with people who have experienced trauma.

Part 2: Exploring Dilemmas in Practice (Pam James)

What is the meaning of trauma and to whom? The dilemma of underlying models

Garland (2004) writes that the meaning of the word *trauma* in the Greek language is a wound, involving the piercing of the skin or breaking of the body envelope. Although describing a physical wound, she draws on Freud's (1920) metaphorical explanation of how the mind can also be pierced or wounded by events. Staying with a psychoanalytic perspective, Garland continues by saying that trauma can override established defensive organisations of the personality so that the person is then exposed to internal anxieties and external perceived threats. Nothing in the world seems safe anymore. There is also a mourning process whereby the traumatised person grieves the lost 'object' (relationship or person) and also grieves the loss of him/herself before the trauma. If this mourning task appears too great, then a person may identify with the lost object and enter a period of melancholia. In therapy, one of the questions posed is whether the elements of the traumatic event can be transformed into something manageable that can be processed mentally. Here, the therapist's capacity is to be a container, i.e. someone who can be present and stay with the distress.

Within psychotherapy, perspectives from cognitive theorists would use language more associated with a shift in core beliefs about the nature and safety of the environment following the trauma: for example, after a road accident where thinking becomes: 'driving in the car on the motorway is not safe and I will be involved in an accident'. This takes a complementary view to the metaphorical position of having a rupture in the protective mind shield. Descriptively, these are different theoretical perspectives and consequentially are associated with different treatments.

The meaning of a trauma event to the psychiatrist will involve whichever category of descriptive symptoms apply, and hence the resulting diagnosis and treatment. The available categories include complex trauma, trauma and post-traumatic stress disorder. It is the latter description with its ongoing symptoms that can have financial recompense in medico-legal settings. In this respect a dilemma or conflict can occur if the symptoms do not reach the criteria for this psychiatric diagnosis, and the client thinks differently. Furthermore, sometimes the client's pre-trauma difficulties become confabulated with the post trauma effects. The issue then is whether the trauma effects are associated with the trauma or just reactivated by it. The relationship between complex trauma and trauma may also create a dilemma if the therapist is unaware of the build-up of different pre-trauma events.

One particular client had a minor car accident after which she found it very hard to return to work. She had sustained no physical injury. She received a referral for therapy through her insurance. In the sessions that followed she gradually revealed that she had experienced a series of losses prior to this accident, none of which she had acknowledged. Her approach was to keep up with the demands on her life. She eventually disclosed the extent of her use of alcohol and her need to keep these ways of coping very secret. She took time to build trust in the therapeutic relationship as she was used to only showing 'the okay side' of her life.

The consequences of a diagnosis: the dilemma of ideographic or nomothetic, which therapeutic response to adopt and use of medication

Taking a personal history is an essential part of the therapy. Hence the need to listen very carefully to the person's experience and to accept that perhaps not all aspects will be immediately apparent. The range of the trauma event itself may be considerable, from fire, earthquake and tsunami, to a minor car accident. Another complexity could arise if the client had experienced an abusive childhood which in itself could be described as traumatic, then in later life had experienced rejection in a close relationship. The latter might appear to be manageable, but when seen in the context of the total life experience the initial abuse makes the process of therapy complex, but perhaps more able to explain the intensity of client feeling. The symptoms expressed may illustrate a borderline personality, whilst PTSD or complex trauma would perhaps be a more appropriate diagnosis.

Some of the symptoms of sleeplessness and hyper-alertness post trauma are particularly difficult and medication to assist with sleep is often prescribed by the GP. However, some sleeping pills (e.g. Zopiclone) can result in nightmares which are the side-effects of the medication itself (see British National Formulary, 2005: 177) rather than the effects of the trauma. Consequently, understanding that this may occur is important for both client and therapist. The traumatised person needs enough sleep to be able to cope, but also needs sufficient awareness of the mental space required to think about the effects of the trauma with the therapist.

The NICE Guidelines (2005) refer to Cognitive Behavioural Therapy (CBT) and Eye Movement Desensitising and Reprocessing (EMDR) as the recommended therapies. The therapist's task – or perhaps dilemma – is to hold the position reflecting the nomothetic and the ideographic position. The NICE Guidelines have arisen from an evidence base where such recommended therapies have produced good results: the casework would strongly suggest that each individual's *particular* perspectives affect recovery. The client may not think that previous events have any relevance to the current trauma, but it's only on the unfolding of their perceptions of life experience that the trauma event itself can begin to be understood. Facilitating the person to articulate and relive the trauma is part of therapy's task, whilst avoiding the possibility of re-traumatisation. Therapists' care and recommended practice anchor the person in the safety of the present, and respect the pace of their unfolding of events. From a neurological perspective, Allison and Rossouw (2013) have shown that building safety is a very significant factor in therapy. Dilemmas may arise if the primary caretaker has been experienced as damaging or unsafe.

What is being considered here is the nature of the created therapeutic space for the traumatised person. It is not about a comparison of which theoretical model to adopt. It is about considering what is included in that model that facilitates the holding space for the client to begin to think with their therapist about what has happened. Can repair occur to the damage to that psychic envelope (Garland, 2004: 11)? And if so is that repair durable?

In attempting to answer these questions, two case examples suggest that it depends. A middle-aged woman had lost her 4 year-old daughter in an accident twenty years previously. Although she had several episodes of different therapies, she grieved constantly for her and the loss had impacted on all subsequent attachments. She formed relationships, but always feared that they would end abruptly. She tried to protect herself from that separation by ending them herself. Therapy for her was a place to speak about her pain: she did not want that opportunity to end, she feared that she would then have nowhere to speak about her loss. It was almost as though the psychic rupture was so great it could not be repaired.

In another example, a woman in later middle age had a car accident in which she was trapped for several hours before being released by the rescue services. In therapy she said that she was coping by trying to put the accident out of her mind, yet her daily experience included strong feelings of panic and recurrent anxieties. Only after some time and the building of safety in the therapy room could she begin to talk about her recollections of the event. Much further on in therapy, she recollected other memories of being trapped in small spaces and looked at the personal meaning this had acquired. In parallel, was the realisation of nearness to death – a fact that she was more able to address than the panic over loss of control when trapped. In therapy which included both cognitive and dynamic elements she worked to repair the psychic envelope, finding that it was possible to understand and control her panic and anxiety.

The dilemma of the consequences of diagnosis: the concept of risk

The concept of risk to self and others must always be considered in therapeutic work. One of the dilemmas arising is that the extent of the upset from the trauma may be masked by the person's self-view that they *should* be coping, whilst another part of them is falling apart. Garland (2004) draws on the Freudian concept of a psychic patch placed over the rupture resulting from the trauma. This patch may present as the abuse of drugs and alcohol or even a psychotic episode, all of which may carry some risk of possible suicide whether intentionally or unintentionally. Risk of this nature may result from complex losses. Further examples include those who have been traumatised by certain types of police work or combat stress who find that their personal relationships become the arena for violent assault and/or the abuse of drugs including alcohol. Repeated exposure to death as in war or disaster recovery work can result in the risk of PTSD. The dilemma of appropriate debriefing as in critical incident work reflects the balance between talking through the event and the risk of re-traumatisation as discussed by Regal (2010).

Furthermore, therapists who repeatedly *listen* to trauma experiences may become traumatised vicariously. Research evidence takes different views about the extent of the negative effect of hearing clients' traumatic events. Dunkley and Whelan (2006) discuss related factors which include therapists' length of experience, personal trauma history and coping style.

Consequences of therapy: the dilemma of care or cure

People who are seeking a complete removal of their trauma memories will be disappointed, as therapy can reduce and remove symptoms but it cannot erase events that have happened. The hope for a cure is realistic and there is no particular dilemma here, once appropriate therapy has been accessed and worked through. A cure can mean different things for different people, not only the reduction and removal of symptoms, but also increased understanding and meaning about the event itself. Von Peter (2009) has suggested that those who work with trauma in eastern cultures (e.g. post tsunami) note that the western concept of recovery that is more focused around individual experience is not helpful in the east. Here, the emphasis is on collective mourning – the community defining and interpreting the traumatic experience, and the self being seen through agency, as in the rebuilding of towns and villages, coherence and subjectivity.

Tedeschi and Calhoun (1995) would suggest that clients who work through trauma may strengthen in adversity. This inner strength is more likely to be available when therapy has allowed an appreciation of vulnerability. It's almost as though a realisation of the likelihood of inevitable death can awaken the attention to life. Hence thinking about death and meaninglessness from an existential perspective may lead to post traumatic growth for some people.

The next part of the chapter looks at the research that underpins post trauma work and traces a hypothetical case which illustrates the stages of therapy in more detail.

Part 3: Exploring Research and Practice with Clients Experiencing Trauma and Post Trauma Stress (Tony Parnell)

Research studies

Trauma and specifically its post trauma consequence, as described in PTSD, emphasises blocks or difficulties in the individual's capacity to process memories and/or their experiencing of the trauma. A key treatment focus is to facilitate trauma processing. The National Institute for Health and Care Excellence (NICE, 2005) recommends Trauma-Focused Cognitive Behavioural Therapy (TF-CBT) and Eye Movement Desensitisation and Reprocessing (EMDR).

Other treatments have been developed to address the therapeutic aim of trauma processing. Foa et al. (2000) identified a number of effective therapies; Horowitz (1998) describes psychodynamic approaches; for a conditioning approach, see Kilpatrick et al. (1985); for schema-based approaches, Janoff-Bulman (1985); for bodywork approaches, Rothschild (2000); and behavioural approaches, Fairbank and Brown (1987).

Iverson et al. (2011) identified various CBT therapies for PTSD that have been systematically researched. These are: EMDR, Shapiro (1995); Stress Inoculation Training (SIT), Meichenbaum (1974) and Kilpatrick et al. (1982); exposure therapy, Foa et al. (2007); and Cognitive Therapy, Beck (1976), Ehlers and Clark (2000), Ehlers et al. (2003) and Tarrier et al. (1999).

Applying the research to practice

This part of the chapter depicts a client's experience which illustrates key concepts in theory, research and practice. Particular focus is given to the nature and structure of the client-therapist relationship with respect to the specific nature and presentation of trauma and post trauma distress. The therapy takes an integrative approach to TF-CBT and centrally the application of Cognitive Therapy for PTSD. The client's individual characteristics will be explored, and how these may influence the process of therapy and the therapeutic relationship. Research indicates that a central factor in the development of PTSD is the client's experiential process – specifically the degree of importance that a particular perception is held over the manner in which a traumatic event is experienced (Ozer et al., 2003). These factors are central to the collaborative formulation and treatment process.

Treatment aims for PTSD

Ehlers and Clark (2000: 335) proposed a cognitive model as follows:

- The trauma memory needs to be elaborated and integrated into the context of the individual's preceding and subsequent experience in order to reduce intrusive re-experiencing.
- Problematic appraisals of the trauma and/or its sequelae that maintain the sense of current threat need to be modified.
- Dysfunctional behavioural and cognitive strategies that prevent memory elaboration, exacerbate symptoms or hinder the reassessment of problematic appraisals need to be dropped.

A central issue here is the sense of 'current threat' that exists within the individual post trauma. Krans et al. (2009: 1079) proposed that 'The sense of current threat exists due to a lack of chronological context in trauma memory so that the threat in the past is not distinguished from the present situation'.

Reflecting on the hypothetical case below, the process of cognitive therapy for PTSD will be explored from a practice application perspective.

Bill's experience: a case study

Pre trauma

Bill was a 30 year-old engineer who had worked within both a factory and construction site environment. He described himself as capable with an ability to overcome difficulties and thrived on challenge. His sense of his capacity to 'adapt and overcome' was a central theme in his sense of self-identity.

Trauma incident

A supervisor had told Bill that he had to meet a deadline for a rush order. He had felt under pressure to complete the machining job. The machine he was working on had been having problems for a couple of days. The safety guard had been sticking: he had reported this, however it had not been repaired. While completing the job his arm was pulled into the machine. His hand and forearm were caught in the moving parts as the faulty safety guard had come down on his arm and trapped it. He shouted for help and a co-worker hit the emergency stop button on the machine.

Bill was wearing gloves and when he took his hand out of the machine the glove, although damaged, was still on his hand. He could not look at the injuries and felt certain he was going to die from the high loss of blood from the wounds. An ambulance was called and he was taken to hospital. The journey was described as 'very distressing' and he was 'in great pain', even though he was medicated. He was 'convinced' he was going to die.

Following admission to Accident and Emergency he had an operation to repair his broken arm and remove two of his badly damaged fingers. He then went on to have a further two operations to repair and reconstruct his hand and arm.

Post trauma/assessment

Bill reported a range of issues at assessment, including:

- spontaneous intrusive imagery relating to the index incident;
- pain-related symptoms;
- hyper-vigilance;
- severe sleep disturbance;
- recurrent dreams (nightmares relating to the index incident);
- situational triggers of anxiety (noise, smells etc.);
- phobic responses (ambulance vehicles and sirens);
- memory and concentration problems;
- irritability issues;
- reduced social activity/detachment from others;
- depressive symptoms.

Proposed treatment

Bill had been assessed by a psychiatrist and met the criteria for PTSD as defined by *DSM-IV-TR* (APA, 2000). It was proposed that 12 sessions of TF-CBT be offered. EMDR was not proposed as dissociation was identified within the assessment.

Assessment

Key aims for the assessment interview are the identification of cognitive themes, the nature of predominant emotions, client problematic appraisals, client problematic behavioural and cognitive strategies, the nature of the trauma memory and spontaneous intrusions (Ehlers and Clark, 2000). Bill was assessed by a psychiatrist as part of his employer's health insurance process: a diagnostic interview structure and range of measures were used. Subsequently, Bill was referred to a psychologist for the commencement of therapy.

The overview of the Cognitive Therapy for PTSD Treatment Plan was as follows (not all of these may be required):

1   Rationale for treatment (psycho-education, discussion/explanation).
2   Reclaiming life work.
3   Memory processing (reliving and/or narrative).
4   Cognitive restructuring (in/out of reliving).
5   Identification of triggers of intrusive memories/emotions (hotspots).
6   In-vivo exposure.

1. Therapy process: formulation/normalisation

Within the first and second sessions a focus was held on formulation and normalisation. This is essential in setting the scene for starting trauma-focused therapy. Central to this process is the development of the client/therapist relationship where emphasis is given to the establishment of trust and creating a sense of safety. The introduction of the aim of revisiting and engagement with the trauma directly is explored and a rationale offered. Discussion of the client's fears and concerns are facilitated and this process offers an opportunity for the client to be understood and begin the process of developing confidence in both the therapist and the process. Fear of re-experiencing the trauma is a common response and coping strategies of avoidance and active disconnection from the trauma are often employed. Client ownership and commitment to the process are important and an individualised formulation and treatment is constructed. Ehlers et al. (2005) identified that discussion and the identification of relevant appraisals – the memory characteristics, triggers and behavioural and cognitive strategies which maintain the PTSD – are central to the development of this individualised therapy.

Normalisation, through psycho-education and discussion, is included at this early stage in the therapy relationship (Talbot et al., 1998). Psycho-education can offer a great deal of relief to clients. Appraisals which cause on-going disturbance can be assisted by information being provided about psychological, medical, physical and institutional processes and procedures. Clarification of the nature of trauma and its effects can enable clients to understand previously unexplainable experiences. Bill had a severe emotional response to intrusive imagery following hearing a specific piece of music. He evaluated this as further evidence of his 'loss of control' and that he was 'going mad'. Discussion of physiological processes and the nature of heightened sensation within a traumatic situation offered some normalisation. He identified that the music that triggered his response was on the radio at the time of the incident. This information, together with the psycho-education of heightened sensory and emotional responding within trauma experience, was key to Bill's ability to re-evaluate his initial response. It is important to note that identifying particular sensory responses and triggers to intrusions and flashbacks enables specific grounding and anchoring techniques to be utilised by clients to promote a sense of control (Kennerley, 1996). These techniques can be initiated from the start of therapy and promote the belief and practical experience that clients can both influence and have a positive impact on their issues.

2. Reclaiming life work

A frequent response is that of being 'stuck' at the time of the trauma. The dominance of the traumatic experience on day-to-day functioning can often detract from previously valued behaviours and activities. Bill reported a sense of self-imposed social isolation due to a desire not to engage in conversation about his accident, injuries and recovery. These conversations enhanced his thoughts and his focus on the trauma: he felt they increased his intrusive thoughts and responses. Helping clients reclaim elements of their former functioning can enhance their sense of normality and provide an increased ability to positively influence their situation. The identification of problematic beliefs, which could negatively impact on the client's ability to enact reclaiming activities, is vital at this point in the therapy process.

3. Memory processing (reliving and/or narrative) and 4. Cognitive restructuring

Central to the aims of a cognitive therapy approach for the treatment of PTSD is the process of imaginal reliving: a key feature of PTSD is the experience of intrusive memories. Expressions of such memories can occur from any of the sensory modalities (smell, taste, touch, hearing, vision), with visual imagery often reported as a primary source (Hackmann et al., 2004). Imaginal reliving has three key functions:

1 It promotes the contextualisation and elaboration of the trauma memory.
2 It holds a focus on the identification of 'hotspots' promoting understanding of the idiosyncratic appraisals of the trauma.
3 It acts as a powerful behavioural experiment to test the client's belief that engaging in thinking about the trauma in detail will cause negative consequences (Ehlers and Clark, 2000).

Regarding reliving, Bill stated his fear of 'opening a can of worms' that he would not be able to control. Vincent (2004, in Shearing et al., 2011) has identified anticipatory anxiety, the re-activation of suppressed memories and re-experiencing associated emotions as key concerns offered by research participants who had undertaken CBT for PTSD.

I asked Bill to identify a 'safe place' – a time or a place where he had felt safe, secure and relaxed. This could be an imaginary or actual memory of a place he had experienced. Key aspects of this 'safe place' are that it has the potential to illicit safety and security. I recorded his safe place description, and offered it as an option if Bill was feeling too overwhelmed by the process. If this were to occur I would stop the revisiting process and recount the description of the safe place, with the intention of reducing his raised anxiety and grounding him. Throughout the process Bill did not use the safe place option.

I restated the process of reliving and invited Bill to adopt a comfortable position in the chair and to close his eyes. Although closed eyes are not essential, sensory response is heightened and the potential for distraction reduced. I invited him to bring to mind and recount the trauma, while holding in focus what he was experiencing. Key emotions, thoughts and feelings were to be noted. I proposed that he should speak in the first person/present tense and describe the events in as much detail as possible, combining sensory and cognitive information. I enhanced this process by asking questions to initiate a focus on sensory and cognitive processes related to his description (Grey et al., 2002). This holds a focus on exposure to the fear experienced during the pre, peri and post trauma events. Ehlers and Clark (2000: 338) proposed that the initial process of reliving 'usually involves the whole event, starting just before the event and continuing until patients knew they were safe'. I used an adapted version of this approach. I had agreed with Bill, before beginning the reliving, that we would start at a point prior to the event and stop just before the trauma occurred. This was in response to his excessive fear of triggering an uncontrolled activation of overwhelming emotions. My rationale for this adapted approach was to enable the process of reliving and the containment of holding to pre-agreed boundaries, while gaining the advantage of accessing and clarifying some aspects of the trauma memory from a 'safer' position. This also acts as a powerful behavioural experiment in line with the third function of imaginal reliving. The process was to be repeated within the session and gaps in memory and 'hotspot' moments would also be identified. Bill went through his recollection of the events, repeating the process four times within the first reliving session. The number of repetitions will be variable and will depend on the amount of information offered and the extent of the cognitive restructuring and re-appraisal work undertaken.

Following each recounting of the reliving, Bill and I discussed problematic thoughts and beliefs associated with key points within the trauma and integrated the re-appraisals and understanding into the next recounting. Cognitive restructuring was offered as well as a re-evaluation and re-appraisal of his belief that 'all' of the trauma was 'out of his control'. He had identified where he had control and had exercised this pre-trauma, and he was able to restructure his appraisal that 'all' of the experience was out of his control. He had also experienced talking about aspects of the traumatic event directly and had not experienced his projected negative consequences. Our discussion confirmed his confidence in the process and his ability to work directly with the memories in a contained manner. The adapted approach had enhanced trust in the therapeutic relationship and the anxiety generated by the thought of discussing the point of the trauma was reduced.

For three weeks, each weekly 90-minute reliving session was characterised by a repetitive recounting process which was enhanced by cognitive restructuring and integration of the re-appraisals. The use of Socratic questioning and systematic discussion of evidence for and against the appraisals were the methods employed.

5. Identification of triggers of intrusive memories/emotions (hotspots)

Gaps in memory were addressed: the process of holding connections with emotions and thoughts, and the integration of hotspots (Grey and Holmes, 2008), were central to the process. Bill had identified five hotspots relating to fear, helplessness and shame. Briere and Scott (2006: 115) have identified that 'client descriptions of past traumatic events often become more detailed, organised, and causally structured as they are repeatedly discussed and explored in therapy'.

The sessions were recorded and offered to Bill to listen to between sessions. He did not want to do this, as he had felt safer engaging with the trauma material within the containment and safety of the therapy environment. The process of listening to the reliving sessions outside of the therapy room can be beneficial to clients and is offered as an option (Grey et al., 2002). Bill's choice not to engage with the recorded sessions did not present an ethical issue, as the use of recorded material outside of the sessions has a function of de-sensitising the client to the trauma material. This would not be effective if the client felt overly anxious and less controlled outside of the session.

A narrative approach can also be employed to elaborate trauma memory by writing a detailed account of the event (Blanchard et al., 2003). This approach is useful when the chronology of events is uncertain. The use of diagrams and visual representations can be helpful in reconstructing events and may also be useful for clients who dissociate when verbally recounting the trauma (Ehlers et al., 2010). Wild (2009) has identified the specific issue of client loss of consciousness within a trauma with resulting gaps in memory. She proposes the construction of a written narrative which may assist in organising the event memory into a sequence and identifying gaps, thus facilitating discussion and a re-evaluation.

6. In vivo exposure

Wilson et al. (2001: 170) identified that prior to *in vivo* exposure the therapist should offer a clear rationale and explain the procedures involved. They also went on to state that 'prolonged and repeated confrontation (i.e. *in vivo* exposure) with situations that are anxiety provoking but not objectively dangerous results in reduction of anxiety'.

Zayfert and Black-Becker (2007: 45) identified that the development of a strong therapeutic relationship was central to the effective practice of cognitive therapy for PTSD. Time taken in psycho-education/normalisation can greatly enhance the development of trust and the client's openness to engagement. A clear explanation of the process and the potential for an initial increase in symptoms with exposure to the trauma is essential, forming the basis of transparency within the therapeutic relationship. Discussing strategies to counteract the sense of loss of control that characterises the client's experience of PTSD is important.

Bill's intense fear of engaging with his traumatic experience was mediated by offering time and explanation of the therapy process. The focus on relationship building enabled him to fully engage. His reported outcome of therapy was characterised by an increase in the intensity of emotional responding during the reliving phase, moving to a gradual but significant reduction in his presenting symptoms. He reported his perception of the trauma had shifted, that he had been able to re-structure his view of the events and his response to them. His presenting symptoms had subsided and he reported a greater sense of control as he adapted to his altered physical capacity.

Although Lee (2009: 235) describes a goal of compassion-focused cognitive therapy, there is relevance for clients and therapists working with post trauma stress: 'One of the fundamental stages of the therapy is to develop the client's deep empathy for the non-intentionality of their difficulties and acts, and the understanding that their struggles, problems and traumatic experiences are not their fault'. The issue of 'non-intentionality' reflects the neuro-biological response system, which produces an unconscious behavioural and emotional reaction in the traumatised individual.

Chapter Summary

Each part of this chapter has explored various aspects of trauma. However, one common thread in particular is woven throughout. Historically embedded, this concerns the importance of meaning – both culturally and to the individual. The therapist's stance, which includes hearing and staying with the individual's particular traumatic experiences both past and current, is a central aspect of evidenced practice. This relational interaction sustains and enables clients to begin to make sense of their shattered personal world.

Think about the chapter's tapestry, woven from historical, theoretical, research and practice perspectives, and consider the reflective questions that follow.

REFLECTION BOX

1 Why might each of versions 1–5 of the *DSM* have incorporated notions of trauma differently?
2 What do you think might be some of the influences on the current high visibility within psychological services of PTSD?
3 When you hear from a client about their recent trauma, what kinds of signals might you perceive that indicate this trauma could be preceded by other traumatic events?
4 How might you answer a client who asks if he or she will recover from their trauma experience?
5 To what extent have you been aware of individual clients' characteristics when processing their traumas?
6 What are your reflections on possible client resistance when meeting the reliving stage of trauma processing?

5

Exploring Psychosis

Introduction

Psychosis has been described as follows:

> A group of severe mental health disorders characterised by the presence of delusions and hallucinations that disrupt a person's perception, thoughts, emotions and behaviour. The main forms of psychosis are schizophrenia (including schizoaffective disorder, schizophreniform disorder and delusional disorder), bipolar disorder or other affective psychosis. (NICE, 2011b: 4)

This description indicates that the term refers not to a single, definable condition but rather to groups of experiences that may be considered out of the ordinary range of human experience. So how have we arrived at a position where there exists a label for groups of experiences which may be very different, have largely unknown causes, progressions and outcomes, but are all characterised by delusions and hallucinations? To examine this question, the next section will consider how the medicalisation of madness during the nineteenth century saw the emergence of the term 'psychosis'. Part 2 will then look at some current dilemmas in working therapeutically with people struggling with such experiences. Finally, Part 3 explores approaches to working with clients experiencing psychotic symptoms, illustrated with particular reference to a phenomenological relational therapeutic stance (PRTS). The reader will note that while bipolar disorder is included within the group of psychoses in classificatory systems, this book includes a separate chapter on exploring bipolar. The rationale for this is to enable the current chapter to focus on the broader notions of psychosis while facilitating a more in-depth discussion of one of the psychoses (i.e. bipolar in Chapter 6).

Part 1: Exploring the Historical Context (Barbara Douglas)

Michel Foucault (1988) argued that each historical period has its own discourse which both produces and confirms the period's perception of unreason. Early conceptualisations include human struggles being externally driven, by various gods and demons, which Porter (2002) illustrates with reference to the early Greek *Iliad* (around 800BC) as having no word for person, and by association, no internal sense of a self that could be troubled. By contrast he argued that the later Hippocratic Corpus (approximately 400BC) evidenced the evolution of a very different conceptualisation of unreason, one of brain disease within a framework of humoral medicine.

The arrival of Christianity to the Roman Empire introduced further conceptual shifts, with existing humoral views increasingly incorporating religious frameworks whereby what we might frame as psychosis was conceived as evidence that tortured souls were battling possession by the devil. Understandably then a fear developed of people considered to be witches and who had the power to spread evil (by inducing illness for example). Cultural responses included seeking out and destroying such people, acceptance of the religious and astrological doctor (e.g. Richard Napier, 1559–1634), and the performance of ritual acts, such as confession, mass and exorcism, to rid folk of these inflictions.

Foucault's argument that madness only emerged as a separately identified construct of unreason requiring social control, classification and observation around the seventeenth century is premised on the developing scientific revolution that took place during the Enlightenment. With its emphasis on scientific method rather than belief as the favoured means of understanding, this period saw the emergence of medicalised views of madness that attempted to understand and classify such experiences and behaviours. The discovery of the network of nerves in the body, for example, led the influential Scottish physician William Cullen (1710–1790) to the conclusion that disruption to the association of ideas was caused by excessive irritation of the nerves (neurosis) and might result in madness, or other illnesses such as diabetes or tetanus depending on the location of the irritation.

Influenced by this notion of neurosis, the Austrian physician von Fuchtersleben (2007 [1846]: 246) introduced the term 'psychosis':

Where psychic phenomena present themselves abnormally we speak of mental illness: it is rooted in the mind and insofar as these phenomena are transmitted through the brain, they are rooted in the body because the brain is the organ of the mind … Every psychosis (disorder of the psyche) is at the same time a neurosis (disorder of the brain), because without the mediation of the nervous system no mental change is able to become manifest but every neurosis is not simultaneously a psychosis.

This evolving medical paradigm surrounding psychosis developed into two quite distinct positions during nineteenth-century psychiatry, defined by German and French psychiatry respectively. The first was a unitary psychosis theory that was developed by various German psychiatrists proposing that only one form of mental illness existed which had varying manifestations depending on individual and environmental factors. The second position, dominated by French psychiatrists and influenced by faculty psychology, considered that psychosis affected different faculties (intellectual, emotional or volitional) and therefore different forms existed (Berrios, 1996).

Fundamental challenge to these positions came with the German psychiatrist Emil Kraepelin (2011 [1904]). Psychiatric classification, Kraepelin argued, could not be undertaken as it had been on the basis of symptoms or behaviours at a given point in time. The same symptoms may be a manifestation of different disease processes and so longitudinal research, based on a model of aetiology and disease process, was the method needed to understand the different manifestations and hence appropriate classifications. Through extensive research with patients across continents, he influentially proposed the existence of two axes of mental illness, referred to as dementia praecox and manic-depressive insanity.

Further weight was given to this emphasis on disease process by the discovery in 1917 of malarial treatment for the previously devastating, and terminal, psychiatric condition known as general paralysis of the insane (GPI), caused by syphilis entering the brain. If syphilitic spirochetes could invade the brain then, it was argued, other psychotic experiences were also likely to have underlying biological causes. Hence, Joel Braslow (1997) argued, the body became the site of twentieth-century psychiatric therapeutics through the treatments for malarial fever therapy, hydrotherapy, prolonged sleep therapy, and later, insulin, cardiazol and electric shock therapies.

This biological perspective subsequently also spearheaded attempts to find an effective drug treatment for patients undergoing psychotic episodes. Although drugs, such as bromides and other sedatives, had previously been available, chlorpromazine, launched in 1952, was the first antipsychotic (neuroleptic) to actively work on the brain's receptor system. It is often suggested that the discovery of these antipsychotics released patients from a lifetime's incarceration on long-stay mental hospital wards. Yet while scientific evidence behind use of antipsychotics appears to indicate their qualified usefulness for many patients in reducing some symptoms of psychosis, such as hallucinations and delusions, it is also evident that with their debilitating effects such as co-ordination and movement problems and blunting of affect, there are often distressing effects for patients in taking these drugs. Additionally, around 30 per cent of patients never respond to these drugs regardless of the dose level (Bentall, 2009). So while drugs may play an important part in easing the distress experienced by some patients, their serious limitations have played a part in more recent explorations of effective psychological interventions.

Alongside the biological emphasis in psychoses discussed above was another strand of psychiatric understanding. Dynamic psychiatry, fundamentally influenced by Freud, conceptualised the individual's difficulties as the manifestations of internal struggles between various parts of a dynamic psychic structure. Within this framework the function of psychosis, Leader (2011) argues, was not one of illness but fundamentally restorative: a means of creating meaning in a ruptured psyche. Within such a dimensional framework evolved the possibility of integrating Kraepelin's two separate categorical psychoses and so the notion of schizoaffective disorder was born. Named by analytic psychiatrist Jacob Kasanin (1933), this blended condition was, he suggested, largely caused by emotional conflicts that could be treated by psychoanalysis.

A range of theoretical schools developed within a psychodynamic tradition, and in addition to intrapsychic models, others considered how the individual psyche was mirrored within, and related to, social systems such as the family. This emphasis can be seen in a 1950s and 60s' systemic turn, in which families were sometimes held to be central to individual problems. The psychotic person was considered to be the individual identified within the family to carry the family problems. These problems were, it was argued, communicated via latent messages behind manifest communications. Psychotic episodes were regarded as being the result of such mixed messages (sometimes termed a double bind) in which the individual could find no understanding or resolution (Leader, 2011). Therapeutic communities, also furthered by the developing anti-psychiatry movement of the 1960s, were conceived as psychologically health-promoting places where individuals could stay while working through such difficulties. Such a framework highlights one origin of the notion of personal journey which is inherent in current recovery approaches to psychosis (Davidson et al., 2010).

Current recovery models promote a view that psychological therapies may be helpful in assisting clients to find more comfortable ways of being. Such approaches, supported by recent research, suggest that hallucinations and delusions may be considered as communication, attribution and reasoning problems where, for example, the individual may attribute voices and/or negative beliefs to external rather than internal sources (Bentall, 2011). Recovery models are discussed further in Part 3 below.

Conclusion

Historical evidence demonstrates that the current term 'psychosis' and its classification within a medical model are relatively recent and represent a specific cultural framework for understanding human experience. Leader (2011) indicates that whatever framework is adopted a dogmatic adherence to a hierarchical expert stance by therapists is unhelpful, and the next two parts of this chapter examine current practice, discussing its dilemmas and illustrating how collaborative and client-centred practice may look in action.

Part 2: Exploring Dilemmas in Practice (Pam James)

What does psychosis mean and to whom? The dilemma of underlying models

While anxiety and depression are words that are used in our everyday language, psychosis is more particular. Amongst mental health professionals the most commonly held understanding is that a person who is described as psychotic has lost touch with the reality of current time and space. They are sometimes also confused about who they are, so identity is also relevant.

The nature of the dilemma here in relation to underlying models lies both between psychology and psychiatry, and within each of these. Within psychiatry these focus around descriptions of symptoms that may accord with more than one diagnostic category, and also with whether the perspective is more biological or psycho-social or an interaction of both of these. Whilst for psychology the dilemmas also reflect some or all of the associated causal factors, whether individual and/or social, this consequently will influences the choice of subsequent treatment model.

Psychiatric descriptors for psychosis are found in the current iteration of the *DSM* for schizophrenia and bipolar disorder. However, for some people a psychotic episode may occur that is associated with neither of these diagnoses. The emergence of a dilemma is possible here, as the person experiencing the psychotic symptoms may or may not eventually receive a diagnosis. Their anticipation is reflected to some extent in the associated professional, most usually a psychiatrist, who is initially unclear how the psychotic state will develop. There could be uncertainty and fear about the development of a long-term condition which may then need to be controlled by medication, most probably for the future.

Hence one of the dilemmas associated with psychosis is its lack of diagnostic clarity. It may be that the early psychosis experienced by the person is not developing into schizophrenia: those who work in the early intervention services will be mindful of this issue and will closely monitor someone in this state. Galeazzi et al. (2006) write about how the conceptions of the professional working with potentially psychotic clients can affect the treatment that might be offered in the pre-psychotic state.

An explanation of psychotic states may have a bio-psychosocial origin, although as Agid et al. (1999) point out, the interaction of development and genetic predisposition with client-perceived social triggers seems hard to disentangle. Observations from the psychological perspective inter-relate with those in psychiatry: the psychotic state itself can be so alarming to the relatives of the person concerned, that they will usually seek medical help and often a period of hospitalisation will be involved. Understanding the situation that has brought about the psychotic symptoms is vital here as only then can the person's reactions be understood. Again, it would seem to be essential to attempt to establish how the current circumstances are perceived by the person themselves, yet one of the dilemmas is that the person is not able to explain what is concerning them due to their temporary loss of current reality. This may render the person silent, angry and withdrawn, very irritable and non-responsive: dissociative states are also relevant here as discussed by Kilcommons and Morrison (2005).

Consequences of a diagnosis: the dilemma of ideographic or nomothetic

The presenting symptoms and underlying experience of each person will be different. Forming or not forming a diagnosis can occur in the early stages of the presenting psychotic symptoms. If these include the threat of violence to another or the physical safety of the person then a response that results in safe containment must follow. However, not all psychotic symptoms can present so acutely.

Consider the experience of a young woman who is approaching important examinations where the successful results will bring about life changes. As the studying intensifies the person begins to sit for long periods of time staring at the wall. She eventually goes out for a long walk but doesn't return, and when she is eventually found she is incoherent and thinks that she is being pursued by strangers. After a few days at home and a visit to the doctor with her concerned parent, she is silent and withdrawn. One morning she is found having overdosed on paracetamol. After hospital accident and emergency treatment and a short interview with the on-call psychiatrist she returns home with anti-depressant prescription. She is determined to continue to study, but now will not take the breaks for meals and sleep. This time she insists that she is being followed when she goes out and wants to get in touch with tutors during night hours. She becomes irrational about taking rest and breaks from study and thinks that the neighbours are watching her. She begins to turn her room into a chaotic mess and refuses to let anyone in. Eventually her concerned parent contacts the psychiatric services, and although a voluntary admission is sought, this is resisted by the young person and she is eventually sectioned for her own safety.

It's almost as though in that inner world the person is telling others to keep out. Extreme perceived shame can be a precursor to a psychotic episode, but anything that progressively or suddenly erodes the perceived self-esteem can provide a trigger. In the writer's experience, this is particularly evident in situations where young people are trying to establish an identity, either in sexual relations or employment. When the person's sense of self is under extreme demands, they may show increased hostility towards others and themselves. The amount of fear that is created for the person experiencing these feelings and thoughts is so excessive that it then creates a further stressor and adds to their confused state. The psychotic episode may represent an extreme defence mechanism that unconsciously functions to protect the person from pain and distress which in themselves would be very damaging. Perry (1993) has proposed a taxonomy where psychotic defences are seen as the least adaptive. Working closely with psychiatric services is essential at this time, as the person's safety may be at risk. They may also need medication to help them to sleep: sometimes sufficient stress reduction can alleviate a psychotic state.

Many dilemmas will arise at this time including the decision to begin anti-psychotic medication. Also, will the person be able to reflect on their own experience so that therapy may bring some understanding? It would seem that the circumstances that precipitated the psychotic state initially are some indication of how difficult the person found it to talk about their situation. In the case mentioned above, the fear and shame associated with impending failure on the one hand and possible success that would involve leaving home to go to college on the other, produced a conflict that seemed inescapable. It was only when this was unpacked in therapy several months later that any understanding came about. In this person's case there was no development into schizophrenia. The psychotic episode was contained by family support and postponing the demands of studying. Salokangas and McGlashan (2008) point out that the prevention of the development of a psychosis may occur with appropriate support.

For some people containment in a safe place (i.e. an acute ward in a psychiatric unit) may be sufficient to allow them to reduce the perceived fear and stress which in themselves will contribute to a return to stability and a non-psychotic state. However, as Tarrier et al. (2007) highlight there may be some stigma post-containment.

If the symptoms alone are seen as the precursors to diagnosis, a person may be given a particular diagnosis, and subsequent medication, only to find that in a few months' time that diagnosis is re-thought, and another one follows. Anecdotal evidence reports the extreme frustration experienced by people with this set of confusing events. Their relatives are often frightened as they are unclear as to what is happening to the person in the family. A resulting dilemma can be that the psychiatric help that was so necessary when the person became psychotic and may have been violent may now be resented. The relatives and the psychotic person are thus held in a power-related relationship with psychiatric services from which they can see no release.

Dilemmas of this kind can be brought about by responding to the person in a way that sees their symptoms and behaviours in the system of the family rather than appreciating the person as an individual who is both separate and alone. This requires individual attention for the person and their family and care in the multidisciplinary team. The work of the Early Intervention Service is indicative here (see Harris et al., 2012, for service users' views): psychologists, psychiatrists, and sometimes social services can work together to rehabilitate the individual. Those who are not able to take up the advantages of this type of care may struggle in the community and have their symptoms controlled by medication.

The consequences of diagnosis: the dilemma of which therapeutic response to adopt, use of medication and the concept of risk

Once an appreciation has been given to underlying associated factors and possibly the introduction of a diagnosis, and if psychological therapy is available, it is usual to work in conjunction with the mental health team. This gives an opportunity for the containment of symptoms using medication, and also some time to think about what has precipitated such an extreme and often frightening reaction.

Renwick et al. (2009) examined the interaction between symptoms and the subjective appraisal of stress. A dilemma can result regarding the extent of mental health service support. People who require medication may continue with the help of the psychiatric services. Those people who manage their symptoms without medication using a stress model may find less service support available in the longer term.

Casework suggests that clients' ability to reflect in therapy on what has happened is very varied. Some can speak more openly than others about their perceptions of the triggers and stressors. Others may be overwhelmed with shame, fear, denial and embarrassment: these feelings may have been part of the factors that precipitated the psychotic episode. Relatives can also be very frightened of psychotic behaviour, and their responses can further stress the client. Medication can be held onto as a defence against the fear of what will happen should this attachment change. Refusal of medication, possibly in an effort to rebel against the perceived dominant and controlling relationship with professionals or family, may also occur. The role of medication or its adjustment requires careful monitoring by the multi-disciplinary team.

Consequences of therapy: the dilemma of care or cure

Perceived underlying models of explanation of the effect of stressors can be related to the dilemma of care or cure. Clients who are able to appreciate that perceived stressors can precipitate psychotic symptoms can begin to take some control over these. This control can only be utilised when awareness has been achieved, often in therapy. There can be a resistance to utilise such awareness as more biologically-based explanations can be put forward in an exclusive manner: these may refer to deficiencies in brain chemistry and seem mysterious and out of the client's control. Disagreeing with a psychiatrist who prescribes a medication that has been so necessary to remove the frightening states of the psychotic world is apparently for some clients too frightening to entertain. The need for psychiatrists and psychologists to work together is essential here to address the possible dilemma resulting in split relationships.

Part 3: Exploring Research and Practice with Clients Experiencing Psychosis (Hamilton Fairfax)

Introduction

> Clients come into NHS psychological therapy for psychosis with the 'ticket' of distress related to psychosis. However, our analysis suggested that the experience of psychosis was not the sole focus of the client or therapists' concern in therapy. Rather, both appeared to be prioritising the client's functioning in the world. (Dilks et al., 2010: 94)

The concept of psychosis is perhaps one of the most widely known and researched terms in psychiatric publications, yet it is also one of the most controversial, associated with some of the most negative and shameful periods of professional practice. Attempts to understand and respond to psychotic phenomena have resulted in extreme forms of surgical interventions, severe medication regimes, life-long incarcerations, dehumanising treatment and social alienation. The popularisation of such experiences by the media, together with the otherworldliness of psychotic presentation, have resulted in suspicion and fear amongst the general public, and the psychiatric and psychological professions (Roe et al., 2004; Nixon et al., 2010). Psychosis is sometimes regarded as a life-long condition with a poor prognosis and little chance of recovery (Carpenter, 2002). Feelings of difference, shame and stigma are also expressed by clients themselves (Dinos et al., 2004).

However, there is also much to be positive about. Research indicates that a significant number of people diagnosed with schizophrenia improve and/or recover over time (Ram et al., 1992; Hopper et al., 2007). Other research has highlighted positive consequences of psychosis: for example, Perry (2005) has commented on how a psychotic experience for some clients enabled underlying issues to be resolved. Psychotic episodes have also been described as states of 'transition', resulting in personal growth and transformation (Bassman, 2007). Far from being a long-term and irresolvable condition, there is good evidence that presentations described as psychotic are amenable to change, and may in themselves provide an opportunity for fundamental growth through addressing underlying difficulties.

Although there is a longstanding debate and considerable tension regarding the term 'psychosis' there is also increasing understanding of the emergence of psychotic symptoms in the wider social context and greater emphasis on the client's authority in the course and direction of treatment. Recent developments in psychosocial and experiential theories place psychosis within the range of all human experience. Research from service user groups, together with clinical evidence, has challenged the traditional view, calling for a more integrated and holistic approach that is informed by the personhood and individual needs of clients (Roberts et al., 2006). Psychosis is not something alien to be studied with suspicion or fear, but an expression that can be understood and helped where necessary.

Recent research points to a Phenomenological Relational Therapeutic Stance (PRTS) that is familiar in many ways to some therapists including counselling psychologists. The Recovery Model and psychological components will be explored to illustrate the need for a meta-perspective such as the PRTS worked from an integrative model of my own design.

I will briefly describe the Cognitive Behavioural model for psychosis to indicate how the PRTS can be integrated and informative. In conclusion I will draw attention to the importance of the relational and phenomenological in the therapeutic process and its role in psychosis.

Elaborating a dimensional model of psychosis

An alternative, dimensional approach assumes that schizophrenia is not a discrete illness entity, but that psychotic symptoms differ in quantitative ways from normal experiences and behaviours (Johns and Van Os, 2001: 1125).

There is growing evidence for psychosis being understood as a dimensional construct, similar to conceptions of other mental health difficulties such as personality disorder (Livesley, 2001). For example, in an extensive twenty-year longitudinal study of general populations Rosser et al. (2007) found that a small group of individuals displayed a stable level of sub-clinical psychotic symptoms throughout the period of investigation.

A dimensional understanding allows the breadth of psychotic phenomena to be understood on a single, shared pole of human experiences, the expression of which is as much related to social, interpersonal and intrapsychic issues as it is to biological causes. It perhaps also provides an explanation for the fluctuating pattern of symptoms or episodes observed in many people with psychosis. It further reduces psychosis to an extreme end of experiences shared by us all, avoiding the categorical approach that requires a number of criteria to be present before an individual is diagnosed and offered help.

However, it is important not to reject the significant contribution that medical interventions can make. There are times when a client may be in such distress that medication may be required, and to deny this on philosophical grounds could be unethical or even dangerous. Medication remains the principal treatment for psychosis, however, between 25 and 50 per cent of clients continue to experience persistent and distressing symptoms and relapse (Grech, 2002). (A detailed discussion about antipsychotic medication exceeds the remit of this chapter but for reviews see Davis et al., 2003). Life events can have a profound effect on an individual's relationship with social, sensory and ultimately intrapersonal realities. Neurobiology offers a physical mechanism for how some experiences may be expressed on the extreme end of the dimension. It is a reminder of the importance of being 'embodied' (namely, sensitive to the physical realities of our clients) which sometimes may be dismissed in a predominantly psychological consideration of a client.

Asserting a dimensional understanding can involve a dialectic whereby synthesis between two opposing views is desired. Vital to the PRTS however is that this synthesis is always defined on an individual basis and constantly negotiated with the client. I find this kind of dialectic approach also helps me to find a balance in not over identifying with either pole. For example, in acknowledging the phenomenological value of a client's experience it is possible to ignore or minimise distress both for the individual and their families. Although we can question the concept of psychosis, it is also crucial to note that these experiences can have a profound and lasting effect on interpersonal relationships, employment and family.

While a dimensional approach may provide a rationale, it is important to review the contextual issues that help contribute to its application in psychosis. Social models of distress have been developed to explore the expression of psychological distress (Beresford et al., 2010). Theories of socially constructed realities form the basis of many psychotherapeutic models (Kelly, 1955) and debates surrounding psychosis (Szasz, 1960). The social model also contributes to the neurological component underlying the need for the wider phenomenological understanding of an individual's social connections. Social issues clearly have a key role in the development, maintenance and severity of psychosis, however they are also equally important in recovery. Recognition of these issues has led to the development of the Recovery Model.

The Recovery Model supports a phenomenological approach as it is based on the centrality of a client as the agent of their own treatment. It has developed over the last thirty years as a result of the combination of developments in rehabilitation practice, human rights and disabilities movements, long-term clinical outcome research and client narratives of personal recovery (Slade, 2009; Davidson et al., 2010; Roberts, 2011). Although there is no single definition of recovery, common issues include 'redefining and accepting illness, overcoming stigma, renewing a sense of hope and commitment, resuming control and responsibility for an individual's life, experiencing citizenship, managing symptoms, being supported by others and being involved in meaningful activities and expanded social roles' (Davidson, 2003: 45). Psychological intervention supports an individualised, co-created response to specific client needs that is defined more by an 'attitude' than specific techniques or strategies.

Psychological component

Psychological interventions have always been offered to some clients with a psychotic diagnosis (Bachmann et al., 2003), however these have attracted more interest in the last thirty years. In the United Kingdom NICE (2009b) has published guidance recommending several evidence-based psychotherapeutic interventions, CBT for psychosis (both individually and group-based), family therapy and art therapy. I will briefly explore the CBT approach for psychosis to show the development of the model in practice as one that is entirely compatible with PRTS. (For further details regarding family therapy see Torrey, 2006, and Smith et al., 2007. For reviews of art therapy see Crawford and Patterson, 2007, and Ruddy and Milnes, 2005.)

CBT in psychosis

Although primarily designed for positive symptoms, CBT in psychosis has developed and been influenced by the 'Third Wave' therapies (e.g. DBT, Mindfulness-Based Cognitive Therapy). Traditional CBT involved behavioural strategies to manage symptoms, such as using ear plugs for auditory hallucinations and anxiety management techniques (Chadwick, 2006). Cognitive techniques were developed to challenge a client's extreme beliefs (such as paranoia and omnipotence) that were not affected by medication. As CBT became more widely used the approach was refined, most notably by Chadwick and Birchwood (1996), who reasserted the belief that psychotic experiences were 'extremely convoluted' expressions of normal experiences (Beck and Rector, 2000). The importance of a therapeutic relationship was also identified whereby a therapist 'agrees to disagree' with a client (Hansen et al., 2006). As opposed to more traditional CBT approaches, the therapist's intention is not to prove the inaccuracy of the client's belief, but instead to enter into and accept the client's belief system as valid.

The development of CBT in psychosis is historically significant as it has helped challenge the traditional psychiatric treatment of psychosis in which the content of symptoms was ignored in favour of controlling and managing expressed distress, mostly through medication (Burgy, 2008). With the use of CBT in both inpatient and outpatient settings, it has become increasingly acceptable to value and acknowledge the content of psychotic phenomena. While CBT is not the first or only therapeutic model to advocate this approach, it does deserve credit for helping to educate the wider psychiatric community.

CBT in psychosis is arguably based on a diathesis model, whereby psychotic experiences are linked to increased individual stress. There is evidence to suggest that individuals with psychosis have a low tolerance for stress which has been associated with genetic and social vulnerabilities, therefore identifying increases in stress as a likely triggering event for a psychotic episode. Techniques which help to manage anxiety are often used in addition to strategies for reality testing. Particular cognitive distortions of personalisation, rigidity and jumping to conclusions are often identified (Hansen et al., 2006). Other techniques are designed to help increase clients' individual control of positive symptoms, such as developing an engagement with voices, and eliciting voices to increase feelings of control. A growing number of outcome studies have found that CBT can have an immediate and longer-term effectiveness (Butler et al., 2006), however long-term success has been associated more with exploring the emotional and relational contributions to psychosis (Messari and Hallam, 2003).

There have been criticisms of CBT. Turkington and McKenna suggested a series of difficulties with the research base, and concluded 'If CBT were a drug, these studies would have been sufficient to consign it to history' (2003: 478). Thomas (2007) has also argued the approach is still based on the establishment of a set of beliefs against which to measure the client's perspective. For example, in reality testing, although the therapists may 'agree to disagree', they will still encourage a client to accept a belief that is more acceptable to their (wider societal) viewpoint.

While not offering a panacea, CBT has established an essential position for psychological therapy in a domain previously controlled by a medical model, thereby facilitating the consideration of other psychotherapeutic approaches. I feel the development of CBT also indicates the growing acceptance of more relational and experiential psychotherapies in CBT, allowing practitioners who were once separated some common ground for collaboration: Person-Based Cognitive Therapy (PBCT) is a good example here (Chadwick, 2006). However, we must be cautious as a profession that the current popularity of CBT does not result in a schism or marginalisation. A union between process and technique, determined by individual client needs, offers the most effective response. A therapeutic attitude and accumulated clinical practice in the totality of therapy are likely to facilitate a connection with our clients' experiences, no matter how unusual these are.

Phenomenological Relational Therapeutic Stance (PRTS): 'Being-With'

The request from clients is for therapists to 'be with them' in a human process. As Hazler and Barwick argue 'It is the therapist's willingness and capacity to experience unique world visions of another that makes it possible to create an environment designed to focus on the perceived world of the client, the phenomenological world' (2001: 73). This quality of Being-With also acknowledges the presence and contribution of the therapist as a participatory human being, ensuring that the process is unique and client defined, and not an attempt to fit their experience into a favoured therapeutic model. Important to the relational process is letting the client know that they 'matter', or that there exists a 'belief that others are aware of, rely on and care about one's presence' (Raque-Bogdan et al., 2011: 272).

The PRTS invites the therapist to find a synthesis between the thesis of 'model-bound' and the antithesis of 'model-less', responding to the request from clients with psychosis to be treated with respect and humanity. The PRTS provides the meta-perspective within which individual distress can be explored by acknowledging the totality of a given person's experience and therefore a greater chance of success.

The dialogue box (Figure 5.1) below details part of a session with a client called 'Hazel'. We have been meeting for eight sessions: she has had two previous admissions with a diagnosis of paranoid schizophrenia and psychotic episodes. Hazel consented to an anonymous recording as she felt it was important to contribute to the de-stigmatisation of mental health issues, particularly psychosis.

HF   I have been thinking about what you told me last week, particularly how quickly your mind was working.

(This was to let Hazel know that she has not been forgotten between sessions, showing that she and what she says is meaningful and matters. This is of course important for all clients but even more so here given her previous experience of services which have made her feel a 'mentally ill' patient.)

Hazel   OK

HF   It sounded, well really sh···.

(Empathising with Hazel through using non professional language to help both enter the reality of the client, but convey a shared humanity as opposed to a relationship purely based on one person being ill and the other not. It also helps to move from the question of what is 'real' by acknowledging the more important reality of her distress.)

Hazel   [laughs]

HF   I suppose what I mean is that it felt to me awful to be you then.

Hazel   It was ... but then I was mad.

(Hazel is still unsure how much she can tell others about what happened to her, she is scared about going back to hospital.)

HF   As we said before I'm not sure what that word really means, I suppose, I think, in one way does it matter if it was real or not, you felt it was real.

Hazel   I was terrified. I really thought they were coming for me, everyone was involved in the plot ... I mean delusion.

(Hazel is using language suggested by a psychiatrist, I feel that she is trying to appear to be 'well' identifying with the illness.)

HF   What percentage of you believes when I say to you that I believe your experiences were real to you and I don't think there is any need for you to go to hospital?

(It is a change in tack but I feel we have a good level of therapeutic relationship and it's important for Hazel to know that this therapeutic process has a different aim than other processes she has experienced. I cannot assume trust particularly as I am part of a service which has been negative for her on some occasions.)

Hazel   I trust you

HF   Really? Completely? After what you've been through with mental health professionals?

Hazel   [pause]

         Okay about 60%

HF   Thank you for that!

(This is not meant sarcastically and Hazel smiles, perhaps feeling relaxed she can be more real in the process. It is a good way of showing her I realise that I need to earn her trust whilst acknowledging that she already has to some extent, which is appreciated!)

HF   How have I earned that?

(This is not just an invitation to review positives in the process so far, but also to emphasise this is a collaborative process that will involve us both discussing the relationship in the process.)

Hazel   You haven't locked me up yet ... and you told me about that weird experience you had. You seem interested.

       (I had previously been discussing the dimensional model and told her an incident when I had become vaguely paranoid about phone calls when under a period of stress.)

HF   I have been thinking about humility, if that's the right word, particularly intellectual humility.

       (There is a slight risk in discussing concepts like 'humility' as religious persecution was also part of some of Hazel's experiences.)

Hazel   What do you mean?

HF   Well, us psychologists and professionals have given you various explanations for your experiences, but what you've said is most of us come back to our favourite models (she nods). I think it can be difficult for us, it definitely is for me, to be uncertain about things, and I wonder if I have to learn to be a bit more flexible about it. I hate to admit not knowing, it scares it me a bit.

Hazel   Me too.

HF   I think it's fair to say that what you experienced was real to you, but I also wonder if all the conclusions you made, for example about what people in cars were doing, are 100% correct. What do you think?

Hazel   Perhaps.

       (Hazel is an intelligent but very self-critical person. Going 'mad' represented a failure to her. We have previously wondered about the rigidity of some of her beliefs and she appeared to be uncomfortable maintaining all parts of her narrative. I felt 'Intellectual Humility' may represent a way of allowing her to reduce the number of theories without feeling she has to 'fail' again.)

Figure 5.1

As the process developed, Hazel was more able to tolerate an alternative explanation of experiences and was less attached to what was 'right' or 'wrong' in her account. She occasionally spoke of experiences that may have been described as possible psychotic phenomena but was able to respond to these in a more flexible way. There were no further episodes requiring admission, her medication was gradually reduced and she started voluntary work. Hazel was eventually discharged from all mental health services.

Conclusion

This section has briefly explored current issues in psychosis and how these influence therapeutic practice. I have suggested that alongside a knowledge of therapeutic models it is particularly vital that we emphasise the human process together with an awareness of the wider context of a client's life. Psychosis is a distressing and destabilising experience, but PRTS offers a way to 'be-with' clients. Perhaps in beginning to 'understand' psychosis, we can acknowledge it is a state of being that can be responded to positively by using psychological therapy.

Chapter Summary

As we endeavour to move forward in trying to understand what is happening for people when psychotic experiences occur, will we be able to take a medico-psychotherapeutic relational stance? And will this be enough to contain this confusing and sometimes violent state? It is likely that mental health professionals may move towards an increasing tendency to consider the individual in context, where safety of self and others will always be of paramount importance.

REFLECTION BOX

1 We tend to think of drug actions in terms of their main and side effects. Might this conceptualisation act to minimise the distress caused by the latter in some clients taking antipsychotic medication?

2 Certain problems appear to attract the gaze of the psychological professions at particular points in time. Why might this be?

3 Have any of your clients experienced psychotic symptoms? What did you think and what did you do?

4 What kinds of dilemmas have occurred when one of your clients has had a psychotic episode?

5 How has the recovery movement contributed to our understanding of psychosis?

6 What challenges could there be for a client, their family, services and a practitioner advocating a dimensional understanding of psychosis?

6

Exploring Bipolar

Introduction

Recent iterations of the *Diagnostic and Statistical Manual of Mental Disorder* include bipolar within a classificatory group of mood disorders. *DSM-5* (APA, 2013a) indicates the following criteria:

- *Bipolar 1 disorder:* characterised by the occurrence of one or more manic episodes or mixed episodes.
- *Bipolar 2 disorder:* characterised by one or more major depressive episode accompanied by at least one hypomanic episode.
- *Cyclothymic disorder:* a chronic fluctuating mood disturbance involving numerous periods of hypomanic symptoms and numerous periods of depressive symptoms.
- *Bipolar disorder not otherwise specified:* includes disorder with bipolar feature that do not meet the criteria for any specific bipolar disorder.

Completed suicide occurs in 10 to 15 per cent of Bipolar 1 sufferers: it is associated with substance and alcohol misuse. There appears to be little gender difference in prevalence and this has been estimated over the lifetime at between 0.4 and 1.6 per cent, with increased prevalence in first-degree relatives. Average age of onset is 20 and most sufferers will have around four episodes per year, with rapid cycling being associated with a poorer prognosis (APA, 2013a).

This portrait is heavily located within a particular discourse – that of a medical model which places experience within the realms of disorder. Healy (2008: 242), however, considers bipolar to be 'a compelling symbol of the current problems of medicine'. Certainly there is evidence that distinctions between bipolar and borderline personality disorder (a term debated in Chapter 7) are disputed. Hatchett (2010) notes that the differences between depression and bipolar may be more about classificatory manufacture than distinct disorders, and that the notion of bipolar is a complex one that may be understood either as experiences lying on a spectrum or as a discrete entity (Paris, 2009). Therapeutic responses for people who are referred to services are usually pharmacological with the central emphasis being on mood stabilisation, although a range of psychosocial interventions may be offered. These are discussed in Parts 2 and 3 of this chapter.

The distress of people who experience what may be termed 'bipolar' is often intense. In addition to struggling with fluctuating mood extremes, painful interactions with the wider social context are regularly experienced. Difficulties, for example, include social isolation and may be compounded by a benefits system that stigmatises sufferers.

So what can histories of the notion of bipolar add to our understanding?

Part 1: Exploring the Historical Context (Barbara Douglas)

Changing languages of classification

How and why particular experiences rise to prominence within particular cultural moments and come to be defined as problems are questions that have meaning for our practice but that we may also tend to overlook. Chapter 2, for example, highlighted how the current notion of depression was constructed within, and reflects, specific culturally determined systems. This holds also for the current notion of bipolar, which links extremes of affective experience and is relatively recent in historical understanding. Mania as a separate construct historically referred to a much broader notion of frenzy which was variously couched within the personas of witches or court jesters. Then in the nineteenth century, there evolved the manic depressive persona concretised by Kraepelin's integration of the separate notions of mania and melancholia into maniacal-depressive insanity.

It is notable that while culturally-framed terminologies change there are still echoes of perceived experiential threads that traverse the centuries. One such perception is a view of melancholy, mania and bipolar as somehow associated – although not necessarily evidenced – with creativity. Aristotle cited Plato, Socrates and Empedocles as examples of gifted and talented people who experienced melancholy (Goodwin and Jamison, 2007), while many centuries later oft-cited authors such as Virginia Woolfe and Sylvia Plath are held up as evidence of such a link. This literary association is similarly highlighted by Claridge et al. (1990) who argued that this link could be demonstrated via the narratives of ten authors, extending from the Middle Ages to the twentieth century, who might be described as psychotic.

Debates have also been had across time as to whether terms such as 'mania' and 'melancholy' should be considered part of the same process or as separate problems. Soranus of Ephisus (circa 100AD), for example, argued that while melancholy and mania were two separate conditions they had a similar onset and required similar treatment. On the other hand, Arataeus (circa 200AD) considered mania as an end stage of melancholy. Centuries later in 1806 Scottish physician William Cullen proposed a similar notion that mania was a higher degree of melancholy, and Griesinger (1867) considered mania as the end stage of melancholy (Goodwin and Jamison, 2007: 4–8). Current empirical research into bipolar remains conflicted, suggesting on the one hand that there is a classificatory distinction to be made between unipolar depression and bipolar, and on the other that bipolar should be considered a spectrum of problems, and that what we term 'borderline personality disorder' is actually a subset of a bipolar spectrum (Hatchett, 2010).

With the Enlightenment (sometimes referred to as the beginning of the Age of Reason) came the emerging study of anatomy, the discovery of nerves and the notion of brain lesions, which underpinned developing medical models of psychiatry. The notion of mania and melancholy as linked problems continued to be debated in the nineteenth century when French psychiatrists Jean-Pierre Falrat and Jules Baillarger respectively termed the succession of mania and melancholia 'circular insanity' and 'double insanity' (Healy, 2008).

Beyond France too this concept of cycling was emerging, with the German psychiatrist Karl Kahlbaum (1882, cited in Baethge et al., 2003) proposing the notion of cyclic insanity. But despite these earlier suggestions, the beginning of the notion of manic-depression is generally credited to Danish physician Carl Lange (1886, cited in Schioldann, 2011) who proposed the term 'periodical depression', which, Healy (2008) suggests, was also the first use of the word 'depression'.

This apparent link between melancholia and mania crystallised in the early twentieth century with Emil Kraepelin's seminal international research. In his proposed twin pillars of psychiatric classification – namely, manic-depressive illness and dementia praecox – Kraepelin (2011 [1904]) argued that diagnosing symptoms at a single moment in time had resulted in mania and depression being wrongly considered to be two separate illnesses. Fundamental to any diagnostic system should be to consider the course of symptoms over time. When undertaken in this way his empirical and longitudinal research indicated that a variety of forms of mania and depression all fell into one classificatory group.

By the mid-twentieth century classificatory tensions around Kraepelin's manic depressive illness were again occurring. The influence of Adolf Meyer, discussed in earlier chapters, is evidenced in the original *Diagnostic and Statistical Manual* (APA, 1952), which coined the term 'manic–depressive reaction' and framed the problem as a biogenetic reaction to psychological and social influences. This was followed in 1957 by German psychiatrist Karl Leonhard's proposed division of mood disorders, into unipolar (more commonly now referred to as major depressive disorder) and bipolar disorders, which he argued were separate conditions. Rogers and Agius (2012) suggest that the doubtful evidence for this division accounts for a resurgence in notions of a continuum of experiences on a spectrum, and for the term first coined by Akiskal in 1977 as 'cyclothymic-bipolar spectrum'.

Research and intervention

The outline above indicates considerable classificatory debate about what is currently termed 'bipolar disorder', but does not address questions about the cause or intervention. In Roman times Galen was largely responsible for embedding the causes of mania and melancholy within a humoral theory of medicine that would last – albeit with increasing religious and superstitious additions – until the Enlightenment. Goodwin and Jamison (2007) describe these long post-Roman years as the Dark Ages as regards the conceptualisation of mental illness, although this may be something of a myth, created by telescoping back in time from within a particular current medicalised world view.

Treatment with lithium salts began, not for mania or melancholy, but for diseases where there was an increase in uric acid – for example, gout – where its alkaline properties were found to be effective. Subsequently trialled for epilepsy it was found to improve patients' mood (Healy, 2008). Treatment for mania and melancholia with lithium carbonate, however, has been seminally credited to psychiatrist Carl Lange (1886) who – discovering that patients with depression tended to produce larger than usual amounts of uric acid – trialled its use, finding it to be beneficial. Although this was the first indication of a possibly effective drug treatment, its use fell into abatement until Australian psychiatrist John Cade's experimental study of patients experiencing manic episodes was reported in 1949. Further research developed by Danish psychiatrist Mogens Schou resulted in increasing publicity for lithium treatment in the scientific press, and with an APA task force into lithium set up in 1969, the drug gained popularity (Healy, 2008).

But what made lithium different from earlier drugs such as bromides which had also been used for the treatment of mania? The answer here is that it was the first drug to introduce the notion of mood stabilisation into psychiatric thinking. As such it defined a treatment aim that would so heavily influence, and link, the futures of both psychiatry and psychopharmacology.

Initial indications of a genetic input to bipolar difficulties came in the late 1960s and early 1970s (see for example Reich et al.,1969), and although the findings remain inconsistent, genetic predisposition was subsequently linked to psychosocial stress in what has become known as the kindling hypothesis (Post, 1992). This suggests that individuals genetically predisposed to bipolar who are exposed to significant psychosocial stress are more likely to experience difficulties. Subsequently, the level of stress needed to trigger further episodes decreases with each event due to the resulting cumulative neurological damage. Thus as resilience reduces over time if recovery is to be a realistic possibility then early intervention is strongly advocated. If we look back at historical psychiatric texts, however, it is also evident that early intervention has been posited as facilitating recovery from mental illness since the early days of moral therapy at the beginning of the nineteenth century. Further analysis of such records might usefully explore further the notion of early intervention.

Conclusion

Bentall (2011) suggests that any Kraepelinean-type clear cut divisions between bipolar and other psychoses are evidentially problematic, leaving us with many current unanswered questions about both classification and intervention. The history of what we term 'bipolar' also indicates that its nature, classification, causation and intervention all remain indeterminate. Many implications for service provision and therapeutic practice are implicit in this confusing picture and some of these are further discussed in the following parts of this chapter.

Part 2: Exploring Dilemmas in Practice (Pam James)

What does the term bipolar mean and to whom? The dilemma of underlying models

The term 'bipolar' has acquired a familiarity in modern everyday conversation, perhaps facilitated by the discussion that has occurred in the media by well-known celebrities who have been given that diagnostic label. A psychiatric diagnosis results when the symptoms are perceived to be present as outlined in the *DSM-5* (APA, 2013a). The psychologist is informed by these diagnostic features and works with clients who are referred for therapy.

As with other diagnoses, the label carries information about the symptoms that present, however there is no clarity about the underlying causation. There can also be confusion with psychosis and borderline personality disorder. More specifically, lists of descriptive symptoms provide no information about the contextual location of the client in his or her life experience. However, most psychiatric perspectives would acknowledge the impact of stressors and life events on the way in which a client copes with these symptoms.

The confusing way in which symptoms can present results in what Little and Richardson (2010) describe as a clinical dilemma. In a thoughtful article they discuss the nature of diagnosis and science, and how the latter is not always totally objective: by this they are suggesting that there are subjective factors that affect which diagnosis will result. It is necessary also to consider the impact on both the client and their subsequent treatment. They argue that for a psychiatrist trying to make an accurate diagnosis, this is a complex and sometimes tentative professional task, and that a way of relating with the client that encourages a shared tentativeness would be a more helpful option.

For clients their diagnosis can have a meaningful consequence, and the way this is perceived by clients may vary. One particular client entered the therapy room saying 'He [the psychiatrist] did think I had bipolar, but now he thinks

I might have a borderline personality'. The client then looked bemused and said 'I was going to "press on" anyway, but shame about changing the meds ... I'd just got used to them'.

Many of the questions arising around the term 'bipolar disorder' have been anticipated and to some extent answered by the British Psychological Society's publication (Jones et al., 2010): this looks across a spectrum of issues including causation, help and treatment (using therapy and/or treatment), and recovery.

Consequences of a diagnosis: the dilemma of ideographic or nomothetic

On looking at two clients' cases, it is possible to see how there are both similarities and differences in their contextual histories. The first client was at a time in her life when her children had left home: when she became depressed it was thought this had been the trigger. However, later that year, she began to go into extreme anger and rage, and threaten family members in an over-excitable manner. This resulted in an admission to an acute ward for a two-week stay, where medication was prescribed and there was a referral for therapy. In taking a personal history, the client spoke about breaks in her early education and time with mental health services. She said that as a teenager she had striven to overcome these gaps in learning, resulting in a successful career development. Currently, though, it was almost as though her present circumstances had triggered her earlier unexplained childhood problems, which had never had the containment of understanding and had been tinged with fear.

Fear again pervaded her thoughts: she strove to return to a more stable present, ashamed that her family should see her in this way. She did not see therapy as an activity that could give her the immediacy of stability that she demanded, and she began to pull away from sessions, eventually saying that she would not continue to attend. She found the diagnosis of bipolar an explanation for her symptoms, although she conceded that this was at the level of matching her symptoms with this diagnosis. Sadly, the next few months were a cycling round of adjustments to medication, depression and uncontrollable excitement changing to rage: she returned periodically to the acute ward. The focus of her concern centred on how much she was being given of each medication and what were its side effects.

Multiple dilemmas can be identified in this brief history. The client's wish to be better as quickly as possible was in conflict with the necessary time that therapy needed to allow a developing awareness of her self-expressed earlier learnt fear of strong feelings. There were dilemmas and uncertainty for the psychologist working therapeutically, as unravelling core beliefs and developing new learning and building client confidence to cope with her irrational impulses to self harm were not quickly achievable in a robust form. As medication could act as a container for her feelings in the short term the psychiatrist's views held sway, and the client was doubtful about her own ability to comfort and understand her often frightening thoughts and feelings. Medication seemed to be 'the only way'.

The second client had also experienced a trauma early on in life when she had been sexually assaulted in her teenage years. This had remained both unreported and not discussed in her family. She had not wanted to burden her mother, and although the client had experienced maternal support during her difficult teenage years with an extended depression, the issue of the sexual assault remained non-disclosed. Eventually in therapy, when this came to be discussed, the client's ambivalence with disclosure was apparent. Again, the relational pattern of not wanting to burden others with her difficulties was shown in the transference with the therapist. Had this relational pattern not only prevented her from disclosing her abuse, but also compounded her depression? Whatever the case, this client had received a diagnosis of bipolar and she was committed to work in therapy. She had never experienced psychotic episodes and gradually developed a trust in her new ability to talk things through. She was keen to use a cognitive framework to see how her core beliefs informed her current thinking. She developed social relationships: for a while she was free from medication.

Sadly, when rejection in a relationship occurred setbacks followed, and she was angry with herself at not being able to cope. She clutched at medication to stop her slipping back and to dull her excitable feelings and sometimes deep depression that she feared might send her back into her late-adolescent depressed state. This client accepted her diagnosis of bipolar: she also read about it on the internet, sometimes confusing herself by focusing on other people's experiences and being influenced by them.

The consequences of a diagnosis: the dilemma of which therapeutic response to adopt, use of medication and the concept of risk

In these two case examples, a diagnosis of bipolar was accepted by the clients. The first client did not persist in therapy – she said that it was hard for her to tolerate the difficult and intense feelings arising from therapy. Contrast that point with the second client's experience, where her feelings were not about self-harm or harming others but about withdrawing into her own internal world.

It is clear that seeing clients' experience of their issues in context is an essential part of finding a way forward in helping them manage their lives. The guidance from NICE (2006) acts as a framework to support therapeutic choices. The psychotic episodes experienced by the first client perhaps highlight the need for medication to return her from the frightening place where impulses seem to overtake rational thought. The dilemma here perhaps is that the client was not able to remain in therapy long enough to understand the possible origins of such strong feelings. If these feelings were acted upon, then there would be a risk both to others and herself. There was no opportunity to learn a little about the sources of that fear that may have started when she was younger, almost as if learning the script that there was no place to discuss painful experiences when they occur.

Part of the client context includes other social contacts with family and friends who play a part in clients' construction of what their diagnosis means to them. As 'bipolar' has become a more commonly known term, does it carry an expectation for close family around the client? For example, if the client becomes particularly excited about a real life event, does this signal to the family that a manic episode may follow? It is possible to extrapolate from this hypothetical scenario to a dilemma position, where on the one hand it can be preventative to anticipate manic times, and on the other it could also deny the client the full range of experience.

Further advantages for clients in experiencing their mood can allow them to follow if there are any actual events that trigger either a manic or a depressed response, and at the extreme of each. Could this in some way be part of a defensive response that prevents a person from facing an issue that is particularly difficult? This kind of explanation is again couched in a dilemma as it does not have sufficient firm evidence on which to base such a hypothesis.

An article by Licinio (2005), in which a person diagnosed with bipolar disorder discussed her experiences, suggests, however, that in this case therapy was not helpful, and from then on she sought to find a medication that would contain the symptoms of her condition. Part of the possible insight into the dilemma of therapy and/or medication may be that it depends on the intensity of clients' symptoms, and the context in which they are living, together with perceived support from family and friends, perceived stressors and their experience of therapy. There are clearly variations with all these factors.

Consequences of therapy: the dilemma of care or cure

Is it possible to recover from what may be termed bipolar? There is no clear evidence on which to base an answer to this question. However, it is possible to say that in therapy, self-awareness and learning could occur that would then support a reduction in the frequency and intensity of extreme responses for some people. Often medication also plays some part. For others who do not persist in therapy, then medication may also act as a stabiliser. One dilemma perhaps is the frustration and sometimes self-anger that some clients feel as they move from one medication to another, and from one therapist to another, in their quest to find a cure. Hammersley (2010) gives the therapist a framework in which to find a place for the role of medication and therapy. Of particular note is her writing about a need for therapist involvement in their ethical responsibility about what will benefit the client and minimise their risk of harm. This last dilemma is of course not restricted to bipolar disorder, but perhaps such issues take on a particular focus when the consequences of not containing the symptoms can become very frightening for the client and their family, something which is further discussed in Part 3 below.

Part 3: Exploring Research and Practice with Clients Experiencing Bipolar (Roly Fletcher)

Introduction

The kinds of difficulties experienced by those who are later deemed to meet the criteria for bipolar disorder[1] can be both extremely distressing and life-changing. Changes in mood, activity, appetite, sleep, motivation, and perception of reality, to name but a few, can begin quickly, over a few weeks (Bentall et al., 2005), at a relatively young age, with the average being 20 (DeRubeis et al., 1998), and reoccur throughout the rest of life (Goodwin and Jamison, 2007). This can have negative consequences on academic and occupational achievement (World Health Organisation, 1992) as well as relationships (Inder et al., 2008) and recreational enjoyment (DelBello et al., 2009). Many individuals will have one or more stays in psychiatric hospitals (voluntarily or compulsorily). Understandably, these experiences can create confusion, contradiction and self-doubt, alongside feelings such as shame (Inder et al., 2008). It is perhaps little wonder that some turn to drugs or alcohol (Regier et al., 1990) or resort to suicide (Goodwin and Jamison, 2007).

It seems important that practitioners have a good understanding of this diagnostic category, particularly because – within contexts such as the National Health Service (NHS) – a psychiatric diagnosis is generally a prerequisite for accessing services (Fletcher, 2012). This chapter outlines the challenges that face both practitioners and clients. Anonymised clinical material is offered where appropriate in order to elucidate the points made.

Clinical examples

Manic episodes

With regard to manic episodes, clients have described their mood as 'the best feeling in the world' and said they felt able to 'do anything', including, for example, storming into their manager's office uninvited, interrupting the meeting in progress, to talk

---

[1]Without meaning to reduce the complexity of the several different bipolar diagnoses, I shall, for the sake of ease, use the singular 'bipolar disorder' to mean any of these diagnoses.

non-stop and enthusiastically about schemes for the business (with their feet on the desk). With hindsight, this particular client had no memory of what these schemes were but was fairly certain they were not sensible. A different kind of example included a shopping spree, adding up to thousands of pounds, for many not-needed items. Another client talked about hearing voices, believing themself to be chosen by some higher power to receive their 'special' messages. At extremes, I have heard of people becoming so caught up in their schemes that they have begun to neglect themselves (eating, drinking, washing, and sleeping). For many, they describe having little insight into these changes at the time, believing nothing was wrong at all, and it was family or significant others who became concerned and contacted mental health services.

Depressive episodes

Unlike manic episodes which seem to be temporary (or at least made so by medication), many individuals continue to experience depression, to varying degrees, on an ongoing basis. Commonly described were low mood, loss of confidence, little motivation to engage in social or occupational activities, feelings of hopelessness and pessimism. In one particular case, fear of the damage that could be done if they were to experience another manic episode led them to feel that they could not afford to become enthusiastic about anything anymore, and fantasies of suicide had become their only means of expressing how desperately they wished to escape their oppressive feelings.

Medicalised thought

The difficulties associated with bipolar disorders are commonly viewed from a medicalised paradigm, within which the 'powerless' client is assumed to have fallen victim to a genetic 'illness' (Royal College of Psychiatry, 2012), implying the difficulties ('symptoms') are therefore located within them. To support this is the observation that 'the prevalence of bipolar disorders are higher in the families of patients with bipolar disorder' (DeRubeis et al., 1998: 346). Studies on adoptees reared away from their biological parents and monozygotic (identical) twins who are reared apart (McGuffin and Katz, 1989) have, arguably, ruled out environmental causes. Environmental stressors are then considered to modulate the timing and intensity of difficulties (Ramana and Bebbington, 1995; Johnson and Miller, 1997). Indeed, many whom I have worked with reported that family conflicts, financial pressures, and work stress – all of which tended to disrupt daily routines – seemed to precede the start of difficulties. Their descriptions of their early lives often also led me to suspect that other family members might well have met the criteria associated with one or other of the mood disorder diagnoses, or at least depression if not bipolar disorder.

Standardised interventions

Medicalised theories of bipolar disorder have then driven the direction of interventions towards 'symptom management' (DeRubeis et al., 1998). Whilst both pharmaceutical and talking therapies are recommended interventions (NICE, 2006), a belief that the behaviour of the manic person 'can be so extreme as to warrant immediate, aggressive medical management … as the first line treatment' (DeRubeis et al., 1998: 359) means that pharmaceutical interventions (sometimes within the context of compulsory hospitalisation) are given the dominant role, 'until the manic episode is past and the premorbid personality is back in view' (Stone, 1978: 437). Whilst depressive 'symptoms' also get treated primarily with medication, there is not the same belief that talking therapies cannot happen alongside this (Havens and Ghaemi, 2005).

Talking therapies are viewed as an adjunct to 'symptom management', encouraging individuals to take prescribed medications (Jones, 2004), and monitor behaviour in the hope that early awareness of changes can serve as a 'warning system [to] have their medications … increased' (DeRubeis et al., 1998: 360).

Talking therapies may also aim to increase resilience to stress by encouraging:

- a limitation of behaviours deemed to exacerbate difficulties or have negative consequences, e.g. limiting over-spending, substance misuse, becoming over-tired (Johnson and Miller, 1997; Jones, 2004);
- strategies to deal with the consequences of a manic episode (DeRubeis et al., 1998), such as debt or job loss;
- strategies for dealing with relational conflict (Frank et al., 1997);
- challenging grandiose or paranoid thinking (DeRubeis et al., 1998).

All of those I have worked with were on medication, regularly reviewed by a psychiatrist, and many had undergone some form of the talking therapies described above (sometimes also with their families recruited into monitoring and working on the techniques).

A word of caution

For those struggling with the difficulties that can be associated with a diagnosis of bipolar disorder, the certainty offered by the medical model might be reassuring. Within health-care settings, diagnostic classifications may offer a language allowing practitioners to communicate complex issues to each other. Hospitalisation can also provide a place of safety, whilst medication can subdue distressing emotions and psychotic processes. Focused interventions can reassure further by telling someone what they should do, offering a concrete challenge to the desperation and powerlessness that the client, those close to them, a practitioner, or even the society around them might feel (Schimmel, 1998).

There is a risk, however, that this certainty blinds us to the fact that we do not yet have a full understanding of these difficulties. Not all clients have a family history of affective disorders which throws doubt upon the exact nature of heritability or specific genes (DelBello et al., 2009). Individuals may also have very different permutations of 'symptoms' which will then throw doubt upon the appropriateness of grouping individuals together if they feel they have little in common with one another. Thus standardised interventions 'may not apply to every individual' (Vetere, 2012: ix). It may therefore be unsurprising that many continue to experience affective episodes, often depressive ones (Havens and Ghaemi, 2005; Judd et al., 2002), alongside ideas of self-harm or suicide (Goodwin, 1999), despite following interventions to the letter. Our certainty in these interventions can limit our capacity to consider alternatives, leading to 'repeated ineffective medication [and talking therapy] trial[s]' (DelBello et al., 2009: 206). Emotional dysregulation is recognised as a key difficulty in bipolar disorders (Inder et al., 2008), and manic-type difficulties may be seen as a means of suppressing or avoiding distressing thoughts or feelings (Neale, 1988; Kramer, 2012). 'Symptom management' interventions can reinforce this by perpetuating the message that these feelings must be treated as if they were too 'abnormal or dangerous' to be expressed. It is perhaps understandable that this leads many to become even more depressed, instilling hopelessness that anyone can, or even wants to, understand or manage their distress (Casement, 1985; Gomez, 1997).

One client I worked with continued to feel depressed, and often suicidal, despite rigidly adhering to medication and the strategies she had learnt. Terrified of repeating or exacerbating the damage she felt she had done during a previous manic episode, this client tried to avoid any stressors that might trigger another. This included her emotional withdrawal from social relationships and activities. Her relationships became characterised by irritation on both sides, with others perceiving the client as 'controlling' and emotionally distant, and the client perceiving them as unsupportive and provocative. She therefore felt isolated, unsupported, anxious, lonely, depressed, angry, and very hopeless. In her despair she would fantasise on the only escape she felt left available to her, that of suicide.

Other clients will resist the idea that there is something 'wrong' with them and the interventions they feel are forced upon them. This can result in their self-esteem being lowered further because their actions are pathologised – 'everyone disbelieves them' (Havens and Ghaemi, 2005: 144) and they feel they are not valued. They can then find themselves isolated and unsupported by those around them. Many of my clients reported that they had stopped taking their medication or discontinued talking therapy at some point, only to find increased pressure from family and healthcare professionals. At times of heightened distress, these clients had then found that the only way to gain support was to comply with the medicalised wishes of those around them, at the cost of their own sense of empowerment. They often reported subsequent feelings of powerlessness and hopelessness, with one client saying that he felt 'broken'.

The relationship

It is argued that a different, less dogmatic, kind of therapeutic relationship is sometimes needed, characterised by more empathic engagement where the practitioner should aim to 'feel, and experience' (Havens and Ghaemi, 2005: 138) – 'being with' what the client brings, in contrast to 'directing' as in the medical model stance.[2] Rather than dismiss the client's perspective as pathological the practitioner attempts to verbalise their 'understanding of what is being encountered' (Casement, 1985: 133), implicitly communicating to the client that their distress is valid and important and thereby reducing self-doubt and feelings such as guilt or shame (Inder et al., 2008). This can be soothing for those still considered to be experiencing the 'symptoms' of mania such as hyperarousal or over-activity, because they do not have to tolerate too much talking (Havens and Ghaemi, 2005). Through respecting and taking seriously the client and their active role in 'discover[ing] what is needed' (Casement, 1985: 26), this also challenges the view of the practitioner as critical, strengthens the therapeutic alliance, reduces the client's sense of difference and isolation, and can thus make it easier for them to consider any alternative views the practitioner might offer (Havens and Ghaemi, 2005). Whilst perhaps providing a less immediate and tangible 'symptom' reduction than focused interventions, this process can ultimately have a greater long-term impact in reducing the intensity of difficult feelings when they arise because both practitioner and client come to realise that they can be tolerated, thought about, and 'survived' (Havens and Ghaemi, 2005). As a result, together with the practitioner, the client can begin to discover their 'capacity for managing life and life's difficulties without continued avoidance or suppression' (Casement, 1985: 133).

For example, one client (whom I shall call Bob) talked non-stop in one session about a social situation which had upset him. There was little space for me to say anything and so I listened carefully for a cue that Bob might need me to intervene. Eventually Bob stopped talking and there was a pause. While I considered all that Bob had said, however, he told me he wished I would say something – that it made him anxious that I had not done so, and that he expected some form of reassurance. In turn, I pointed out to Bob that whilst I understood he was upset, the situation sounded like the kind of 'up and down' that we can all experience from time to time, and that could well resolve itself given time. Bob seemed to relax. He told me that it was a surprise to him that someone would react so calmly to his emotions. When we explored this a little more, he described his fear that his thoughts and feelings

---

[2]Whilst my work is often informed by the psychodynamic model, such a therapeutic stance is not specific to this and more accepting stances can be found within all of the major models of therapy, including existential, humanistic and cognitive-behavioural (particularly the mindfulness school).

were generally grounds for punishment if they did not fit in with the expectations of others. Certainly this had been the case with his father when he was growing up, and he recalled that his fear had led him to suppress his feelings, only showing others a happy, 'entertaining' persona as far as possible, whilst often really feeling lonely and depressed when alone. At a time of particular life stress, however, his 'entertainer' persona had got out of hand in his attempt to ward off his distress. His socialising interfered with sleep. Others noticed that he talked rapidly, often laughing inappropriately, and began to spend large amounts of money on items related to socialising. The extremity of this led to his first hospital admission, a diagnosis of bipolar disorder, medication, and management strategies. He told me that all of this had intensified and reinforced his fear of the consequences of his feelings. He also said that, by not acting in a manner that colluded with his fear, I had challenged his perception that his feelings were dangerous and this had allowed him to begin to feel less anxious and calmer.

This was the beginning of a different kind of relationship for Bob and me, and he began to risk bringing more of his feelings – comfortable and less comfortable – into our sessions, including, at times, some which might be considered psychotic or risky. Bob explained that he had begun to find it easier to tolerate these as they seemed less distressing. He said he was able to express himself more in social situations, and to his surprise had found that others understood and shared many of his feelings. He thus felt more supported and less abnormal. Although medicalised interventions had clearly provided much needed intervention at a time of crisis, it was through the development of a therapeutic relationship (within which he could gain a deeper understanding of himself and his emotions) that he finally began to feel less afraid. This is not to say that Bob did not continue to experience difficulties, particularly when life was stressful. However, he told me that being able to share his feelings with others, rather than hide them, meant he had more social support and he did not feel such an urge to resort to 'entertaining'. This reduced his fear that he would end up 'out of control'. He was not re-admitted to inpatient services in the time I knew him. He also continued on medication, managing the levels of this with his psychiatrist who eventually became so confident in Bob's ability to seek appropriate support when needed, that he discharged him back into the care of his GP, allowing them to manage the levels from then on. At the end of our work, I hoped that Bob would continue to build on the work we had begun, challenging his fear that others would criticise his distress, and instead asking for support when needed with his feelings, hopefully thus avoiding future crises.

Dilemma and risk

The decision whether to provide 'symptom' management interventions, thereby remaining allied with the dominant medicalised perspective, or whether to move away from this is not necessarily an easy one. There may be times when staying 'with' the emotion means facing extremes of, for example, suicidal despair, frustration, anger, grandiosity, paranoia, denial, and rigidity. It requires a great deal of practitioner judgement, insight, skill and support to be able to tolerate this and what it evokes in them, let alone to continue to make sense of what is emerging and ensure they work in a way that continues to be effective and in the clients' best interests. This kind of work also requires client participation. For some, practitioners and client alike, the emotional difficulties that such a way of working can evoke can be too much to bear, particularly when the benefits of doing so have not yet become apparent. In such a case this can lead to conflict, disengagement, and/or perhaps a heightening of potentially harmful behaviours that have been used in the past to cope with emotional distress (e.g. drugs or suicide). Take, for example, my work with Bob. Despite my assurances, he may not have trusted that my lack of criticism would last. Instead of continuing to risk sharing his distress with me, Bob's fears could have led him back to hiding these, presenting me with his 'entertainer' persona instead.

This risk is present within the work, and it can be seen that the practitioner needs to carefully consider the dilemmas that such work can evoke, especially given how damaging some behaviours can become to the individual or to others. Within contexts such as the NHS inadequate resources also limit the organisation's ability to support those who work in this way. The potential associated risks can significantly increase the difficulty involved (Fletcher, 2012). It may be beneficial to minimise such risks by favouring the focused interventions that are deemed to be less 'risky' under such circumstances. However, to do so may then make it incredibly difficult to avoid acting in a manner that perpetuates a client's fear of their feelings and thus their ability to tolerate or manage these in the longer term, hence creating a vicious circle.

Conclusion

In describing the diagnostic category of bipolar disorder, and the current thinking associated with it, I have outlined some of the confusing difficulties that face both clients and practitioners. I have argued that 'symptom management' interventions (pharmaceutical and focused talking therapies) can provide valuable relief from extremely distressing states and the potentially damaging or harmful behaviours that can be associated with these. This medicalised view of the problem fits well within health-care services such as the NHS, where reduced resources has driven the search for short-term, focused interventions that can be standardised and measured in terms of outcomes for 'target' issues.

However, I have also argued that 'symptom management' interventions can inadvertently reinforce clients' underlying anxieties about their own emotional distress, thereby perpetuating an avoidance of these, potentially through the damaging behaviours that gave rise to their diagnosis in the first place. Instead, a less directive approach, within which the client's emotional states are 'allowed' by the practitioner – who experientially demonstrates that these can be tolerated – can begin to challenge that client's anxieties about the 'danger' of their own feelings, and thus a reliance upon damaging coping strategies. Yet this way of working can elicit extremely distressing emotional states that may be too difficult to tolerate for any variety of reason. There is therefore the risk that it can also potentially trigger risk behaviours. Currently, there seems to be no firm answers to the questions that I have raised within this chapter. It therefore seems important that practitioners have a good level of knowledge about the current approaches to bipolar disorder, while also remaining open to the uniqueness of each individual client, such that alternatives can be considered if appropriate.

Chapter Summary

There are two central themes which run through this chapter, both of which impact on the therapist and client in relation to their work together. Firstly, what bipolar is or is not remains confusing, and clients who attract the label may vary considerably in their range of experienced symptoms. Whether such experiences should all be grouped under one label, albeit with subsets, has been historically, and currently remains, very much debated. Secondly, there is an issue about whether the focus of the work should concern symptom management or tolerance of intensely difficult feelings. Are these mutually exclusive, and if so, where the focus should lie may depend on client, therapist, and the context in which they work together. Safety and what this means is an issue for all.

Both these issues serve to remind ourselves that as therapists to adopt an expert stance in working with clients who attract the label 'bipolar' would be to lay claim to a degree of certainty that is not evidenced in the shifting sands of the associated research. Understanding and enabling clients to find a more comfortable way of being in the world may lie in the evolving process between therapist and client and the meaning that is co-created between them.

REFLECTION BOX

1 What do you consider to be the relevance of historical understandings of mania and melancholia to the current notion of bipolar?
2 There are suggestions that the bipolar spectrum may include experiences currently labelled 'borderline personality disorder'. Does this influence your understanding of the classification of psychological distress?
3 Reflect on your clients' attitudes to their medication and beliefs about causal factors in their diagnosis.

4 What kinds of dilemmas have you experienced when working psychotherapeutically with clients diagnosed with bipolar disorder?
5 How reliable is the diagnosis 'bipolar'? Is your impression of the person that they do
   seem to meet the criteria for this diagnostic category, or do you end up questioning it?
6 How useful or otherwise would it be to 'buy into' this diagnosis with this
   particular client?

7

Exploring the Borderline

Introduction

Borderline personality disorder is characterised by significant instability of interpersonal relationships, self-image and mood, and impulsive behaviour. There is a pattern of sometimes rapid fluctuation from periods of confidence to despair, with fear of abandonment and rejection, and a strong tendency towards suicidal thinking and self-harm. Transient psychotic symptoms, including brief delusions and hallucinations, may also be present. (National Institute for Health and Care Excellence, 2009a: 4)

Within the general population of Britain, NICE suggests, around 0.7 per cent may meet these criteria, as may 4 to 6 per cent of primary GP attenders, and the majority of those meeting the criteria are women (NICE, 2009a: 20).

The phrase *borderline personality disorder*, however, suggests some underpinning assumptions. Firstly, a borderline suggests a delineation between two or more structures or territories; secondly, that the notion of personality itself may need to be considered; and finally, that the notions of disorder and classification are unproblematic. The noted historian of psychiatric nosology, Berrios (1993), considered diagnostic accounts of personality disorder to be palimpsests – that is, accounts akin to the surface layer of a painting superimposed on a previously painted canvas.

This chapter will begin by considering the influence of historical layers on the current portrait. It will then examine some of the dilemmas in working with people whose experience meets the criteria for a borderline diagnosis, and finally, it will consider two contexts in which current psychotherapeutic practice takes place (i.e. a specialist NHS service and an employment context).

Part 1: Exploring the Historical Context (Barbara Douglas)

Borderline

In any field 'borderline' suggests a delineation between two or more structures or territories and psychiatry and psychotherapy are no exception. A borderline form of distress was first formally delineated within early twentieth-century under-standings of neurosis or psychosis. Prior to this, notions of neurosis and psychosis had meanings in which there was little place for a borderline construct. For exam-ple, the influential Scottish physician William Cullen argued that neurosis referred to any illness which was brought about by excessive physical nerve activity. This *might* include mental illnesses, which he termed vesaniae, but *equally* might result in illnesses such as diabetes or tetanus (Cullen, 1777, cited in Shorter, 2005). Although a reconfiguration of psychiatric problems during the nineteenth century into those which affected intelligence and those which affected emotions was the fertile soil in which the idea of a borderline began to take shape, this remained embryonic. In the 1890s, for example, Irving Rosse, Professor of Nervous Diseases at Georgetown University (1986 [1890]: 32), wrote of 'a class of persons standing in the twilight of right reason and despair'.

But it was the early twentieth-century conceptualisation of the neuroses – with their theoretical basis located in Freud's psychic structural organisation – that par-ticularly paved the path for the concept of a borderline personality. This is usually formally credited as emerging in a seminal paper given by New York psychoanalyst Adolph Stern in 1938, in which he stated:

> There is a degree of immaturity and insecurity that is not present in the ordinary transference neurosis with which we are familiar ... so intense an affective involve-ment can this attachment become that attention to this aspect of the transference takes up an inordinate amount of time. (1938: 63)

Stern's paper was representative of contemporary analytic discussions concerning the emergence of the 'new patient' – namely, the apparently increasing numbers of clients who did not fit contemporary understandings of neuroses but demon-strated difficulties that resulted in problematic transferences. Thus the rationale for the uncoupling of a borderline concept from the neuroses was located firmly within psychodynamic theory and the transference relationship. This developing relational conceptualisation of the borderline was furthered by Main (1957), whose influential object relations research paper 'The Ailment' focused less on the characteristics of an individual deemed to be 'borderline' and concentrated instead on the interaction between client and therapist. This intersubjective space was, he suggested, the loca-tion where relational complexities evolved and 'sentimental appeal from the patient enmeshed with arousal of omnipotence' in the nurse (1957: 136).

Although the borderline emerged in this way as a means of considering its suitability for analysis, alongside this uncoupling from neurosis a borderline concept was also detaching from psychosis within more institutionally-based psychiatry. Here too we can see how terminologies used to delineate this rather fuzzy patient/ condition concept were framed by dominant epistemologies of the early and mid-twentieth century. Glover (1932), for example, described the behaviours as 'incipient schizophrenia', Zilboorg (1941) as 'ambulatory schizophrenia', and Hoch and Polatin (1986 [1949]) 'pseudoneurotic schizophrenia'.

Personality

As part of a wider psychological world view that witnessed a developing interest in the notion of personality structures, the 1940s saw the beginnings of a shift from borderline viewed as a territory between neurosis and psychosis to its re-emergence as one of personality structure. The gradual translation of theories of personality dominated by psychoanalytic thinking, into an emphasis on the empirical examination of traits and the construction of tests to measure personality differences between individuals, can be seen in the following ways in which borderline issues were referred to.

Deutch (1986 [1942]), for example, conceptualised the borderline patient in terms of 'as if personalities', and Rapaport et al. (1946) as having a 'preschizophrenic personality structure'. Continuing into the 1950s and 60s, Schmideberg (1993 [1959]) introduced the idea of the patient as 'stably unstable', and Kernberg (1986 [1967]) developed the notion of 'borderline personality organisation'. The notion of personality problem was reflected in, and given further weight by, its inclusion in the first edition of the *Diagnostic and Statistical Manual of Mental Disorders* (APA, 1952) as 'pathological trends in the personality structure'. These shifting sands of the study of personality were echoed in the birth of descriptive psychiatry and *DSM-III* (APA, 1980), which described borderline personality as a stable, longstanding personality structure that was largely intractable. *DSM-III-R* (APA, 1987) further emphasised the longevity of the problems in the description of clusters of 'personality traits [that] are inflexible and maladaptive' (1987: 339). Thus the borderline personality morphed from one of 'organisation' into one of 'disorder', from a framework of continuum into one of categorisation, and from a theory-driven understanding into what has been termed 'a descriptive approach' as discussed below.

Disorder

Medical models of distress, associated therapies, and their research bases, are currently premised on the notion of disorder and its classification. Yet such constructs, as the above outlines, are changing and contested sites which represent the confla-tion of many stakeholder agendas, both past and present. Lunbeck (2006) asserts that the study of borderline personality disorder acts as an exemplar for the shifting paradigms of psychiatry, psychoanalysis and psychology. Its conceptualisation has moved during the course of the twentieth century from a boundary between neurosis and psychosis, from organisation within a dynamic conceptualisation of personal-ity, to disorder within what is referred to as 'descriptive psychiatric classification'. Recent *psychological* approaches are adopting a life-course perspective in which such clusters are understood as problems of psychological development (Winston, 2000), with markers in abuse, neglect or otherwise traumatic childhood events that trigger disturbances of identity and selfhood. Peter Fonagy argues that in adopting a developmental framework:

> We are likely to see behavioural organisations that we currently term personality disorders as age specific adaptations to biopsychosocial pressures, which are best treated by developmentally specific interventions. (2007: 3)

Within this developmental framework Fonagy (2007: 3) also concludes that 'the behaviours and experiences clustered around the notion of borderline personality disorder do *not* comprise an intractable, stable organisation but rather they remit in relatively short periods' – a statement supported by ongoing research over the last twenty-five years (see for example Zanarini et al., 2003). The *naming* of the concept as a personality disorder may therefore be problematic. It invites anxiety in health-care professionals, and although optimism and therapeutic persistence are known to be important in working with clients deemed to meet the criteria for borderline per-sonality disorder (Linehan, 1993a; Markham, 2003), it has been demonstrated that optimism is lower for clients deemed to meet the criteria for borderline personality disorder, than either depression or schizophrenia. Thus, a Catch-22 situation arises whereby the labelling of someone as meeting the criteria for such a disorder may in itself become a predictor of a likely poorer outcome for the client.

Conclusion

The above discussion has focused on the movable clinical paradigms around the notion of borderline personality, although we should not forget that social and legal factors have also influenced the *visibility* – and thereby the perceived incidence – of patterns of experience that are labelled 'borderline personality disorder'. Changing service structures from hospital- to community-based provision offers one example. Vassilev and Pilgrim (2007: 350) suggest that 'there is no single theory that can tell us everything about a phenomenon; the best we can hope for is to zoom in and out and change the angles of our observation to improve our understanding'. Part 1 has briefly zoomed in on a historical perspective on borderline personality disorder and the impact of these influences on current therapeutic thinking and practice. Part 2 looks at practice settings where dilemmas may occur, arising from those situations with which borderline personality may be associated.

Part 2: Exploring Dilemmas in Practice (Pam James)

What does borderline personality mean and to whom?
The dilemma of underlying models

The concept of the borderline has possibly acquired a tendency towards exclusivity regarding descriptive grouping, yet this can also include those who have eating disorders, depression, and on occasion, psychotic symptoms. More recently, Chmielewski et al. (2011) have concluded that it is a multi-dimensional construct and should be taken into account when pursuing appropriate treatments. Considering the associated issues with this terminology is relevant for those for whom the dilemma exists, and Meares et al. (2011) have asked whether self disturbance is at the core of the upset.

In looking at a particular client's case, in addition to presenting as very depressed, the extent of her emotional instability – particularly involving over-dosing, cutting and attempted self-harm – was such that the psychiatrist spoke about an *initial* diagnosis of depression, and *later*, borderline personality disorder. This was perceived by the client as not helpful in her planned profession. This served to increase the client's sense of hopelessness and despair: she looked it up on the internet and saw the ongoing nature of the diagnosis. She was vulnerable to suicide attempts. It was almost as though the diagnosis itself produced the behaviours. Eventually, for the client, as her self-harm by cutting stopped, then self-harm by exercise and dieting came more to the fore. However, each client's response to their diagnosis will be different. In another example, the client was not distressed: instead she said that it was useful to have a diagnosis as it gave her some relief that there were other people who also experienced life in this way.

A central concept underlying the whole group of personality disorders is that of a trait-based enduring quality to the descriptors, which could accompany a possibility of resistance to change in therapy. However, recent research reflects a different viewpoint that the beliefs and behaviours can be changed in therapy and this is reinforced in the (2009a) NICE Guidelines. Zanarini (2009) reports on four different successful therapies, stating that mentalisation, transference-focused therapy, dialectic-behaviour therapy and schema-focused therapy can all produce successful outcomes, but the therapy is long term. There is a dilemma here, and this is concentrated around the availability of services that can meet this requirement, as well as the length of time in therapy.

Before a diagnosis has occurred, clients can report feelings of abandonment and insecurity from which they find it difficult or impossible to be comforted. McDonald et al. (2010) write about the ontological insecurity that is experienced by people who eventually acquire the description of borderline. One dilemma lies in the experience of aloneness and the lack of ability to self-comfort. Feelings are reported to be very intense and almost impossible to calm and contain. In this state, clients may attempt to self-medicate by using alcohol and illegal substances to dull their awareness. Such attempts can increase a person's risk of harm and result in further on-going problems. An associated dilemma can be working with a client to reduce their substance abuse, whilst at the same time providing another way to comfort distressing and despairing feelings that seem overwhelming.

Consequences of symptom identification and diagnosis: the dilemma of ideographic and nomothetic when working therapeutically

The (2009a) NICE Guidelines indicate that the evidenced treatment response refers to more than one helpful therapy. Dilemmas arise in the application of the Guidelines as individual patient experiences contain their own particular descriptions. The advantages of working psychologically aim to understand the particular person in context: a rational explanation for feeling anxious or depressed can be understood, rather than just responding to this as a set of symptoms.

One particular client with a diagnosis of borderline personality had been referred for therapy by her psychiatrist. This had been triggered by a suicide attempt some months previously, a chronic eating disorder and the rejection of a previous male therapist, after which the client had indicated her preference for a female. Emotional instability was the focus, perhaps arising from her past learning and experience of insecure attachment and abusive relating. When a person has been abused, this often becomes internalised to become self-abusive.

At our first meeting she did not look at me at all, but kept her head down, so that her hair covered her face almost entirely. There were long periods of silence. She seemed that she was more comfortable when I didn't try to engage eye contact. It was almost as though she was shy, defended, embarrassed. Yet towards the end of the session she challenged me by saying 'You don't want to work with me … everyone says I'm no good'. When this was reflected to her, the door opened to hearing about her previous experiences of others who had described her as such. She seemed to be generally not believed, particularly around her past relationships with men when she said that they had abused her, both emotionally and sexually.

In the session, I spoke tentatively about the need for support around her during the therapeutic process. We discussed the use of the crisis lines and having community psychiatric nurse contact. I was holding the knowledge of her resentment towards support from previous experiences, and also my knowledge that a team around her could assist to provide an external container for her feelings and thoughts arising both from therapy and everyday living. To be able to work with this person, there was a need to build some containment. External containing systems could be put in place, but would she use them? The building of internal containment was much more challenging and long term.

Meanwhile, in the sessions she spoke of her use of alcohol and cannabis, self-harm by cutting and her lack of eating. She had the capacity to make me extremely concerned for her safety and wellbeing. In supervision I worked to try to understand my counter-transference, and also to stay congruent. This gave me a framework in which to work.

The client appeared to have developed a sense of trusting me, which was emerging from a history of a lack of trust of significant others, including mental health professionals who hadn't believed her regarding sexual abuse. She spoke about much of her previous life experiences with hesitancy and caution. I too felt this caution as I needed to take care that she should not become so distressed, leave the session, and have no container for her emotions.

Commenting on the dilemmas of casework with this client focuses around the time taken to build any therapeutic relationship so that the therapies recommended in the NICE Guidelines could commence. The beginning of trust needs time to develop: the transference relationship with the therapist can strongly mirror early relating, especially when under stress, and needs to be understood. Containment for feelings also needs to be established – therapy that involves exploration is not recommended due to the arousal of strong feeling which cannot be contained and may result in self-harm. The possible dilemma for the practitioner is to use knowledge of the concept of transference to understand the relationship, whilst working to build and learn a safe and different way of responding to strong upsetting feelings rather than self-harm.

Consequences of a diagnosis or symptom recognition: the dilemma of which therapeutic response to adopt, use of medication and the concept of risk

The therapeutic model that is preferred for people with a borderline personality is associated with cognition and behaviour – dialectical behaviour therapy (DBT). Linehan (1993b) discusses DBT which works in an educative way to allow the person to safely learn about their emotions, so that they are not overwhelmed by strong anger or emotional pain. The rationale here is not to use exploratory therapies that open up emotions and then have no 'container'. The risk of suicide can be considerable if strong feelings emerge which cannot be contained. The concept of a container comes from psychodynamic working where the developing child learns that it is acceptable to get upset and be comforted. This is in contrast to the developing child who gets upset and has no comforter, only their own terror of what has occurred. Defences are then unconsciously used to protect the young psyche and these can include detachment and denial. A response to being angry with another may be anger with the self, as anger with another would be too frightening.

Although working within a DBT framework, if the concepts of transference and counter-transference are understood by the therapist, it is then possible to understand the client's behaviours. Examples present in many ways – in missed appointments if the client wants to avoid emotional pain, in anger shown after an unexpected break in planned sessions. Consequently, although it would not be helpful to work only psychodynamically, it is helpful for the therapist to be aware of the possible effects of the client's presenting past.

This makes working therapeutically with borderline personality a process that involves caution. Suicide attempts can occur frequently, whether as a learnt response to distress, a need to be noticed, or a sense that there is no hope that things will be better in the future. It seems that in stress and distress, using alcohol and drugs can be an attempt to self-medicate to remove the feelings of despair and isolation. In these inebriated states, any rational thinking becomes less possible and self-harm becomes more likely. In some cases it is almost as though psychotic symptoms are present. However, the extended use of prescribed medication is not recommended by the NICE Guidelines. Furthermore, stored medication can be used to over-dose: if prescribed this is usually for a seven-day period only.

The response of the mental health professional to self-harm and attempted suicide can also produce a dilemma as different reactions can occur. Anecdotal reports suggest that Accident and Emergency departments do not always respond sympathetically, and therapists can feel concerned and protective about their clients, whilst also fearful that further attempts may occur. There can be different ways of understanding clients' behaviours in multi-professional teams and these may create inter-professional conflict. It is almost as though the client behaviours recreate the dysfunctional family which was part of their childhood experience.

Consequences of therapy: the dilemma of care or cure

Zanarini et al. (2010) report that therapeutic change can occur. If factors associated with clients' experience are seen as arising from severe difficulties in childhood, then is it possible in therapy to construct *lasting* change?

Casework suggests that relapses occur, that long periods of therapy are required to produce change. Relapses can be triggered by perceived interpersonal conflicts and relationship breakdowns. The service design to support such clients refers to having a revolving door. Further upset can be triggered by staff changes, precipitating early feelings of being abandoned and abused. Therapists and psychiatrists will move job, but in a good working environment change is best when anticipated and worked through. Clients need time to build up their defences against loss and change. The dilemma of a potential ongoing client relapse must to be understood when designing services to meet the needs of this client group.

The chapter now turns to examine research evidence when working with clients with borderline personality, and also to consider the experiences of working with clients with this presenting issue in the context of employment.

Part 3: Exploring Research and Practice with Clients Experiencing Borderline Personality Issues

A: Working with borderline issues in the National Health Service (Claire John)

Introduction

The NHS is often the starting point for working with people who have a cluster of symptoms that are expressed as Borderline Personality Disorder (BPD): there is a growing evidence base for psychological interventions. The value of psychological formulation, in addition to diagnosis, is central to understand a shifting, complex and often socially and emotionally challenging group of people, and also pivotal to successful outcomes.

Reports issued by the National Institute for Mental Health in England (2003) cite that people with personality disorder should not be excluded from services. In 2009 the National Institute for Health and Care Report included DBT as an evidence base for the treatment of BPD. The British Psychological Society's report published in 2006 also recognised personality disorder as amenable to treatment provided the chosen intervention is used in a coherent and consistent manner. A number of treatment modalities are outlined, including DBT.

Modern practice within the NHS is informed by evidence – the gold standard being quality research using randomised control trials – but well-informed clinical opinion is also valued. DBT enjoyed good research outcomes when Linehan et al. (1991, 1993a, 1993b) investigated its efficacy, although Scheel (2000) noted some methodological difficulties with some of the findings. Feigenbaum (2007) has also reviewed the literature for DBT and concluded that there is a growing evidence base, including co-morbid presentations.

The Australian-based Hunter Project was evaluated by Carter (2010) and found that DBT had a beneficial effect on quality of life, but did not have any demonstrable differences on deliberate self-harm and hospitalisation compared to treatment as usual and being on a waiting list. However, they also qualify their findings, noticing that admissions and self-harm were not as prevalent in the control groups as they would have anticipated. General clinical improvement and greater retention rates than general therapy groups were also noted by Soler (2008). A 60 per cent drop-out rate can be anticipated in most psychotherapy groups – this was 40 per cent for DBT.

Working with dialectical behaviour therapy in the NHS

While acknowledging its American origins the DBT model can be modified to accommodate cultural differences in the British NHS. Potential candidates for a DBT programme need to understand the commitment and rationale for the programme, and experience has shown that a good period of pre-treatment enhances successful completion. Pre-treatment offers the opportunity to experience DBT while enabling both parties to work collaboratively toward effective treatment options. During the pre-treatment phase target hierarchies are established, and both parties are then aware in which order behaviours will be addressed. The most life-threatening behaviours are prioritised. Using a system of chain analysis – i.e. recalling all events immediately prior to the life-threatening act – the client and therapist can try to determine ways of managing high levels of emotional arousal. They will attempt to identify stages in the chain where the client could do something differently to lower their distress while also getting their needs met. The client is given an opportunity to see both how DBT will work and its limitations.

Traditional DBT requires access to an individual therapist 24 hours a day, seven days a week. Although challenging, it may be replicated in the public sector by using agencies such as home treatment teams. One of the roles of the individual therapist is to provide coaching and encourage the person to use any skills they have acquired. Home treatment teams can provide out-of-hours care and meet between session coaching needs.

Clinicians will meet in parallel to the group programme: its supervisory quality encourages therapists to think about their contribution to shaping behaviour in a validating, if also challenging, environment. Group members will notice any prejudice, judgement, and indeed opposing thoughts that arise, and seek a synthesis between entrenched opinions. This process continues throughout the life of the treatment programme, including any ongoing individual work. Whilst providing supervision it can also lend support and potentially be a training forum to non-DBT-trained clinicians. Promoting a transparent and well-understood philosophy enables multi-disciplinary teams to consistently manage the erratic nature of clients. A methodologically coherent model is endorsed by all published guidelines (Alwin et al., 2006; NICE, 2009a).

The group is comprised of three modules: Interpersonal Effectiveness; Emotional Regulation; and Distress Tolerance. Each is preceded by Mindfulness Training. Unlike other therapy groups, DBT skill training requires therapists to offer their own material as examples. This is done prudently using 'safe material' which functions to normalise reactions to emotionally arousing situations while demonstrating the effectiveness of the skills. Using three facilitators means that the group can continue even if a client runs into crisis and needs immediate attention. One facilitator assists, while the two remaining clinicians continue teaching.

The acquisition of skills varies according to the participant's emotional arousal. If the participant is feeling emotionally stable, skills will feel unnecessary, as though they have come naturally, but at times of heightened distress their effectiveness could be impaired. Drawing on aspects from all modules enables the person to respond to their crises using the most effective skill at the time. Noticing opposing opinions and being able to work through to a synthesis without judgement are vital parts of the work. Tensions can arise both between individual participants and participants and facilitators. DBT embraces challenge and noticing that therapists are flawed ('all therapists are jerks') gives grist to the mill. Everyone in the group works toward finding solid solutions to emotionally fraught situations while acknowledging no one has the right answer.

Case study

Jayne is a 30 year-old married woman with three children. She had had no contact with mental health services until the birth of her third child. She had struggled through pregnancy, had felt confused and afraid. Post-partum she responded turbulently, was admitted to psychiatric hospital and was diagnosed with post-natal depression. She was referred to the Psychological Therapies Service. A bright and intelligent young lady, she was also fearful and guarded. She was concerned about her abilities as a mother, and quickly disclosed difficult early relationships in her own formative years. Her own experience of parenting had been confusing, invalidating, and very often frightening. She had been expected to care for her younger siblings: her mother was a prominent but frightening figure, and her father was unavailable to her through his work. Relationships with her wider family were confusing, and sexual in nature. She had struggled to separate from her family, and had dropped out of university, doubting herself, and afraid of unwanted sexual attention.

Despite all the difficultness she managed to find employment, and succeeded in developing a successful career for herself. She entered a solid relationship and married. Her mental health varied but she was able to maintain her relationship and home until the birth of her third child. At this point she described feeling out of control, unable to establish whether her experiences were real or imagined, and once again fear and mistrust pervaded her lived experience. She frequently had thoughts of dying, and indeed had acted on these thoughts by self-poisoning. However, her desire to be available to her own children, to be a good mother, meant that she could never follow through on her actions and she would seek help.

By turns angry and distressed she entered the DBT group, unsure of its ability to help her. She found that mindfulness came easily and she was able to engage with the process. She was an avid student, wanting to get the most out of the programme, but began to recognise that some of her efforts were aimed at pleasing others rather than establishing a different way of coping with her rollercoaster emotions. She began to develop insight and find strategies that enabled her to cope.

Although her life was extremely stressful, taking many unexpected and challenging turns, she was able to use her skills and share her experiences with the group. When she was asked to resume some family responsibility Jayne found the pressure increasing. The strategy has been to reinforce her skills. Although there had been settled times via the group, the success of the programme could only be gauged by her response to 'real-life' situations. There are times when Jayne feels she has not coped as well as she should, and she has harmed, but she has also thought about using her skills. She has managed very difficult situations effectively, thinking of solutions even if she has not been able to implement them at the time.

Future developments

Running DBT programmes can be inspirational but consideration must be given to other ways of working. Anecdotally, running the programmes has not 'cured' the participants, but each one has gained something: here the question may be is the cost of the programme justified in producing partial success? Other ways of working might complement DBT services: for example, using a mentalisation stance with clients on a one-to-one basis post completion of the programme is being piloted. The rationale for this is that once clients have a stable emotional basis to work from they may be able to mentalise more effectively.

Bateman and Fonagy (2000) developed Mentalisation Based Therapy (MBT): a programme of one-to-one and group therapy. In essence clients learn to think about their thinking so they are able to understand the thoughts of others, a skill learnt in childhood. However, if a client's childhood had been disrupted in some way the ability to mentalise will not have been established. Unhelpful ways of thinking will have developed that do not allow the client to empathise with others or develop flexible ways of thinking within themselves. Focusing on the here and now, the group experience offers rich examples of non-mentalising which can be worked with as they occur. If a client has successfully managed to contain their emotional arousal through DBT it is possible that they can readily enter into MBT. In a strained NHS it is not always possible to offer full MBT or DBT programmes at the same time. Being able to offer an integrated service may enable clients to enjoy the benefits of both programmes. Actively mentalising whilst delivering DBT appears to enhance the delivery of the programme, which leads all parties to reach a dialectic more easily.

Further interventions, such as Systems Training for Emotional Predictability and Problem Solving (Bloom et al., 2002), complement a personality disorder service. This programme is didactic: using a group format it teaches a step-by-step method of coping with overwhelming thoughts and feelings. Drawing on cognitive behavioural therapy and systemic models it enables clients to recognise the often rapid shift in emotions and thoughts, identify negative filters (adapted from Young's

Schema Therapy, 1994), and learn a system of skills to manage the arousal. The programme relies on people within a client's life to reinforce skills, and so they are invited to training sessions to allow them to appreciate and support the skills being taught to the clients. Although its efficacy in reducing suicidal thoughts has yet to be proven (Harvey et al., 2010), STEPPS is a useful programme for those engaging in lower risk behaviours.

The final part of this chapter is concerned with the employment context and considers issues that occur in connection with people associated with having a borderline personality.

B. Working with borderline personality issues in employment settings (Nicola Gale)

Mental health and work

Mental health has for some time been at the forefront of the current employment agenda. Perkins et al. (2009) called for a reversal in the trend of worklessness for people with a mental health condition and more support in negotiating the social world of work. In relation to the provision of health services, the government introduced Improving Access to Psychological Therapies. The Department of Health also introduced SHiFT (closed March 2011), a programme to reduce discrimination against people with mental health conditions in work. For the NHS, with over one million employees, Boorman (2009) published an analysis of the current state of wellbeing of NHS staff and a blueprint for investment, including early access to effective health-care interventions. These kinds of employment-related initiatives have, however, paid little attention to the impact on individuals and employers of personality difficulties, such as the presenting issues of borderline personality.

The employment context

This part of the chapter dealing with people who have aspects of (or a diagnosis of) BPD in the workplace derives from the author's work and experience as clinical lead in a staff psychological service in an NHS Trust. In the employment context individuals rarely present having undergone a formal assessment and diagnosis of BPD from mental health services. Presentation is likely to result from an accumulation of difficulties which are perceived by the individual and others to be pervasive, and are causing individual distress and organisational disruption. Considerable efforts are made to support staff with mental health conditions to stay in work. At the same time, the presentation of borderline personality disorder symptoms can give rise to the need for a consideration of fitness for clinical practice, depending on the role and context. Issues also arise in relation to the welfare of others in teams, supervisory duties if the individual is in a management position, and in managing the risk and impact of behaviours that may occur within and outside the workplace.

Individuals in the workplace

Work may act as a source of support, consistency, boundaries and containment. It may also give rise to challenges that exacerbate the features of the disorder. Table 7.1 below summarises some of the challenges individuals may face.

Table 7.1

DSM-IV-TR criteria Borderline Personality Disorder	Common Workplace Issues for the Individual
Abandonment	Organisational change and changes of line management / colleague relationships
Unstable interpersonal relationships	Close friendships quickly formed deteriorating and causing distress / sense of alienation
Identity disturbance	Difficulties managing work and private self and assigned work roles
Impulsivity	Personal debt problems, sexual boundaries in work relationships
Suicidal / self-harming behaviour	Being 'sent' for help / assessment
Affective instability	Distress at ups and downs of working day, moods of colleagues, demands of service users
Chronic emptiness	Career /role dissatisfaction /indecision
Anger	Sense of grievance over treatment at work
Paranoid ideation / dissociation	Feeling persecuted at work

Issues for management and colleagues

A staff member experiencing issues associated with borderline personality can be seen as excessively needy and difficult to manage. For example, if management need to make changes in the work environment, these may be taken overly personally. The fallout of impulsive behaviours can also be time-consuming to manage. The unstable interpersonal relationships that characterise someone with these presenting issues can leave colleagues experiencing them as unpredictable. Team activities such as clinical supervision and reflective practice may suffer from the diminution of trust that can be a consequence of unstable team relationships, conflict and impulsive behaviours. Behaviours may happen in the public gaze, which risks bringing the organisation and possibly the individual's profession into disrepute.

An individual with borderline personality disorder behaviours may well become a manager or leader with a consequent negative impact on the team culture. Equality and a sense of fairness in the workplace can suffer due to the close bonds that this person may form with certain staff members at the expense of others. Often they come across as confusing as leaders, due to the identify disturbance that is a part of their issues, so team members do not receive the constancy and reliability that are expected of a team leader.

So how can BPD manifest in the workplace? What follows is a hybrid case study made from themes that have typically arisen over many years: note that it is not a representation of individual clinical material.

Samantha is a staff nurse in her late thirties. Her behaviour at work has been problematic, with unreliable attendance and emotional outbursts including in front of patients who complained. She is now subject to disciplinary action. She is no longer speaking to the deputy ward sister who had temporarily to suspend her from work: beforehand she used to idolise her. Management were concerned that these ruptures in working relationships were putting patient care at risk.

Samantha is seen for a psychological assessment. She describes problematic patterns in personal relationships: getting out of control on evenings out; spending more than she could afford; and chronic emptiness. The subject of the diagnosis was broached with careful and sensitive timing, talking in terms of a continuum, and of personality structures. Samantha, who had long thought there was something wrong, recognised the borderline criteria as features of her own experience and found the diagnosis containing.

Samantha's difficulties were not sufficiently great to warrant referral to specialist services. Work was therefore begun with Samantha on skills in emotion regulation, distress tolerance, and interpersonal effectiveness, aimed at achieving greater stability and a consistent performance at work. She was offered welfare support over the disciplinary and debt. Mediation helped to restore appropriate working relationships on the ward. Conversations with the ward management assisted with strategies to maintain appropriate boundaries at work, consistency of line management, and to refocus team behaviours on patient care.

Issues in assessment

Specific routes to assessment in the workplace context can be line managers or Human Resources personnel, frequently following an incident in a ward/department that will often have had its origins in relationship problems or a behavioural incident. Occupational Health departments may also refer, having been asked to assess if there is an underlying health condition that may be affecting an individual in the workplace.

Assessment will consider a diagnosis, and may involve structured interview tools and seeking information from multiple sources. In addition a formulation will be developed. Alwin et al. (2006) give an overview of the relevant considerations. The assessment in the workplace will require understanding the organisational role of the individual, and any particular risks that that role presents. There is a need to distinguish the borderline pattern from the normal ups and downs and occasional incidents that happen as part of working life. As the assessment is taking place in a work context, confidentiality policies and protocols must be clear in order to address any apprehension that there could be adverse consequences. As is usual with this presentation there is often a history of failed attempts to get help.

Interventions for the individual

Where individuals either do not need more specialist services or are unlikely to be considered appropriate for referrals to more specialist care, interventions taken from DBT and mentalisation can supply some of the core skills that are lacking in those presenting with borderline personality symptoms. A programme of individual skills development can be effective in achieving greater stability and a consistent performance at work (McKay et al., 2007). The toolbox approach (Krawitz and Jackson, 2008) can also be useful, including a capacity to reflect, a planned behaviour change, changing negative self talk, and building a tolerance towards emotional distress, as well as ways of applying these (for example, in dealing with difficult emotions, relating to others, and work on personal identity).

Often the role of the specialist workplace psychological service is to undertake an extended assessment, understanding patterns of behaviour, and generate a psychological formulation. As Davidson (2008) points out, formulation provides a shared and comprehensive understanding of the person's current difficulties, their origin and maintenance, and is a cornerstone for psychological treatment using a cognitive model. Longer-term work is generally indicated for borderline personality disorder treatment, however, and an appropriate service needs to be structured to manage crises. Where other services are involved, collaboration on a crisis plan specifically for workplace issues should be considered. Krawitz and Jackson (2008) emphasise the importance of the individual committing to prepare for future crises, in order to increase the likelihood of healthy solutions and reduce the risk of making things worse. The extent to which this involves other people at work requires careful negotiation.

There is a need, if treatment and support is going to be referred on to another service, to manage the presentation of the borderline structure in the assessment (NICE, 2009a). Individuals will typically attach quite strongly once they feel understood, and in demonstrating extremes of idealisation may say things like 'this is the first time anyone's really understood ...'. Fears of rejection and abandonment can easily be activated by talk of referral however early in the assessment process. There can be difficulties too in finding an appropriate service. While these individuals have the need and clinical features they are often seen as too high functioning for relevant services. There can be a stigma for health professionals and employment implications to be managed, and services are often not set up to be accessible at hours which will support the maintenance of employment.

Interventions for the organisation

Coaching for line managers and HR personnel can be useful in relation to understanding the importance of consistency and maintaining boundaried and work-focused relationships at work. Support with managing organisational processes in a way that does not exacerbate the difficulties is important, so that the attempted solutions do not exacerbate and create further problems. Sampson (2006) refers to this issue facing Community Mental Health Teams (CMHTs) in managing people with a diagnosis of borderline personality disorder.

The way forward

The issue of how personality structures and disorders affect work needs to be part of the agenda for mental health support in the workplace. In practical terms, awareness needs to be raised about recognising some of the early warning signs of challenging personality structures before there is an adverse impact on individuals or the workplace, and also recognising when a clinical referral to psychology services is indicated for assessment and advice.

Chapter Summary

The location of the borderline personality in its historical context was followed by examples of some of the dilemmas that arise in current practice. These were then followed by a closer look at research studies carrying optimism for working with people with these presenting issues, and focusing also on the workplace. The following reflective questions invite you to think about your own practice experience.

REFLECTION BOX

1   How does the term 'borderline personality disorder' impact on your therapeutic work?
2   There are suggestions that we might reframe some diagnostic categories because they do not recognise the experience of complex trauma that underlies

(Continued)

(Continued)

them but focus instead on the personality of the person. Might it be useful to reframe the construct of borderline personality towards one of complex trauma?

3 Reflecting on your casework have there been clients who have shown the behaviours of borderline personality and yet not been diagnosed as such? In what way might their progress in therapy have been different if a diagnosis had occurred?

4 This chapter has discussed some of the dilemmas posed by working with people described as having a borderline personality disorder. What kind of dilemmas have you encountered in your casework?

5 How would you in your clinical capacity enable all professionals to maintain a validating stance when working with clients who meet the criteria for borderline personality disorder?

6 If you were the team manager for someone with a diagnosis of borderline personality, how would you support them and ensure the team was working well?

8

Exploring Eating Disorders

Introduction

Generally, eating disorders, including anorexia, bulimia and binge eating, are regarded as responses to a combination of factors which may include attachment issues, low self-esteem, family relationship issues, loss, problems with study or work, bullying or abuse, and in some instances a suggested genetic or neurological predisposition. These may occur when food is used to cope with feelings such as anxiety, anger, loneliness, boredom, shame, failure, a loss of control or sadness. They are regularly associated with other responses to distress. In terms of a medical model, these include obsessive compulsive disorder, borderline personality disorder, and depression. Conditions, protocols and treatments of choice, particularly evidence-based self-help programmes, include cognitive behavioural therapy (CBT), cognitive analytic therapy (CAT) and interpersonal psychotherapy (IPT). Specialist services have emerged, albeit patchily, across Great Britain, and can be found within the national health, voluntary and private sectors.

For the client, however, there are many meanings to eating difficulties. Many describe the experience as an addiction, others as an identity. Some engage with an all-encompassing daily weight loss and food control that will be heavily defended from anyone perceived as attempting to subvert this. Fear encompasses much of the experience of relating to food and weight: fear of losing the battle, of losing identity, of losing control, or of being without the means for existing in the world.

Just as the nature, causes and experiences of eating disorders are numerous and complex so there is also a range of models put forward to offer frameworks for understanding these. Most recently, for example, neuropsychological models have considered eating disorders in relation to early trauma, attachment and neurological pathways in the formation of attachment bonds (Lask and Frampton, 2011). Other biomedical models may investigate genetic predispositions to eating problems.

Psychosocial models tend to focus on an evaluation of the individual's negative self-evaluation and may investigate links to eating problems with (for example) parental depression, adverse childhood experiences, or the impact of bullying. Social constructionist models may consider the concept of disorder itself as historical, cultural, and/or gendered, and ask, for example, why we have constructed a gendered disorder which emphasises a drive for thinness rather than a drive for muscularity.

Research into eating disorders is immensely important because they cause considerable, and life threatening, distress both to the individual experiencing them and to families. One in 200 females and one in 2,000 males will suffer from anorexia, which also has the highest mortality rate of any of the psychiatric classifications. Five times as many people suffer from bulimia and, in addition, long-term problems are not uncommon in both (NICE, 2004: 7).

Part 1 of this chapter now turns to a historical contextualisation of our current understanding and treatment of eating disorders, and considers how a historical examination contributes to thinking about these issues and the perspectives that are taken when working with clients.

Part 1: Exploring the Historical Context (Barbara Douglas)

There was a perceived increase in eating disorders within western society in the 1980s and 1990s and a resulting proliferation of work examining their history (Bell, 1987; Brumberg, 1988; Vandereycken and van Deth, 1994). Whether this was the result of increased incidence or increased publicity (or both) was the question being asked. Research explored the role of television in the relative increase in both the incidence and visibility of eating disorders as well as a globalisation of a drive for thinness (Gordon, 2000). Questions also focused on whether the medieval notion of saintly fasting was continuous or discontinuous with anorexia as we understand it (Habermas, 2005). Thus historical research is one driver towards our better understanding of the cultural and biologic causative factors of eating problems.

Notions of disease specificity emerged in western medicine largely during the last couple of hundred years (Scull, 2009). Before this, ideas around body and mind problems, including emaciation, were largely part of a systemic world view in which body, mind and environment were holistically seen as interrelated. Humoral medicine, the mainstay of western medical understandings for centuries, framed ideologies within a concept of balance, both between nature and body and within the body. So while Pearce (2004: 191) details what may be the first recorded death from anorexia in 383AD amongst a group of ascetics 'who had spurned the corporeal world', and a Renaissance case in which St Theresa of Avila used olive sticks to induce vomiting, the notion of specifying a delineated disorder construct such as we refer to as anorexia or bulimia would be a misconception.

The first description of what might sound familiar to us as anorexia is regarded as being that of English physician Richard Morton (1694, cited in Pearce, 2004). At a time when science, and particularly anatomy, focused interest on the body, the impetus for Morton in describing cases of emaciation was part of an attempt to understand the causes of consumption:

> A nervous atrophy, or consumption, is a wasting of the body without any remarkable fever, cough or shortness of breath, but it is attended by want of appetite and a bad digestion, upon which there follows a languishing weakness of nature and a falling away of the flesh every day more and more. (2004: 191–192)

Morton's statement of nervous consumption as a need to 'shake off all sadness' and as 'difficult because it first flatters and deceives the patient' is something that might well be recognised currently in experiences of anorexia (Bhanji and Newton, 1985: 591).

But the authors generally credited with defining anorexia as a specific form of self starvation were, in France, Ernest Lasegue in 1873, and in Britain, Sir William Gull in 1868 and 1873 (Pearce, 2004). Neurological physician Lasegue (1816–1883) described the emotional causations and family involvement in *l'anorexie hysterique*: 'the family has but two methods at its service which it always exhausts – entreaties and menaces – and which both serve as a touchstone' (Brumberg, 1988: 128). At the same time, in a move away from a somatic understanding of the problem contained in his initial terminology of *apepsia hysterica* (1868), the notable English physician Gull coined the term 'anorexia nervosa' (1873) as 'a particular form of disease characterised by extreme emaciation and often referred to as latent tubercle and mesenteric disease' (Pearce, 2004: 192). Maddon (2004) suggests that Gull's anorexia nervosa is important because it is the first to consider psychological factors. That neither identified fear of weight gain or abnormal body image in their descriptions suggests a discontinuity in what anorexia is, and means, in different times/cultures. These aspects (weight phobia, fear of fatness and abnormal body image) are perhaps culturally and historically specific features confined to a later cult of thinness.

Gull, Lasegue and others in the late nineteenth century progressively delineated anorexia as a separate condition from either hysteria or neurasthenia (Shorter, 2005). The treatment was considered to be similar, however, requiring rest and isolation, and evidenced by the French neurologist Charcot (1889). He suggested two fundamentally important treatment factors to be removal from the place in which the disease originated and the primary authority of the physician in its management. It is interesting to note that mid to late twentieth-century behavioural treatments for eating disorders followed similar regimes with hospitalisation and bed rest, being followed by progressive privileges only on the resumption of an increased and regularised food intake.

The early twentieth century saw the emphasis placed firmly on weight loss and emaciation. Biological theories centred on the work of German pathologist Morris Simmonds (1855–1925) and the role of a pituitary disorder. Simmonds proposed that pituitary insufficiency led to weight loss in some patients and for a period of around thirty years theories of wasting diseases turned to endocrinology rather than psychiatry for answers. Vandereyken and van Deth (1994: 180) concluded that this caused mistreatment that 'throws a dark shadow on this episode in the history of anorexia'. Other drug treatments that emerged from this endocrine model of emaciation included thyroid extract and insulin with chlorpromazine.

Interest in the somatic causes of emaciation dwindled following the realisation that malnutrition was not usually a part of pituitary problems. The space was filled by a shifting emphasis towards psychogenic and psychosomatic approaches to eating disorders, in particular with the work of German psychiatrist Hilde Bruch (1904–1984). Bruch fled Germany in the wake of anti-Semitism, first to Britain and then to America where her psychoanalytic interests lay first in obesity. Obesity, she argued, was a manifestation of the child's struggle to develop autonomy within the family (Gilman, 2010). Turning her interests to anorexia her highly influential work proposed that the nature of eating disorders represented a struggle with selfhood within the family (Bruch, 1978, 1979). Her empathic writing and emphasis on the nature of the therapeutic relationship spurred on, and made known within the psychotherapeutic field, work with this client group. Skarderud (2009) argues that consigning Bruch to the historical annals of the period is a mistake as her focus on the needs of therapy to work with the self of the client is now being confirmed in theories of, and research into, attachment and mentalisation (Fonagy et al., 2011a).

It was psychoanalytic constructs that influenced the emergence of early iterations of the *Diagnostic and Statistical Manual of Mental Disorders* (APA, 1952) and *DSM-II* (APA, 1968), within a framework of individual reaction, a continuum of experience and behaviours as manifestations of unconscious conflict. Only with the *DSM-III* (APA, 1980) was there a paradigmatic shift towards descriptive categorical classification of mental disorder, sometimes referred to as the rise of the second biological psychiatry (Shorter, 1997: 239). In this evolving framework the focus shifted from understanding the cause and process to delineating disorder criteria and the treatment outcome. This was associated with the development of measurement scales, such as the Stirling Eating Disorders Scale and the Eating Disorders Inventory, as well as randomised controlled trials of therapeutic interventions with eating disorders clients. It was within this context that Gerald Russell (1979) influentially detailed bulimia as *an ominous variant of anorexia* in a paper of that title, resulting in the delineation of *bulimia nervosa* as a separate disorder.

Conclusion

Vandereycken and van Deth (2000: 183) write that 'culture is regarded as the soil from which self starvation grows into a sign of sanctity, a kind of spectacle, or a specific illness'. This brief section has outlined some of these cultures. Until a couple of hundred years ago holistic concepts of the person and environment dominated, with concepts of disorder specificity only emerging more recently. At this point the focus turned towards self starvation as it uncoupled itself from the overlapping and feared conditions of tuberculosis on the one hand, and hysteria on the other.

Since the Victorian period conceptual understandings of eating disorders have mirrored those of general psychiatry, being located within notions of hysteria, neurology, and psychodynamic theories of development, and with ever-increasing specificity within the dominant descriptive psychiatry of the late twentieth and early twenty-first centuries. Further delineation is evident in the *DSM-5* (APA, 2013a) where binge-eating disorder merits a full categorical code. Simultaneously, however, this specificity is being challenged in the realms of client work itself where the majority of clients being seen with eating problems appear to sit within a framework of eating disorders not otherwise specified (EDNOS) because their experiences cross currently defined categorical borders (Busko, 2007). On this note it is timely to lead into considering some of the current dilemmas in understanding and working with clients who experience eating problems.

Part 2: Exploring Dilemmas in Practice (Pam James)

What does the term 'eating disorder' mean and to whom?

There are two main presenting issues that are under the umbrella of this term: anorexia nervosa and bulimia nervosa. These descriptions signify to all that something is 'wrong' with the pattern of eating, to the extent that it has become labelled as a disorder. If the regulation of eating is described as existing on a continuum, at some point the diet/non-diet, indulge/starve self, indulge/self deny approach to eating has become such that it is now described as an eating *disorder*. Psychological explanations vary according to which theoretical base gains predominance, although the (2004) NICE Guidelines recommend CBT as the treatment of choice. Fairburn et al.'s (2008) transdiagnostic model has gained wide acceptance. Williams (2003) focuses on the psychodynamics of the process of eating and its association within the context of dependent relationships. Slade (1982) puts forward a formulation that culminates in seeing this presenting problem as particular psychosocial stimuli that become associated with bodily control through eating. Dilemmas can occur when therapists find that clients do not make progress as expected using the recommended approach. Whichever psychological model is used to explain the pattern of a relationship with food, there is a need to recognise this so that at least the physical health of the person can be maintained.

Other presenting problems often occur at the same time, such as depression, obsessional behaviour including the need to be perfect, anxiety, low self-esteem and self-harm. These conditions can produce symptoms that are often first seen by the GP who refers on to the psychiatric services to maintain the person's physical and mental health: this will frequently involve medication and a referral for therapy. A symptom overlap may result in confusion about which psychotherapy to implement, when disordered eating is one of a number of presenting issues.

Psychologists aim to try to understand something about the client's overall life experience. This involves a balance between working with the person to often hear discreet aspects of their pain and inner world whilst maintaining a confidential balance with the multi-professional team.

For the person experiencing the eating disorder, confusion and shame may inhibit their expression and understanding of what is going on. Someone with bulimia can be trying to mask their vomiting and cope without telling anyone. Goss and Allan (2009) provided a literature review in this area. Controlling eating is often associated with an idealised body size which comes to take on an irrational importance. Legenbauer et al. (2011) highlight the body image concept as an integral factor in therapeutic work with eating disordered clients. What is clear from casework is that individuals' experiences of their eating disorder vary widely.

One of the practice dilemmas is the time taken in regular communication amongst the multi-professional team. The person may be in therapy with a psychologist and also in the care of a psychiatrist, either as an out-patient or in extreme cases in a residential unit. Physical and psychological health are inter-related. The checks on weight by the GP become a necessary focus to monitor sufficient body weight and blood tests to check for the presence of essential minerals. It follows therefore that it is likely that psychiatric models of care and causality will meet up with psychological models of understanding quite early on in the case history of the person.

Dilemmas of the consequences of a diagnosis: nomothetic and idiographic aspects

The NICE Guidelines (2004) provide evidence for the preferred therapeutic response, yet any therapist who has worked with these presenting issues will appreciate the diversity of individual presentations: the need to listen to the client, the need to work in a multi-professional team, and the need to maintain physical health. There is a certain tension also regarding who should monitor the *body mass index*, whether GP, psychiatrist or CPN. All these options are external to the client and in some way this could suggest that there is reluctance in the person themselves to self-care.

Preferred approaches are cognitive therapy and family therapy: the latter involves the participation of family members. NICE recommends that cognitive therapy is located in the context of the family, perhaps as eating disorders are more likely to present in adolescence. However, dilemmas arising from the complexity of present-ing issues can be seen. In the following case example, one client had experienced fam-ily relationship problems whilst growing up whereby she felt she needed to protect and defend her mother in parental arguments. She was conscientious and quiet: she also simultaneously feared and loved her father. The change in her relationship with food was triggered by a sexual assault. Her overall behaviour became less confident and she stopped her job and only went out occasionally. She began to reduce her food intake, believing that she was overweight. This control over food persisted until she became extremely thin: she was referred to psychology with a mix of presenting issues, including PTSD symptoms, self-harming and self-starving. Within the multi-professional community mental health team, the psychologist sought to apply cogni-tive therapy to work with perceptions and beliefs about body shape and the need to reduce food intake. However, the dilemma of working with this client's overall trau-matic life events was further understood in supervision by consideration from the psychodynamic perspective. Williams' (2003) chapter entitled the 'No-entry system of defences' provides a possible explanation of how this client was unable to allow any 'entry' into her body. This included changes to thinking processes that might arise from the use of cognitive therapy, and discussions about family relationships and in particular food. It was almost as though the only way in which control of her world could occur was through food. Progress in the sense of working to get better was not possible for this client for a while and further dilemmas focused around her care when she was not able to use therapy. She still needed to be looked after regarding her weight and the ongoing deterioration of her physical health.

When talking about interpersonal family relationships was eventually possible, this was hindered by embarrassment: the protection of family members (as it was not com-fortable to speak about them in any way except positively) became one of the issues. The client refused family therapy. overall the family did not want to sit down together and face difficulties that up until then had not been expressed or understood.

Dilemmas of the consequences of a diagnosis: the concept of risk

One of the central dilemmas concerns the extent to which a particular person's physical health may be at risk. Lock et al. (2001) found more risks to physical health between adolescent girls and boys with disordered eating and those without such eating behaviours. There were also differences between genders: boys and girls had other associated mental health issues.

A bulimic client appears at the table to be eating enough food, but when this is mixed with vomiting in private, then there may be periods of time when their body is without sufficient minerals for the action of vital organs. The same may occur with anorexic clients, but the eating behaviour is more observable and so appropriate physical checks can be made.

The shame and embarrassment of individuals' experience of their eating disorder can prevent them coming forward for help. By the time that help is forthcoming the person may have developed a more extended aspect of their problem and a more extreme response is now essential to maintain life. It is almost as though the relationship with food has become the one way by which control can be maintained. This relationship can be controlled by themselves for themselves, the dilemma being that the thinking about consequences of behaviour has become almost obscured. Thinking about the effects of not eating is apparently irrational. This is a further dilemma as conversations about the serious effects on physical health become sterile. At this point, the interpretation of themselves in their world has become orientated towards the presentation of the self as governed by their body size and shape. The agenda for a carer is sufficient self-nourishment, but for the person with an eating disorder, that agenda is to control their body weight and probably reduce it in a systematic way.

Without paying attention to the underlying psychological factors, the risk of not returning to a healthy eating pattern remains a threat. Without the appropriate care of all family members in family therapy, there may be family breakdown which itself brings further distress. The therapist's quest in working to help a client may lie with understanding the possible antecedents of the eating disorder, whether with family relationship difficulty and/or with the person's self-perception that becomes distorted. The client's quest may be to maintain or reduce their body weight. Hence different perspectives will occur.

Whichever is the case, it seems that in the state of less intake of food that the person's rational reflexive capacity to consider the threat to their health, their food intake and the connection between these is not possible. Working with clients with an eating disorder can give therapists a counter-transferential feeling of exasperation and frustration that the person with the eating disorder can be so illogical and irrational. From clients' views, the casework would suggest that there is no choice as they are compelled to have less food, to exercise for long periods of time and just be unable to undertake any logical thinking about this behaviour.

The dilemmas of the concept of care or cure

The lasting return of the client to a healthier pattern of eating needs to consider the context and other associated factors that underlie the presenting issue of the eating disorder. Another case example reflects the importance of establishing trust between the therapist and client and beginning to look at a more nurturing pattern of eating. A client who had multiple issues that had resulted in a diagnosis of borderline personality disorder was self-harming on occasion and had a low *body mass index* which had been under review by her GP. Meetings over several months were necessary to establish a pattern of trust, during which time chaotic eating patterns and self-harming occurred. It was only when the client had developed trust in the therapist that she was then able to begin to self-nurture which was also reflected in her eating. However, as soon as the perceived environmental stressors re-appeared, she began to self-doubt, self-harm, and starve herself further. The latter could perhaps be understood as a need to once again put up her defences and try to create a perceived body shape that would be more acceptable. Williams (2003: 25), writing about thinking and learning in deprived children, is helpful in understanding some of the dilemmas in sustaining the helpful effects of therapy in providing sufficient thinking space where painful experiences can be contained and acquire meaning.

Part 3: Exploring Research and Practice with Clients Experiencing Eating Disorders (Amanda Hall)

Introduction

Eating disorders are perplexing and challenging. Moreover, there is often a crossover in the spectrum with sufferers moving from restricted eating to binge eating, followed by purging behaviours. This can lead to individuals attracting multiple diagnoses, and confusion in relation to appropriate therapy programmes.

The curiously titled 'eating disorder not otherwise specified' (EDNOS) is the most prevalent diagnostic description, accounting for some 50 to 75 per cent of the population with an eating disorder. However, in a recent study by Thomas et al. (2009) random effects analyses indicated that whereas EDNOS did not differ significantly from anorexia nervosa and binge eating disorder on eating pathology or general psychopathology, bulimia nervosa exhibited greater eating and general psychopathology than EDNOS.

With an emphasis on evidence-based practice within the NHS, the jury is still out in relation to cohesive models of effective psychotherapy or combinations of therapy that are easily translatable from research trials to real-life practice. This results in idiosyncratic therapy programmes which are duly aligned to individual presentation, but often in the absence of a formally sanctioned evidence base.

Most services offer multi-theoretical and multi-modal psychotherapeutic programmes to address presenting issues directly. This range might include behavioural approaches to address eating and weight gain, or the reduction of self-induced vomiting; cognitive approaches to address body image disturbance and a preoccupation with shape and weight; family approaches to address systemic management of the condition; psychodynamic approaches to ameliorate underlying issues such as shame and unresolved childhood conflict; and neuro-cognitive approaches to reduce rigidity of thinking and perfectionism. Individualised holistic packages of therapy attempt to address the multiple aspects of the individual's difficulties. However, due to the insidious nature of the eating disorder, individuals often struggle with a motivation to change, with resulting difficulties and challenges for those supporting them.

Experience in the field suggests that an individually devised programme of care is most effective if the client is involved at all levels in its design, evaluation and construction. An individual with an eating disorder is often caught in the grip of an all pervasive desire for control accompanied by an obsession with an eternal drive toward attention to detail (for example, in relation to calorie intake, food variety increase or minute changes in weight). Characteristically, then, the view of the individual is unlikely to concur with the professional opinion and recommendations, resulting in tensions within an effective therapeutic process. Battles often abound in relation to a necessary increased calorific intake or the reduction of purging behaviours.

Set against the backdrop of the NHS community services, this section will address practice with individuals experiencing this perplexing condition and its accompanying challenges in the field.

Background

Whilst explanations for developing an eating disorder are complex and multi-factorial, the pervading issue for sufferers is a tyrannical and relentless preoccupation with food, body shape and weight which is invariably a displacement for other troubling issues. Eventually, this develops into a pathological obsession leading to a complete narrowness of perspective, to the degree that very little else interests the individual.

Simon, an athletic young male with extraordinary talent in his field of exercise physiology, was paralysed by his continual drive to stay thin. His skeletal form appeared to go unnoticed by his college tutors who continued to place physical demands upon him as he strove to stay on course for his first-class degree. At that time much of the therapy involved him giving himself permission to take additional protein drinks and fluids to ensure he was able to stay fit enough to perform, even though his internal voice created constant dissonance. After time, once he had achieved his degree, Simon was able to re-position himself in relation to his eating restrictions. He also loosened his need to prove himself once he had fully understood his drive for perfection.

In low weight anorexia nervosa in particular, due to the effects of starvation, there is often a reduction in creative higher order thinking capacity. Steinglass et al. (2006) explored a 'set shifting deficit'. They discovered that individuals diagnosed with anorexia nervosa did not differ from healthy controls on five measures of neuropsychological function, but were much worse on one which suggested cognitive rigidity and 'a problem in set shifting'. The authors suggest that this narrowed thinking is associated with brain abnormalities which may be attributed to prolonged starvation.

While there are many therapies available, most have not achieved support from NICE due to both a dearth of research and the methodological preferences of NICE, which are ever present in the field of psychological therapies. Two examples of current therapeutic approaches, which have emerging evidence bases from working with clients with eating disorders and their accompanying features, are described below.

To address cognitive rigidity and inflexibility of thought both before and after weight gain, a recent addition to a therapist's repertoire of skills is Cognitive Remediation Therapy (CRT) developed by Kate Tchanturia and colleagues (Tchanturia et al., 2007). This approach has been shown to be effective as part of a therapy programme in acute anorexia nervosa. It aims to stimulate mental activities and improve thinking skills and information-processing systems when other therapies, for example cognitive behavioural therapy (CBT), may be too complex and intense for the individual.

A second approach in the field is Cognitive Behaviour Therapy – Bulimia Nervosa (CBT-BN), devised by Chris Fairburn (1981), which is one of the most accepted evidence-based models for treatment for bulimia nervosa (as recommended by NICE). In recent years a generic form, Cognitive Behaviour Therapy – Enhanced (CBT-E), has gained more eminence as a treatment for EDNOS. This treatment was designed for use in all types of eating disorders on the basis that anorexia nervosa, bulimia nervosa and EDNOS all have a number of consistent clinical traits. This enhanced CBT also concentrates on four additional maintaining mechanisms: clinical perfectionism, core low self-esteem, difficulty in coping with intense mood states, and interpersonal difficulties (Byrne et al., 2011).

In relation to recovery rates a recent study looking at the success of Transdiagnostic CBT by Helverskov et al. (2010), the overall outcome of 43 per cent having no eating disorder after 30 months was in concordance with, or better than, previous findings. Relapse in treatment for eating disorders is commonplace and many of the therapy programmes are designed to incorporate and ameliorate relapse.

Rhiannon knew she was thin, however most of the time she did not know how thin she was (apart from occasional unaware or off-guard glimpses in a mirror or a shop window). She attended for therapy each week and appeared to be engaged, even grateful, for the help but improvements were slow. She struggled to add extra food each week, not even allowing a scraping of butter on her crispbread. Her anorexic thoughts told her 'Too many calories, too much fat – can't do fat. Not this week. Next week'. However, the following week she would plan to increase her exercise to counter the perceived fat acquisition. In spite of feeling tired, cold and lethargic, next week rarely came. Rhiannon checked her body hundreds of times a day to make sure she could feel her bones. She was unable to look at food as she was so hungry and the sight or smell of food would trigger cravings. Rhiannon believed it was best to keep walking and sleeping, as she was always tired, in preference to thinking (which was problematic as she always felt confused). She struggled with her anorexic thoughts, relentless thoughts of food and satiation: these focused on how to curb the appetite that would overwhelm her, that would ruin her plan for staying in control and which, if she indulged in them, would result in a total lack of control. She feared that as she was so hungry, if she gave in to such thoughts, she would never stop eating.

In therapy CRT helped slow Rhiannon's thinking. It challenged her thoughts and perspectives and began to break down the rigidity of her thinking and the concreteness of her thought processes. It allowed for alternatives and enabled her to begin to think perhaps she could manage some yoghurt or that eating more calories might not immediately result in her getting fat. CBT-E gave her a new way of approaching what felt like internal and external chaos. It provided structure, safety and hope. It addressed the body checking (which reinforces the thoughts and behaviours) and provided an arena in which to evaluate the irrational quality of her beliefs. It also allowed careful management of the fears of increased food intake and weight regain. Over time, Rhiannon learnt to trust herself in relation to hunger and food intake, and she devised new ways of being within a trusting therapeutic relationship which had provided her with a healthier sense of control over her life.

However, even the most effective interventions for bulimia nervosa and binge-eating disorder will fail to help a substantial number of patients. Moreover chronic cases of anorexia nervosa are rarely included in research trials due to the intractable and complex nature of their clinical presentation alongside a lack of good prognosis in relation to the individual's capacity to engage.

Ambivalence, poor engagement and issues of control

Individuals like Simon and Rhiannon are often highly articulate, determined and intelligent, and this focused approach to life often leads to challenges which feel insurmountable as regards the therapeutic process. Most mental health therapists and health-care systems are generally attuned to working with people with higher levels of engagement, flexibility and the motivation to change. Frequently, during the early stages of the development of an eating disorder there is an unhealthy combination of a denial of symptoms, high levels of resolution of cognitive dissonance and a reluctance to seek treatment, all of which makes recognition and early intervention especially challenging. This in turn leads to entrenched and unchallenged behaviour accompanied by ingrained and credible cognitions and an immutable future plan to gain comfort or relief from discomfort via dietary intake control.

As the condition progresses, high levels of ambivalence and reluctance to change combined with rigidity of thinking present an insuperable hurdle for recovery or therapeutic success. Working with ambivalence represents an enormous task in the therapeutic engagement process and creates tensions between the therapist/family/service and the individual. The therapeutic goals, at times, will appear at odds, particularly during times of low weight and high risk physically. In these situations the therapist (or team) will have to undertake a risk analysis in order to ensure the client remains out of life-threatening danger. This can place a tremendous strain on the therapeutic relationship.

The ambivalence and lack of flexibility in making changes or healthier choices (i.e. eating or drinking more) play out as a battle for maintaining control and autonomy. This battle for control, which is often unconscious or unspoken and unacknowledged by the sufferer, leads to boundary setting about what should be done in times of risk, and most services will insist on setting 'non-negotiables' (Geller et al., 2001) in order to ensure that a contract has been agreed at the outset of treatment. This contract enables a clear discussion and communication of control and the legal aspects of duty of care issues early on in the therapy (which, ironically, is often agreed on with high levels of ambivalence).

At their lowest weight, due to the related health risks, both Rhiannon and Simon were mortified when I advised them that it was likely they might have to be sectioned under the Mental Health Act if they continued to lose weight. This is always a possibility for individuals who have a dangerously low BMI and are not regaining their weight, but it should be remembered that this action is not treated lightly and will always be done within the greater mental health (usually multi-disciplinary) care planning procedures. They both believed that they were invincible, and in control, and were distressed that they might lose their liberty should they fail to regain a small yet highly significant amount of weight in order to reduce the risk of requiring urgent medical re-feeding. Within the therapy programme they were disappointed that I might betray them, and yet were also reassured that I would maintain a boundary which meant that I was simply not willing nor able to watch them starve themselves to death.

Given that explanations for eating disorders often focus on insidious issues in regard to the need for control, it is not difficult to see how these play out in the therapeutic arena and impede success. Therefore any therapy plan, by necessity, will require attention to be paid this dynamic. The motivational enhancement model allows practitioners to evaluate where individuals are in relation to the stages of change cycle.

As described by Prochaska and Velicer (1997), this trans-theoretical model conceptualises psychotherapeutic change along three dimensions: firstly, the 'stages of change' (or the *when* of change) and readiness to work towards a goal; secondly, the 'processes' of change (the *how* of change) and activities brought into play to modify thinking, behaviour or affect in relation to a problem; thirdly, the 'level' of change (the *what* of change) or the domain in which change will occur. There is some evidence that these factors predict movement through the stages.

Perfectionism

Another dominant theme in eating disorders is perfectionism. Research has long shown that this personality trait is present in a high percentage of sufferers. It has an enormous impact upon both the development and the maintenance of the condition. The main issue with perfectionism is the individual's attention to detail and thus the drive is often a motivation to perfect their body shape and slimness via their eating restrictions and/or purging in the case of bulimia nervosa. This is the holy grail of an eating disorder, and the quest in search of happiness or a better life should always be held in the therapist's mind as sublimation of the need for control or an escape from unhappiness or even the mundane. Many individuals spend their time preoccupied with achieving a perfect body or working towards the mythical and mercurial *perfect* weight, combined with a belief that once perfected and maintained therein lies happiness or a sense of profound achievement.

However, add to this the dimension of cognitive dissonance (most sufferers will have insight into the potential risks associated with their behaviours) and the result will be a constant state of dis-ease (albeit often at an unconscious level), as the sufferer battles internally between a perpetual fantasy of success against the insidious knowledge of risk and danger. It is widely accepted that in general people with eating disorders are not deliberately attempting to kill themselves. Moreover, they are almost certainly aware of the double jeopardy nature of their condition (given the wide exposure to the risks via health information systems, professionals and widespread media coverage). Ironically, many often believe that they have not succeeded in their quest unless they have been referred to a specialist eating disorder unit, which adds danger to the picture as referrals to inpatient 'specialist' units on the NHS are reserved for those with intractable conditions and those most at risk of death. Furthermore, largely due to a combination of financial constraints, geographical distance and a lack of proven efficacy in relation to in-patient treatment, local services work hard to provide community/out-patient treatment packages. Unless community and specialist units work closely together, adaptation from such in-patient units to real life is often very difficult and relapse is predicted and expected, leading to disillusionment on the part of the sufferer, their family, and therapists and other professionals.

Risk and ethics

Eating disorder sufferers frequently present with complex mental and physical health issues which cause high levels of concern within health-care systems. The low body weight/BMI associated with anorexia nervosa in particular, and the electrolyte imbalance and associated risks associated with bulimia nervosa (and purging in EDNOS), create specific risk management and ethical dilemmas. There are a number of guidelines to assist the practitioner in making decisions in relation to this: for example, guidance known as MARSIPAN (Royal College of Psychiatrists, 2010) advises on best practice in terms of medical intervention, and Paul Robinson's (2009) work on severe and enduring eating disorders (SEED) provides advice on the management of long-term enduring conditions.

There is always a tension at the interface between the Mental Health Act (MHA) and the Mental Capacity Act (MCA). The use of the MHA is preferred over the latter, and if an individual who is deemed not to have capacity required treatment then this should be conducted under Section 3 of the MHA rather than the Deprivation of Liberty Safeguards under the MCA.

However, the issue of capacity must always be taken into consideration. Many sufferers from eating disorders will have well-rehearsed (and somewhat convincing) reasons and explanations for continuing along their seemingly chosen path: these will have internal validity for each sufferer and will be hard to challenge using logic.

In recent years Jacinta Tan has developed a body of research utilising a qualitative approach exploring the ethics of eating disorders and compulsion. While the results of her research were unequivocal in clear life-threatening situations there was much less agreement about whether sufferers with anorexia nervosa should be made to have treatment in other situations. Tan et al. (2010) reported that respondents concurred that it had to be the individual's decision to get better, and that treatment needed collaboration with the therapist. However, some respondents felt that sufferers should be coerced into treatment initially until they were able to make informed choices for themselves once they had improved.

Maria was referred to therapy by her parents. She was vomiting at home after every meal and hiding her vomit in bags under her bed. Her parents were beside themselves and pleaded with her to stop, but more than anything they wanted her to resume being the perfect child she had always been. Maria was confused: she stated she did not know why she was behaving in this way and yet she related it to the time she realised she was not able to continue being the child protégée she had been when she was much younger, (when she was a very talented gymnast) due largely to her changing shape. It proved difficult to separate out whose needs were being met by attending for therapy. Her parents, desperate for improvement, exerted pressure on Maria which led to perpetual feelings of letting them down and increased vomiting and secretiveness. Family therapy sessions helped unravel and loosen expectations and disappointments and also helped Maria regain some sense of a future without the pressure of brilliance. Her recovery continues but she now has the support of a family who are able to understand her difficulties (even if they are still unable to *comprehend* them) and, more importantly, Maria is able to express her feelings in a safer manner and her family are able to receive these in a different way.

Conclusion

This part of the chapter has attempted to disentangle the intricacies of eating disorders and the therapeutic approaches in place to address them. While there have been some clear developments in the field there are still enormous gaps in our knowledge in relation to what helps people overcome the distress which underpins and drives eating disorders, and which might lead to healthier attitudes and behaviours towards food and eating. However, therapists in the field of eating disorders will have to be prepared to commit to working with people in the longer term and will need to hold a robust sense of hope on behalf of clients who may have lost it for themselves.

Chapter Summary

This chapter has examined the conceptual models and therapeutic approaches taken to eating problems. It has considered some of the serious dilemmas and perplexities in practice and has illustrated these through case studies. Perhaps what has become evident across the chapter is the extent to which, despite considerable research and service development, eating difficulties remain serious problems of complexity, confusion and delineation.

> **REFLECTION BOX**
>
> 1 The 1980s and 1990s saw a perceived rise in the incidence of eating disorders. What do you consider might have been contributory factors in this?
> 2 Eating problems have historically been considered to be socially constructed concepts, manifestations of biological attribution and problems in selfhood and identity. How do and your clients understand their eating difficulties?

3 What factors do you think explain the persistence of clients' concern with their body size and weight?

4 In your work with clients with an eating disorder what dilemmas have arisen that have affected clients' progress?

5 Why are individually devised packages of care in agreement with the client *especially* important for people with eating disorders?

6 Why does *ambivalence* present such a problem in the therapeutic relationship for people with eating disorders?

9

Conclusion

Part 1: Reflections on Historical Contexts (Barbara Douglas)

The preceding chapters have illustrated psychotherapeutic practice taking place in a range of contexts and involving therapeutic relationships with people who are trying to make sense of their experiences of psychological distress. Practice contexts play an integral part in the development of this therapeutic work but there tends to be less awareness of how the historical context also plays an important part in the way we view the world and, in the context of this book, experiences that might be described as common presenting issues. Part 1 of each chapter has explored the ways in which particular conceptualisations of psychological distress and difference have dominated particular historical periods, including religious, supernatural, moral, medical and psychological discourses. Each of these discourses has framed the way societies have attempted to make sense of difference, with each one giving rise to its own classificatory systems as a means of imposing order and understanding on the unfamiliar, the different, the frightening and the distressing (Douglas, 2010). Such discourses have included:

- humoral approaches, which survived in one form or another across many centuries;
- potent mixes of humoral and religious notions of human suffering in early Christian western cultures;
- Enlightenment science underpinned by the study of human anatomy and the nervous system;
- the biological classificatory systems of Linnaeus and Darwin from which emerged attempts at similar classifications of psychological distress within medicine;
- psychoanalytic constructs from which emerged notions of distress resulting from a disturbed dynamic psyche rather than biologically-based disease entities;
- the development of a more socially-based view of mental illness, in which individual experiences were described as reactions, or responses to, individual circumstances, rather than biologically-based disease entities;

- the development of a descriptive position that suggests the construction of categories of psychological disorders should be based not on causation or theory but on a description of experiences and symptoms.

These historical ideological frameworks are reflected in autobiographical accounts of people's lived experience of psychological distress and its treatment. Examples include, but are no means limited to, narratives of possession by the devil in Christoph Haizmann's diary of 1677 and 1678 (Haizmann, cited in Peterson, 1981), John Perceval's (1838) account of admission to a private lunatic asylum (also in Peterson, 1981), and the emergence of psychiatry as a science in Daniel Schreber's (2002 [1903]) account. Later accounts include Hannah Green's (1964) narrative which highlights the dichotomy between somatic and dynamic psychiatry in mid twentieth-century America; Mary Barnes (Barnes and Berke, 1973) who describes her experience of, and treatment within, an English therapeutic community during the 1970s, based on anti-psychiatry philosophies; and Lauren Slater's (1998) account which reflects more recent pharmaco-psychiatric experiences.

The history is of necessity simplified and the reader is offered an outline of largely western historical conceptualisations of human distress. But in summary, the intention has been to demonstrate that experiences, symptoms and classifications of what we might term 'psychiatric' or 'psychological' disorders do not stand alone in a vacuum: rather, each conceptualisation represents a dominant ideological framework for understanding human experience of the period. Ahistoricism that is oblivious to a notion of world view can give rise to acceptance of dominant concepts as statements of fact rather than as culturally-situated tools that represent attempts to create understanding and meaning. How we view the resulting meaning will vary according to our interpretation of the evidence, the values and philosophies we hold, our informed evaluation of the nature of truth, and the personal impact on each individual of experiences of the classificatory process. Part 2 of each chapter examined dilemmas in working with clients who experienced each of these common presenting issues and explored some of these varied experiences of the powerful experiential implications. These are reflected on in Part 2 of this chapter.

Categorising distress, within whatever framework, in attempts to impose sense on the environment (Haslam, 2000), tends to locate problems within the individual. However, the ways in which particular clusters of behaviours are problematised at particular times are not located within the individual but are socially and historically constructed. It is not in any way our intention to deny the experienced distress of the client and a desire to help in the best way possible, but, rather, the focus on historical perspectives in this book invites the reader to critically evaluate and debate the nature and construction of the common presenting issues we have detailed, and to examine whether and/or how this impacts on the nature of the reader's therapeutic processes, practices and relationships.

Part 2: Reflections on Dilemmas in Practice (Pam James)

Perhaps the essence of a dilemma is that it poses different (usually two) pathways, whether of stance, choice or action. The pathways available are usually equally unfavourable if considered as the only route, and experiencing this difference creates a tension. As the chapters describe, a dilemma has an 'in the eyes of the perceiver' perspective. Dilemmas may exist in the foreground against an evolving contextual background, for example the dilemmas associated with diagnosis continue as the *DSM-5* evolves from the *DSM-IV-TR* (APA, 2013a and 2000).

The therapist as both academic and reflective practitioner travels across terrain that is marked with information points that give shape to the landscape. The NICE Guidelines provide clusters of knowledge about common presenting issues relevant to their treatment. Recognition of symptoms leads to a diagnosis which precedes guidance towards appropriate therapeutic models. The vigilant practitioner examines these evidence bases for their potential applicability and uses professional judgment to see how that therapeutic approach might help that particular client. Conversely, as Johnstone and Dallos (2006) suggest, using formulation, a particular client's experience sits within the nomothetic evidence from controlled studies. Formulation and diagnosis could then co-exist, perhaps reducing the tension of choice.

Therapists' continuous training and supervision guide the passage of multiple meetings with clients, lighting up the pathways across the labyrinth of their internal and perceived external worlds. One guide that is inherent in the therapeutic process is the interactive relationship between therapist and client: how absurd would it be if a therapist worked through stages of therapy (whether prescribed or exploratory) without listening to or noticing client feedback? A conversation would result where neither could hear the other.

So the practitioner needs to be vigilant in crossing the terrain of human experience, having a duty of care to look after their 'other' whilst travelling with the belief and hope that a less distressing place can be reached or at least tolerated. In parallel with this metaphor of a journey there lie on-going dilemmas. There is a need to categorise, diagnose and create order, perhaps driven by fear of the presenting issue itself, or maybe just to generate a system of control from which management can follow. This categorisation may spawn dilemmas as illustrated in the preceding chapters.

Thinking back to times past, how might an encounter take place between two people pre-history? Imagine such a meeting, where one recounted to the other their narrative of a distressing, perhaps even traumatic event: the listening other might have provided a place in which to hear the person's story or may even have shared their own experiences. This would have been in the absence of the landmarks of present knowledge including diagnoses and consequential treatments. Obviously there have been other socially-constructed groupings of presenting issues as illustrated in the parts of this text concerned with historical perspectives: perhaps complex frameworks of social construction would detract from the potential healing of an encounter.

In an over-simplification, could the expression of experience which is heard by another in a receptive manner facilitate a manageable assimilation of that distress into the conceptual memory of the distressed person? This apparent simplicity is clouded by human constructs of shame and embarrassment ('I should be able to cope'), guilt ('I shouldn't feel or think this way'), regret ('If only I hadn't done that'), fear ('I will be punished now'), and pride ('I can't face that person now'). Losses and the pain of separation also inter-weave within a person's experience. All are connected to the interface between self and other, where the self strives (whether within or without awareness) to self-protect by creating defences from pain and distress. Waddell's (2002: 4) description of the developmental journey from infancy to the last years describes the ways in which 'the defensive measures which one may adopt for psychic survival at one point in his life may imprison him within that regressive or self-protective mode. Or else they may become part of a holding operation, in which case they can be relaxed in the light of later, more positive experiences'. Perhaps this quote could be relevant to common presenting issues in this text.

Much of the narrative of ongoing human distress is positioned here. In observing the development of the personality in young children it is possible to see the exploring infant withdraw when ashamed and frightened if told off repeatedly by an angry parent. Such withdrawing behaviour can include somatising, thumb-sucking and hiding, suggesting self-protection by closing down painful communication. Bevington et al. (2013) highlight the therapeutic importance of establishing an epistemic highway with the child where there is trust and an open communication channel: the emphasis was not on a comparison of theories but on cross-therapeutic concepts in the working alliance.

Another dilemma is that our initial learning is out of the control of each of us, creating first-family interaction patterns. These neuronal connections lay out our templates for later responding. If these patterns continue to be used in adult situations they may be helpful or unhelpful, as seen in the work of Hofer (2006) who discusses the effects of early interactions on subsequent interpersonal experiences. Fonagy et al. (2011b) continue the theme of neurobiology together with a therapeutic stance when considering borderline personality and the practice of mentalisation. They use the concept of diagnosis while emphasising non-pathology, taking a developmental relational perspective. Therapy can create self-awareness, and new intra- and inter-personal learning. The challenge is that all of this will be sustained.

Finally, this book moves towards its concluding section which invites the reader to take a reflective stance on the text's main recurring themes, while also considering the challenge of humane relating in a professional context.

Part 3: Concluding Reflections (Sheelagh Strawbridge)

This book has explored ways of working creatively with the various approaches to psychological distress represented as 'psychotherapy' and 'psychopathology'. In reflecting on the philosophies associated with these approaches, philosophy is interpreted broadly as a world-view and not in a technical academic sense. Nevertheless, philosophy points to an exploration of presuppositions, values and implications, here relating to perceptions of psychological distress, the ways in which we seek to understand it, and the consequent ways in which we seek its alleviation.

One of the things I value about the book is its historical perspective. However, there are differing approaches to history, and histories of ideas – including scientific ideas. These have often been cast in the mould of 'whig' histories with a built-in assumption of progress, 'seen as a series of victories over pre-scientific thinking', (Burrow, 2009: 474). Here, on the contrary, the historical perspective is used to promote critical reflection, indicating how current concepts are socio-culturally situated and far from being politically neutral.

So the character of any exploration is shaped within a specific socio-historical context and guided by assumptions, explicit or implicit, about its nature and purpose. These direct the development of theories, or maps of the territory, that suggest further explorations. As Macfarlane notes, naming places and map-making give meaning and structure to a landscape, placing a particular territory within a wider matrix of significance and making the unknown known (2003: 191). And so it is with our maps of psychological distress, but as Macfarlane warns 'on a map the weather is always good, the visibility always perfect. A map offers the power of perspective over a landscape: reading one is like flying over the country in an aeroplane – a deodorized, pressurized, temperature controlled survey. But a map can never replicate the ground itself' (ibid.: 184).

The theoretical maps of psychological distress explored in this book represent in part two main and contrasting traditions: both locate the territory of human psychology within a broader landscape of 'science', but one claims a place within the 'natural sciences' whereas the other claims a distinction for the 'human sciences'.

Psychopathological approaches are linked with medical practice rooted in a view of natural science that evolved from the 'scientific revolution' of the seventeenth century and the eighteenth-century 'Enlightenment'. The expansion of human knowledge was sought by rational empirical inquiry that was free from religious dogma. The emphasis was on knowledge claims based on objectively observable 'facts', free of values, and the belief in the power of science was coupled with equally strong beliefs in technological and social progress. As psychology emerged as a discipline it was shaped by the philosophies of empiricism and positivism aiming to apply scientific methods to the study of human beings. The emphasis on objectivity and observability favoured a focus on behaviour rather than subjectivity. It was nomothetic, assuming that discoverable laws could constitute a body of knowledge that allowed the prediction and control of human behaviour. Such laws could then be applied to the treatment of criminality and mental illness, the assessment of abilities and aptitudes, the education of children, the organisation of the workplace, and so on.

Of course, knowledge is not static and the early stress on behavioural psychology and behaviour modification has shifted significantly, towards a re-conceptualisation as cognitive-behavioural psychology and therapy (Bergin and Garfield, 1994: 824). The picture becomes increasingly complex as practitioners of differing approaches continue to learn from each other, but cognitive-behavioural psychology and CBT still incline towards a natural science perspective and research based in this tradition, with randomised controlled trials seen as the 'gold standard'.

There is then an affinity between medical science, the medical contexts of practice, psychopathological approaches to psychological distress rooted in psychiatry, and a 'natural science' view of psychology. The approach is technical-rational, its goal to diagnose problems and develop techniques to solve them with the expertise and balance of responsibility lying with the practitioner. This natural science perspective is inherently deterministic, seeking explanations in terms of cause and effect. Though aiming to be value-free, its thrust is conformist, towards individual adjustment and adaptation. Interestingly, later editions of the *Diagnostic and Statistical Manual* have become less scientific in this sense, discarding the search for causes fundamental to scientific medicine, which recognises that symptoms (e.g. persistent headaches or diarrhoea) have a variety of causes and that a failure to investigate can lead to inappropriate treatments and even death.

In contrast, psychotherapeutic approaches can be located within a 'human science' tradition, claiming that the subject matter of disciplines such as psychology, history and sociology is crucially different from that of the natural sciences and that they rest on a theory of understanding and research into human consciousness, meaning and subjective experience. Consciousness and human agency are emphasised and values are inseparable from the assumption that human beings have the capacity for choice and personal responsibility. The exploration and interpretation of experience owe much to phenomenological philosophy and studies of language and discourses, which have unlocked possibilities for studying conscious and unconscious meanings and their social contexts. The resulting qualitative research methods tend to be idiographic – more focused on the detail of individual experience than on general laws.

From this perspective it is acknowledged that people react to interpretive and explanatory concepts and change in response to being classified or diagnosed. Psychotherapeutic approaches therefore stress the exploration and understanding of individual experiences and responses. Formulation in contrast to diagnosis emphasises the complexity of an individual's distress and a more collaborative approach between practitioner and client is favoured. Personal qualities, choices and relationships are seen as central to the work, and the therapeutic significance of the personal and intimate nature of the client/practitioner relationship is recognised.

There are then significant differences in the assumptions, values and methods between a tradition which is technical in its approach – searching for causal explanations and remedial techniques – and one which explores and interprets meanings embedded in subjective experience. Nevertheless, both traditions claim the legitimacy bestowed in the modern world by being 'scientific'. Just as in the medieval world knowledge claims deemed incompatible with the contemporary religious world view could be outlawed as heresy, today ways of knowing that cannot be encompassed within a current scientific world view can be easily dismissed. However, Polanyi (1967) demonstrated the legitimacy of ways of knowing beyond the explicit, exact and testable. He explored our capacity to 'know more than we can tell' – the unspecifiability of much implicit knowledge and skilled activity – which he termed 'the tacit dimension', and saw as crucial in discovery, including scientific discovery.

There is in psychotherapeutic approaches an acknowledgement of the vital interpersonal connection between client and practitioner and the possibility of 'knowing [and communicating] more than we can tell', of entering the world of another not encompassed within cause and effect explanations or explicit interpretations. The work of Rogers (e.g., 1996) has been central in drawing attention to the therapeutic significance of interpersonal contact between practitioner and client, the importance of 'being-with' rather than 'doing-to' another, and Buber's (1971) distinction between the 'I–It' and 'I–Thou'. More recently, Stern (2004) has also explored the profound impact of 'moments of meeting' distinguished from 'moments of interpretation' from within a psychoanalytic perspective. Whatever the explanation may be – mirror neurones or empathy circuits in the brain perhaps – most of us will have experienced our capacity for deep empathic connection in our close relationships: a more direct understanding of another than can be put into words.

We have a capacity of knowing from the inside rather than the outside that has something to do with our common humanity. The contrast between the heroic fictional detective Sherlock Holmes and the self-effacing but equally successful Father Brown illustrates this well. Holmes is a man of action, an amateur scientist and logician. He is an acute observer with remarkable powers of deduction. In contrast, Brown puts himself imaginatively into the minds of criminals and in discovering them through his empathy, grounded in their shared humanity, discovers his own capacity for sin. In disclosing Father Brown's secret, Chesterton (1981: 461–467) tells us something about his art as a writer, excavating his own experience to enter the lives of his characters.

Empathic identification and genuine contact are as significant in psychotherapy as scientific ways of knowing and such meetings between persons are rooted in valuing the other. This essentially moral and interpersonal character of psychotherapy is explored in some depth by Lomas (1999) and Gordon (1999), and is just as vital as a foundation in scientific ways of knowing: 'To interpret human life requires unending observation, profound sympathy, wide reading, the ability to open yourself to strange and unexplored areas of your personality and to penetrate deep into the lives of others' (Callow, 2004: 230). No one kind of knowledge is sufficient and this reflection on acting applies equally to psychotherapy.

The authors of this book have demonstrated the importance of this open-minded attitude to inquiry in their creative syntheses of psychopathological and psychotherapeutic approaches to distress. The tension between diagnosis and interpretation has focused much of the discussion, and within the current highly technical parameters of health service provision, the intangible 'tacit' dimensions of psychotherapeutic approaches are more difficult to highlight explicitly. The values and human contact at the heart of psychotherapy are, by their very nature, resistant to specification in terms defined by resource conscious managerial demands for evidence-based practice.

In medicine the benefits of science and technology are so clear that there is a reluctance to look beyond the search for technical solutions to our problems. Technical rationality is powerful and seductive, but failing to recognise its limitations is dangerous. Weber linked it with the development of industrial capitalism, markets, bureaucratisation and the demand for calculable economic efficiency – a process he termed 'rationalisation'. I have explored this elsewhere, together with Ritzer's linked metaphor of 'Macdonaldisation', in relation to the effects of medical contexts of practice on psychotherapy (e.g. Strawbridge, 2002). Much in our world can be seen as a realisation of this socio-historical process towards a market-driven society of 'specialists without spirit, sensualists without heart' (Weber, 1974: 82).

It is, therefore, heartening that the approaches described here demonstrate possibilities, within health settings, of encountering clients in their meaningful worlds. The recent emphasis on compassion within traditionally more technical approaches to psychotherapy is also encouraging (e.g. Gilbert, 2010). Even within physical medicine, as Helman (2006) argues, the stress on its technical aspects can result in a loss of caring contact with patients and attending to their stories that can be detrimental to effective treatment. The acknowledgement in the NHS that the neglect and death of significant numbers of patients have resulted from a lack of compassion further bears this out.

Taking a broader view, ethical debates are beginning to surface about the appropriate limits of markets. Sandel (2012), for example, argues that – while we have drifted from having a market economy to being a market society – the financial crisis has prompted debates about the moral failings of markets, and he asks how we can protect 'what money can't buy'. So within this context and that of the explorations in this book we might hope for a re-introduction of humane values into medicine, where they have been lost, and to defend and maintain the emphasis on caring contact and relationships that is central to psychotherapeutic practice.

References

Agid, O., Shapira, B., Zislin, J., Ritsner, M., Hanin, B., Murad, H., Troudart, T., Bloch, M., Heresco-Levy, U. and Lerer, B. (1999) 'Environment and vulnerability to major psychiatric illness: a case control study of early parental loss in major depression, bipolar disorder and schizophrenia', *Molecular Psychiatry*, 4 (2): 163–173.

Akiskal, H. (1977) 'Cyclothymic disorder: validating criteria for inclusion in the bipolar affective group', *American Journal of Psychiatry*, 134: 1227–1233.

Allison, K. and Rossouw, P. (2013) 'Exploring the concept of safety from a neuro-psychotherapeutic perspective', Australian Psychological Society: Counselling Psychology Conference, 21–24 February, Melbourne.

Alonso, J. and Lepine, J. (2007) 'Overview of the key data from the European study of the epidemiology of mental disorders', *Journal of Clinical Psychiatry*, 68 (S2): 3–9.

Alwin, N., Blackburn, R., Davidson, K., Hilton, M., Logan, C. and Shine, J. (2006) *Understanding Personality Disorder*. Leicester: The British Psychological Society.

American Psychiatric Association (1952) *Diagnostic and Statistical Manual of Mental Disorders*. Washington, DC: American Psychiatric Association.

American Psychiatric Association (1968) *Diagnostic and Statistical Manual of Mental Disorders*, 2nd edition. Washington, DC: American Psychiatric Association.

American Psychiatric Association (1980) *Diagnostic and Statistical Manual of Mental Disorders*, 3rd edition. Washington, DC: American Psychiatric Association.

American Psychiatric Association (2000) *Diagnostic and Statistical Manual of Mental Disorders*, 4th edition, Text Revision. Washington, DC: American Psychiatric Association.

American Psychiatric Association (2013a) *Diagnostic and Statistical Manual of Mental Disorders*, 5th edition. Washington, DC: American Psychiatric Association.

American Psychiatric Association (2013b) *Post traumatic Stress Disorder*, available at www.psychiatry.org/File%20Library/Practice/DSM/DSM-5/DSM-5-PTSD.pdf (last accessed 4 April 2013).

Appignanesi, L. (2008) *Mad, Bad and Sad: A History of Women and the Mad Doctors from 1800*. London: Virago.

Auden, W.H. (1948) *The Age of Anxiety: A Baroque Eclogue*. London: Faber and Faber.

Bachmann, S., Resch, F. and Mundt, C. (2003) 'Psychological treatments for psychosis: history and overview', *Journal of American Academy of Psychoanalysis and Dynamic Therapy*, 31: 155 176.

Baethge, C., Salvatore, P. and Baldessarini, R. (2003) '"On cyclic insanity" by Karl Ludwig Kahlbaum MD: a translation and commentary', *Harvard Review of Psychiatry*, 11: 78–90.

Barham, P. (2004) *Forgotten Lunatics of the Great War*. New Haven: Yale University Press.

Barnes, M. and Berke, J. (1973) *Two Accounts of a Journey through Madness*. London: Penguin.

Bassman, R. (2007) *A Fight To Be: A Psychologist's Experience From Both Sides of the Locked Door*. Albany: Tantamount.

Bateman, A. and Fonagy, P. (2000) 'Effectiveness of psychotherapeutic treatment of personality disorder', *British Journal of Psychiatry*, 177: 138–143.

Beck, A. (1976) *Cognitive Therapy and the Emotional Disorders*. New York: International Universities Press.

Beck, A. and Rector, N. (2000) 'Cognitive therapy of schizophrenia', *American Journal of Psychotherapy*, 54: 291–300.

Behar, E., DiMarco, I., Hekler, E., Mohlman, J. and Staples, A. (2009) 'Current theoretical models of generalized anxiety disorder (GAD): conceptual review and treatment implications', *Journal of Anxiety Disorders*, 23: 1011–1023.

Bell, R. (1987) *Holy Anorexia*. Chicago: University of Chicago Press.

Bentall, R. (2009) *Doctoring the Mind: Why Psychiatric Treatments Fail*. London: Allan Lane.

Bentall, R. (2011) 'The psychology of psychosis', in D. Pilgrim, A. Rogers and B. Pescosolido (eds), *The Sage Handbook of Mental Health and Illness*. London: Sage. pp. 313–334.

Bentall, R., Kinderman, P. and Manson, K. (2005) 'Self-discrepancies in bipolar disorder: comparison of manic, depressed, remitted and normal participants', *British Journal of Clinical Psychology*, 44: 457–473.

Bentley, S. (2005) 'A Short History of PTSD: From Thermopylae to Hue', *The VVA Veteran*, available at www.vva.org/archive/TheVeteran/2005_03/feature_HistoryPTSD.htm (last accessed 30 March 2013).

Beresford, P., Nettle, M. and Perring, R. (2010) *Towards a Social Model of Madness and Distress?* Joseph Rowntree Foundation, available at www.jrf.org.uk/sites/files/jrf/mental-health-service-models-full.pdf (last accessed 28 October 2011).

Bergin, A. and Garfield, S. (1994) *Handbook of Psychotherapy and Behaviour Change*, 4th edition. Chichester: Wiley.

Berrios, G. (1993) 'European view on personality disorders: a conceptual history', *Comprehensive Psychiatry*, 34 (1): 14–30.

Berrios, G. (1996) *The History of Mental Symptoms: Descriptive Psychopathology Since the Nineteenth Century*. Cambridge: Cambridge University Press.

Berrios, G. (1999) 'Anxiety disorders: a conceptual history', *Journal of Affective Disorders*, 56: 83–94.

Bevington, D., Fuggle, P., Fonagy, P., Target, M. and Asen, E. (2013) 'Innovations in practice: adolescent mentalisation-based integrative therapy (AMBIT): a new integrated approach to working with the most hard to reach adolescents with severe complex mental health needs', *Child and Adolescent Mental Health*, 18 (1): 46–51.

Bhanji, S. and Newton, V. (1985) 'Richard Morton's account of "nervous consumption"', *International Journal of Eating Disorders*, 4 (4): 589–595.

Blanchard, E., Hickling, E., Devineni, T., Veazey, C., Galovski, T., Mundy, E. and Buckley, T. (2003) 'A controlled evaluation of cognitive behavioral therapy for post-traumatic stress in motor vehicle accident survivors', *Behaviour Research and Therapy*, 421: 79–96.

Bloom, N., Bartels, N., St. John, D., and Pfohl, B. (2002) *STEPPS: Systems Training for Emotional Predictability and Problem Solving: Group Treatment for Borderline Personality Disorder.* Coralville: Blums' Books.

Boardman, J., Craig, T., Goddard, C., Henderson, C., McCarthy, J., McInerny, T., Cohen, A., Potter, M., Rinaldi, M. and Whicher, E. (2010) *Recovery is for All: Hope, Agency and Opportunity in Psychiatry.* London: South London and Maudsley NHS Foundation Trust and South West London and St George's Mental Health NHS Trust.

Bögels, S., Alden, L., Beidel, D., Clark, L., Pine, D., Stein, M. and Voncken, M. (2010) 'Social anxiety disorder: questions and answers for the DSM-V', *Depression and Anxiety*, 27 (2): 168–189.

Boorman, S. (2009) *NHS Health and Wellbeing: Final Report.* London: COI for the Department of Health.

Boyle, M. (2011) 'Making the world go away, and how psychology and psychiatry benefit', in M. Rapley, J. Moncrieff and J. Dillon (eds), *De-medicalising Misery: Psychiatry, Psychology and the Human Condition.* Basingstoke: Palgrave Macmillan. pp. 27–43.

Braslow, J. (1997) *Mental Ills, Bodily Cures: Psychiatric Treatment in the First Half of the Twentieth Century.* California: University of California Press.

Brewin, C. (2003) *Post-traumatic Stress Disorder: Malady or Myth?* New Haven, CT: Yale University Press.

Briere, J. and Scott, C. (2006) *Principles of Trauma Therapy: A Guide to Symptoms, Evaluation and Treatment.* London: Sage.

British National Formulary (2005) London: British Medical Association Publishing Group Ltd and the Royal Pharmaceutical Society of Great Britain.

British Psychological Society (2007) *New Ways of Working for Applied Psychologists in Health and Social Care.* Leicester: British Psychological Society.

Brown, C. (2005) *Postmodernism for Historians.* Harlow: Pearson Longman.

Brown, G. and Harris, T. (1978) *Social Origins of Depression: A Study of Psychiatric Disorder in Women.* London: Tavistock.

Bruch, H. (1978) *The Golden Cage: The Enigma of Anorexia Nervosa.* Massachusetts: Harvard University Press.

Bruch, H. (1979) *Eating Disorders: Obesity, Anorexia and the Person Within*. New York: Basic Books.

Brumberg, J. (1988) *Fasting Girls: The History of Anorexia Nervosa*. New York: First Vintage Books.

Buber, M. (1971) *I and Thou*. London: Simon and Schuster.

Burgy, M. (2008) 'The concept of psychosis: historical and phenomenological aspects', *Schizophrenia Bulletin*, 34 (6): 1200–1210.

Burrow, J. (2009) *A History of Histories*. London: Penguin.

Burton, R. (2001 [1621]) *The Anatomy of Melancholy*. New York: New York Review Books Classic.

Busfield, J. (1986) *Managing Madness: Changing Ideas and Practice*. London: Routledge.

Busko, M. (2007) 'DSM-IV Diagnostic Criteria for Eating Disorders May Be Too Stringent'. American Psychiatric Association Annual meeting: Abstract NR683.

Butler, A., Chapman, J., Forman, E. and Beck, A. (2006) 'The empirical status of cognitive-behavioral therapy: a review of meta-analyses', *Clinical Psychology Review*, 26 (1): 17–31.

Butler, G., Fennell, M. and Hackman, A. (2008) *Cognitive-Behavioural Therapy for Anxiety Disorders*. London: Guilford.

Butler, G. and Mathews, A. (1987) 'Anticipatory anxiety and risk perception', *Cognitive Therapy and Research*, 11 (5): 551–565.

Byrne, S., Fursland, A., Allen, K. and Watson, H. (2011) 'The effectiveness of enhanced cognitive behavioural therapy for eating disorders: an open trial', *Behavioural Research and Therapy*, 49: 219–226.

Callow, S. (2004) *Being an Actor*. London: Vintage.

Cape, J., Chan, M., Lovell, K., Leibowitz, J. and Kendall, T. (2011) 'Management of generalised anxiety disorder: the updated NICE guideline', *Healthcare Counselling & Psychotherapy Journal*, 11 (2): 12–16.

Carpenter, J. (2002) 'Mental health recovery paradigm: implications for social work', *Health and Social Work*, 27: 86–94.

Carter, G. (2010) 'Hunter DBT project: randomised controlled trial of dialectical behaviour therapy in women with borderline personality disorder', *Australian & New Zealand Journal of Psychiatry*, 44 (2): 162–173.

Casement, P. (1985) *On Learning from the Patient*. London: Routledge.

Cashdan, S. (1988) *Object Relations Therapy: Using the Relationship*. New York: Norton.

Chadwick, P. (2006) *Person-Based Cognitive Therapy for Distressing Psychosis*. Chichester: Wiley.

Chadwick, P. and Birchwood, M. (1996) 'Cognitive therapy for voices', in G. Haddock and P. Slade (eds), *Cognitive-behavioural Interventions with Psychotic Disorders*. London: Routledge. pp. 75–85.

Charcot, J.-M. (1889) 'Isolation in the treatment of hysteria', *Clinical Lectures on Diseases of the Nervous System*, 3, The New Sydenham Society. pp. 207–219.

Chesterton, G.K. (1981) *The Complete Father Brown*. London: Penguin.

Chmielewski, M., Bagby, R., Quilty, L., Paxton, R., and Ng, S. (2011) 'A (re)-evaluation of the symptom structure of borderline personality disorder', *Canadian Journal of Psychiatry*, 56 (9): 530–539.

Claridge, G., Pryor, R. and Watkins, G. (1990) *Sounds from the Bell Jar: Ten Psychotic Authors*. Basingstoke: Macmillan.

Clarke, J. and van Amerom, G. (2008) 'A comparison of blogs by depressed men and women', *Journal of Mental Health Nursing*, 29: 243–264.

Clarkson, P. (2003) *The Therapeutic Relationship*. London: Whurr.

Cornwall County Asylum (1907) *Probable Causes of Insanity*, Bodmin Asylum Reports 1907–1919 (HC1/1/3/9). Bodmin: Cornwall County Record Office.

Corrie, S. (2010) 'What is evidence?', in R. Woolfe, S. Strawbridge, B. Douglas and W. Dryden (eds), *The Sage Handbook of Counselling Psychology*, 3rd edition. London: Sage.

Costa, N. and Weems, C. (2005) 'Maternal and child anxiety: do attachment beliefs or children's perceptions of maternal control mediate their association?', *Social Development*, 14 (4): 574–590.

Craske, M. and Hazlett-Stevens, H. (2002) 'Facilitating symptom reduction and behavior change in GAD: the issue of control', *Clinical Psychology: Science and Practice*, 9: 69–75.

Crawford, M. and Patterson, S. (2007) 'Arts therapies for people with schizophrenia: an emerging evidence base', *Evidence Based Mental Health*, 10: 69–70.

Cullen, W. (1769) *Synopsis Nosologiae Methodicae*. Edinburgh: n.p.

Cullen, W. (1777) 'First lines of the practice of physic', in E. Shorter (2005) *A Historical Dictionary of Psychiatry*. New York: Oxford University Press. p.192.

Davidson, K. (2008) *Cognitive Therapy for Personality Disorders: A Guide for Clinicians*, 2nd edition. London: Routledge.

Davidson, L. (2003) *Living Outside Mental Illness: Qualitative Studies of Recovery in Schizophrenia*. New York: New York University.

Davidson, L., Rakfeldt, J. and Struass, J. (2010) *The Roots of the Recovery Movement in Psychiatry: Lessons Learned*. London: Wiley-Blackwell.

Davis, J., Chen, N. and Glick, I. (2003) 'A meta-analysis of the efficacy of second-generation antipsychotics', *Archives of General Psychiatry*, 60: 553–564.

DelBello, M., Adler, C., Cerullo, M., Fleck, D. and Strakowski, S. (2009) 'Bipolar Disorder', *Encyclopedia of Neuroscience*: 201–207.

Department of Health (2012) *Any Qualified Provider*, available at http://healthandcare.dh.gov.uk/any-qualified-provider-2/ (last accessed 2 May 2013).

DeRubeis, R., Young, P. and Dahlsgaard, K. (1998) 'Affective disorders', in A. Bellack and M. Herscn (eds), *Comprehensive Clinical Psychology*, 6. Oxford: Pergamon. pp. 339–366.

Deutch, H. (1986 [1942]) 'Some forms of emotional disturbance and their relationship to schizophrenia', in M. Stone (ed.), *Essential Papers on Borderline Disorders: One Hundred Years at the Border*. New York: New York University Press.

Dilks, S., Tasker, F. and Wren, B. (2010) 'Managing the impact of psychosis: a grounded theory of recovery process in psychosis', *British Journal of Psychology*, 49: 87–107.

Dinos, S., Stevens, S., Serfacty, M., Weich, S. and King, M. (2004) 'Stigma: the feelings and experiences of 46 people with mental illness', *The British Journal of Psychiatry*, 184: 176–181.

Douglas, B. (2010) 'Disorder and its discontents', in R. Woolfe, S. Strawbridge, B. Douglas and W. Dryden (eds), *The Sage Handbook of Counselling Psychology*, 3rd edition. London: Sage. pp. 23–43.

Dowbiggin, I. (1985) 'Degeneration and hereditarianism in French mental medicine 1840–1890', in W. Bynum, R. Porter. and M. Shepherd (eds), *The Anatomy of Madness: Essays in the History of Psychiatry 1*. London: Routledge.

Dowrick, C. (2004) *Beyond Depression: A New Approach to Understanding and Management*. Oxford: Oxford University Press.

Dowrick, C., Kokanovic, R., Hegarty, K., Griffiths, F. and Gunn, J. (2008) 'Resilience and depression: perspectives from primary care', *Health: An Interdisciplinary Journal for the Social Study of Health, Illness and Medicine*, 12 (4): 439–452.

Dugas, M., Gagnon, F., Ladouceur, R. and Freeston, M. (1998) 'Generalised anxiety disorder: a preliminary test of a conceptual model', *Behaviour, Research and Therapy*, 36: 215–226.

Dunkley, J. and Whelan, T. (2006) 'Vicarious Traumatisation: current status and future directions', *British Journal of Guidance and Counselling*, 34 (1): 107–116.

Ehlers, A. and Clark, D. (2000) 'A cognitive model of post-traumatic stress disorder', *Behaviour, Research and Therapy*, 38: 319–345.

Ehlers, A., Clark, D., Hackmann, A. and McManus, F. (2010) 'Intensive cognitive therapy for PTSD: a feasibility study', *Behavioural and Cognitive Psychotherapy*, 38: 383–398.

Ehlers, A., Clark, D., Hackmann, A., McManus, F. and Fennell, M. (2005) 'Cognitive therapy for post-traumatic stress disorder: development and evaluation', *Behaviour Research and Therapy*, 43: 413–431.

Ehlers, A., Clark, D., Hackmann, A., McManus, F., Fennell, M., Herbert, C. and Mayou, R. (2003) 'A randomised controlled trial of cognitive therapy, a self-help booklet and repeated assessment as early interventions for post-traumatic stress disorder', *Archive of General Psychiatry*, 60: 1024–1032.

Elkins, D. (2009) *Humanistic Psychology: A Clinical Manifesto: A Critique of Clinical Psychology and the Need for Progressive Alternatives*. Colorado Springs: University of the Rockies Press.

Ellenberger, H. (1981) *The Discovery of the Unconscious: The Evolution of Dynamic Psychiatry*. New York: Basic Books.

Elliott, R., Greenberg, L. and Lietaer, G. (2004) 'Research on experiential therapies', in M. Lambert (ed.), *Bergin and Garfield's Handbook of Psychotherapy and Behaviour Change*, 5th edition. Chicago, IL: Wiley. pp. 393–446.

Exeter City Lunatic Asylum, Male and Female Patient Case Books 1886–1911, ECA/4034A/UH/2/1-15. Exeter: Devon Record Office.

Fairbank, J. and Brown, T. (1987) 'Current behavioural approaches to the treatment of post-traumatic stress disorder', *The Behaviour Therapist*, 10 (3): 57–64.

Fairburn, C. (1981) 'A cognitive behavioral approach to the management of bulimia', *Psychological Medicine*, 11: 707–711.

Fairburn, C., Cooper, Z., Shafran, R., Wilson, G. and Barlow, D. (eds) (2008) *Clinical Handbook of Psychological Disorders: A Step-by-Step Treatment Manual*, 4th edition. New York: Guilford.

Feigenbaum, J. (2007) 'Dialectical behaviour therapy: an increasing evidence base', *Journal of Mental Health*, 16 (1): 51–68.

Fletcher, R. (2012) 'Dealing with diagnosis', in M. Milton (ed.), *Diagnosis and Beyond: Counselling Psychology Contributions to Understanding Human Distress*. Ross-on-Wye: PCCS Books. pp. 1–10.

Foa, E., Hembree, E. and Rothbaum, B. (2007) *Prolonged Exposure Therapy for PTSD: Emotional Processing of Traumatic Experiences*. New York: Oxford University Press.

Foa, E., Kean, T. and Friedman, M. (2000) 'Guidelines for the treatment of PTSD', *Journal of Traumatic Stress*, 13: 539–588.

Fonagy, P. (2007) 'Editorial: personality disorder', *Journal of Mental Health*, 16 (1): 1–4.

Fonagy, P., Bateman, A. and Bateman, A. (2011a) 'The widening scope of mentalizing: a discussion', *Psychology and Psychotherapy: Theory, Research and Practice*, 84 (1): 1–112.

Fonagy, P., Luyton, P. and Strathearn, L. (2011b) 'Borderline personality disorder, mentalisation and the neurobiology of attachment', *Infant Mental Health Journal*, 32 (1): 47–69.

Foucault, M. (1988) *Madness and Civilization: A History of Insanity in the Age of Reason*. London: Vintage.

Frank, E., Hlastala, S., Ritenour, A., Houck, P., Tu, X., Monk, T., Mallinger, A. and Kupfer, D. (1997) 'Inducing lifestyle regularity in recovering bipolar disorder patients: results from the maintenance therapies of bipolar disorder protocol', *Biological Psychiatry*, 41: 1165–1173.

Freud, S. (1894) 'On the grounds for detaching a particular syndrome from neurasthenia under the description "anxiety neurosis"', *The Standard Edition of the Complete Psychological Works of Sigmund Freud*, 3: 85–115. London: Hogarth Press.

Freud, S. (1917) 'Mourning and melancholia', *The Standard Edition of the Complete Psychological Works of Sigmund Freud*, 14: 237–258. London: Hogarth Press.

Freud, S. (1920) 'Beyond the pleasure principle', *The Standard Edition of the Complete Psychological Works of Sigmund Freud*, 18: 7. London: Hogarth Press.

Galeazzi, G., Elkins, K., Pingani, L. and Rigatelli, M. (2006) 'Views on psychosis and judgment of appropriateness of early interventions in pre-psychotic phase: a survey of members of the International Early Psychosis Association', *Journal of Mental Health*, 15 (5): 569–576.

Garland, C. (ed.) (2004) *Understanding Trauma: A Psychoanalytic Approach*. London: Karnac.

Geller, J., Cockell, S. and Drab, D. (2001) 'Assessing readiness for change in the eating disorders: the psychometric properties of the readiness and motivation interview', *Psychological Assessment*, 13 (1): 189–198.

Gilbert, P. (2010) *The Compassionate Mind*. London: Constable.

Gilman, S. (2010) *Obesity: The Biography*. Oxford: Oxford University Press.

Glover, E. (1932) 'A psychoanalytical approach to the classification of mental disorders', *Journal of Mental Science*, 78: 819–842.

Gomez, L. (1997) *An Introduction to Object Relations*. London: Free Association.

Goodwin, F. (1999) 'Anticonvulsant therapy and suicide risk in affective disorders', *Journal of Clinical Psychiatry*, 60 (2): 89–93.

Goodwin, F. and Jamison, K. (2007) *Manic Depressive Illness: Bipolar Disorders and Recurrent Depression*, 2nd edition. New York: Oxford University Press.

Gordon, P. (1999) *Face to Face: Therapy as Ethics*. London: Constable.

Gordon, R. (2000) *Eating Disorders: Anatomy of a Social Epidemic*. Oxford: Blackwell.

Goss, K. and Allan, S. (2009) 'Shame, pride and eating disorders', *Clinical Psychology & Psychotherapy*, 16 (4): 303–316.

Grech, E. (2002) 'A review of the current evidence for the use of psychological interventions in psychosis', *International Journal of Psychosocial Rehabilitation*, 6: 79–88.

Green, H. (1964) *I Never Promised You a Rose Garden*. London: Pan.

Greene, T. (2007) 'The Kraepelinian dichotomy: are the twin pillars crumbling?', *History of Psychiatry*, 18 (3): 361–379.

Grey, N. and Holmes, E. (2008) '"Hotspots" in trauma memories in the treatment of post-traumatic stress disorder: a replication', *Memory*, 16 (7): 788–796.

Grey, N., Young, K. and Holmes, E. (2002) 'Cognitive restructuring within reliving: a treatment for peritraumatic emotional "hotspots" in post-traumatic stress disorder', *Behavioural and Cognitive Psychotherapy*, 30: 37–56.

Gull, W. (1874) 'Anorexia nervosa (apepsia hysterica, anorexia hysterica)', *Transactions of the Clinical Society of London*, 7: 22–28.

Habermas, T. (2005) 'On the uses of history in psychiatry: diagnostic implications for anorexia nervosa', *International Journal of Eating Disorder*, 38: 167–182.

Hackmann, A., Ehlers, A., Speckens, A. and Clark, D. (2004) 'Characteristics and content of intrusive memories in PTSD and their changes with treatment', *Journal of Traumatic Stress*, 17: 231–240.

Haizmann, C. (1981 [1678]) 'The diary of Christoph Haizmann', in D. Peterson (ed.), *A Mad People's History of Madness*. Pittsburgh: University of Pittsburgh Press. pp. 19–25.

Hall, J. and Marzillier, J. (2009) 'Alternative ways of working', *The Psychologist*, 22 (5): 406–408.

Hammersley, D. (2010) 'The interface between psychopharmacology and psychotherapeutic approaches', in R. Woolfe, S. Strawbridge, B. Douglas and W. Dryden (eds), *The Sage Handbook of Counselling Psychology*, 3rd edition. London: Sage. pp. 630–652.

Hansen, L., Kingdon, D. and Turkington, D. (2006) 'The ABCs of cognitive-behavioral therapy for schizophrenia', *Psychiatric Times*, 23, available at www.psychiatrictimes. com/schizophrenia/content/article/10168/51321 (last accessed 17 May 2013).

Harris, K., Collinson, C. and Roshan, das Nair (2012) 'Service users' experiences of an early intervention in psychosis service', *Psychology and Psychotherapy: Theory, Research and Practice*, 85 (4): 456–469.

Harvey, R., Black, D. and Blum, N. (2010) 'Systems training for emotional predictability and problem solving (STEPPS) in the United Kingdom: a preliminary report', *Journal of Contemporary Psychotherapy*, 40: 225–232.

Haslam, N. (2000) 'Psychiatric categories as natural kinds: essentialist thinking about mental disorders', *Social Research*, 67 (4): 1031–1058.

Hatchett, G. (2010) 'Differential diagnosis of bipolar personality disorder from bipolar disorder', *Journal of Mental Health Counselling*, 32 (3): 189–205.

Havens, L. and Nassir Ghaemi, S. (2005) 'Existential despair and bipolar disorder: the therapeutic alliance as a mood stabilizer', *American Journal of Psychotherapy*, 59 (2): 137–147.

Hayes, S., Wilson, K., Gifford, E., Follette, V. and Strosahl, K. (1996) 'Experiential avoidance and behavioral disorders: a functional dimensional approach to diagnosis and treatment', *Journal of Consulting and Clinical Psychology*, 64 (6): 1152–1168.

Hayward, P. and Bright, J.(1997) 'Stigma and mental illness: a review and critique', *Journal of Mental Health*, 6: 345–354.

Hazler, R. and Barwick, N. (2001) *The Therapeutic Environment*. Philadelphia: Open University Press.

Healy, D. (2004) *Let Them Eat Prozac: The Unhealthy Relationship between the Pharmaceutical Industry and Depression*. New York: New York University Press.

Healy, D. (2008) *Mania: A Short History of Bipolar Disorder*. Baltimore: Johns Hopkins University Press.

Helman, C. (2006) *Suburban Shaman: Tales from Medicine's Frontline*. London: Hammersmith.

Helverskov, J., Clausen, L., Mors, O., Frydenberg, M., Thomsen, P. and Rokkedal, K. (2010) 'Trans-diagnostic outcome of eating disorders: a 30 month follow-up of 629 patients', *European Eating Disorders Review*, 18 (6): 453–463.

Hoch, P. and Polatin, P. (1986 [1949]) 'Pseudoneurotic forms of schizophrenia', in M. Stone (ed.), *Essential Papers on Borderline Disorders: One Hundred Years at the Border*. New York: New York University Press. pp. 119–147.

Hofer, M. (2006) 'Psychobiological roots of early attachment', *Current Directions in Psychological Science*, 15 (2): 84–88.

Hoffman, D., Dukes, E. and Wittchen, H. (2008) 'Human and economic burden of generalized anxiety disorder', *Depression and Anxiety*, 25: 72–90.

Hopper, K., Harrison, G., Janca, A. and Sartorius, N. (2007) *Recovery from Schizophrenia: An International Inquiry.* New York: Oxford University Press.

Horowitz, M. (1998) *Cognitive Psychodynamics: From Conflict to Character.* New York: Wiley.

Horvath, A. and Symonds, B. (1991) 'The relationship between the working alliance and outcome in psychotherapy: a meta-analysis', *Journal of Counselling Psychology*, 38 (2): 139–149.

Horwitz, A. and Wakefield, J. (2007) *The Loss of Sadness: How Psychiatry Transformed Normal Sorrow into Depressive Disorder.* Oxford: Oxford University Press.

House, J., Landis, K. and Umberson, D. (1988) 'Social relationships and health', *Science*, 241: 540–545.

Hunot, V., Churchill, R., Teixeira, V. and Silva de Lima, M. (2010) *Psychological Therapies for Generalised Anxiety Disorder (A Review)*, The Cochrane Library, 4, available at http://onlinelibrary.wiley.com/doi/10.1002/14651858.CD001848.pub4/pdf (last accessed 17 May 2013).

IAPT Programme (2011) *Counselling for Depression (CfD)*, available at www.iapt.nhs.uk/workforce/high-intensity/counselling-for-depression/ (last accessed 2 May 2013).

Inder, M., Crowe, M., Moor, S., Luty, S., Carter, J. and Joyce, P. (2008) '"I actually don't know who I am": the impact of bipolar disorder on the development of self', *Psychiatry*, 71 (2): 123–133.

Iverson, K., Lester, K. and Resick, P. (2011) 'Psychosocial treatments', in D. Benedeck and G. Wynn (eds), *Clinical Manual for Management of PTSD*. Washington, DC: American Psychiatric Publishing. pp. 157–203.

Janoff-Bulman, R. (1985) 'The aftermath of victimization: rebuilding shattered assumptions', in C. Figley (ed.), *Trauma and its Wake: The Study and Treatment of Post-traumatic Stress Disorder*. New York: Brunner/Mazel. pp. 15–35.

Johns, L. and Van Os, J. (2001) 'The continuity of psychotic experiences in the general community', *Clinical Psychology Review*, 21: 1125–1141.

Johnson, S. and Miller, I. (1997) 'Negative life events and time to recovery from episodes of bipolar disorder', *Journal of Abnormal Psychology*, 106 (3): 449–457.

Johnstone, L. and Dallos, R. (2006) 'Introduction to formulation', in L. Johnstone and R. Dallos (eds), *Formulation in Psychology and Psychotherapy: Making Sense of People's Problems*. London: Routledge. pp. 1–15.

Jones, S. (2004) 'A review of psychotherapeutic interventions for bipolar disorder', *Journal of Affective Disorders*, 80: 101–114.

Jones, S., Lobban, F. and Cooke, A. (2010) *Understanding Bipolar Disorder: Why Some People Experience Extreme Mood States And What Can Help*. London: Division of Clinical Psychology British Psychological Society.

Judd, L., Akiskal, H., Schettler, P., Enicott, J., Maser, J., Solomon, D. et al. (2002) 'The long-term natural history of the weekly symptomatic status of bipolar I disorder', *Archives of General Psychiatry*, 59: 530–537.

Kabat-Zinn, J., Segal, Z., Williams, M., and Teasdale, J. (2002) *Mindfulness-based Cognitive Therapy for Depression: A New Approach to Preventing Relapse*. London: Guildford.

Kasanin, J. (1933) 'The acute schizoaffective psychoses', *American Journal of Psychiatry*, 13: 97–126.

Kelly, G. (1955) *The Psychology of Personal Constructs*. New York: Norton.

Kennerley, H. (1996) 'Cognitive therapy of dissociative symptoms associated with trauma', *British Journal of Clinical Psychology*, 35: 325–340.

Kernberg, O. (1986 [1967]) 'Borderline personality organisation', in M. Stone (ed.), *Essential Papers on Borderline Disorders: One Hundred Years at the Border*. New York: New York University Press. pp. 279–319.

Kilcommons, A. and Morrison, A. (2005) 'Relationships between trauma and psychosis: an exploration of cognitive and dissociative factors', *Acta Psychiatrica Scandinavica*, 112 (5): 351–359.

Kilpatrick, D., Veronen, L. and Best, C. (1985) 'Factors predicting psychological distress among rape victims', in C. Figley (ed.), *Trauma and its Wake*. New York: Brunner/Mazel. pp. 113–141.

Kilpatrick, D., Veronen, L. and Resick, P. (1982) 'Psychological sequelae to rape: assessment and treatment strategies', in D. Doleys, R. Meredith and A. Ciminero (eds), *Behavioural Medicine: Assessment and Treatment Strategies*. New York: Plenum. pp. 473–497.

Kirsch, I. (2009) *The Emperor's New Drugs: Exploding the Antidepressant Myth*. London: Bodley Head.

Kirschenbaum, H. and Henderson V. (1990) *The Carl Rogers Reader*. London: Robinson.

Kraepelin, E. (2011 [1904]) *Lectures on Clinical Psychiatry*. Milton Keynes: Lightening Source UK.

Kramer, U. (2012) 'Defence and coping in bipolar affective disorder: stability and change of adaptional processes', *British Journal of Clinical Psychology*, 49: 291–306.

Krans, J., Näring, G., Becker, E. and Holmes, E. (2009) 'Intrusive trauma memory: a review and functional analysis', *Applied Cognitive Psychology*, 23: 1076–1088.

Krawitz, R. and Jackson, W. (2008) *Borderline Personality Disorder: The Facts*. New York: Oxford University Press.

Kristeva, J. (1999) *Stranger to Our Selves*. Hemel Hempstead: Harvester Wheatsheaf.

Krohne, H. (1993) 'Vigilance and cognitive avoidance as concepts in coping research', in H. Krohne (ed.), *Attention and Avoidance: Strategies in Coping with Aversiveness*. Seattle: Hogrefe and Huber. pp. 19–50.

Lane, C. (2007) *Shyness: How Normal Behaviour Became a Sickness*. London: Yale University Press.

Lasègue, C. (1873) 'De l'anorexie hystérique [on hysterical anorexia]', *Archive Géneral de Médicine*, 21: 385–403.

Lask, B. and Frampton, I. (2011) *Eating Disorders and the Brain*. Oxford: Wiley-Blackwell.

Layard, R. (2006*) The Depression Report; A New Deal for Depression and Anxiety Disorders*. London: London School of Economics, Centre for Economic Performance Mental Health Policy Group.

Leader, D. (2011) *What is Madness?* London: Hamish Hamilton.

Leahy, R. (2010) 'Emotional schemas in treatment-resistant anxiety', in D. Sookman and R. Leahy (eds), *Treatment Resistant Anxiety Disorders*. New York: Routledge. pp. 135–160.

Lee, D. (2009) 'Compassion-focused cognitive therapy for shame-based trauma memories and flashbacks in post-traumatic stress disorder', in N. Grey (ed.), *A Casebook of Cognitive Therapy for Traumatic Stress Reactions*. London: Routledge. pp. 230–246.

Legenbauer, T., Schütt-Strömel, S., Hiller, W. and Vocks, S. (2011) 'Predictors of improved eating behaviour following body image therapy: a pilot study', *European Eating Disorders Review*, 19 (2): 129–137.

Lexis, M., Jansen, N., Huibers, M., van Amelsvoort, L., Berkouwer, A., Tjin, A., Ton, G., van den Brandt, P. and Kant, I. (2011) 'Prevention of long-term sickness absence and major depression in high-risk employees: a randomised controlled trial', *Occupational Environmental Medicine*, 68 (6): 400–407.

Licinio, J. (2005) 'The experience of bipolar disorder: a personal perspective on the impact of mood disorder symptoms', *Molecular Psychiatry*, 10: 827–830.

Linehan, M. (1993a) *Cognitive-Behavioural Treatment for Borderline Personality Disorder: The Dialectics of Effective Treatment*. New York: Guildford.

Linehan, M. (1993b) *The Skills Training Manual for Treating Borderline Personality Disorder*. New York: Guildford.

Linehan, M., Armstrong, H., Suarez, A., Allmon, D. and Heard, H. (1991) 'Cognitive behavioural treatment of chronically parasuicidal borderline patients', *Archives of General Psychiatry*, 48: 1060–1064.

Little, J. and Richardson, K. (2010) 'The clinician's dilemma: borderline personality disorder or bipolar spectrum disorder?', *Australian Psychiatry*, 18 (4): 303–308.

Livesley, W. (2001) *Handbook of Personality Disorders*. New York: Guilford.

Lock, J., Reisel, B. and Steiner, H. (2001) 'Associated health risks of adolescents with disordered eating: how different are they from their peers? Results from a high school survey', *Child Psychiatry and Human Development*, 31 (3): 249–265.

Lomas, P. (1999) *Doing Good? Psychotherapy Out of its Depth*. Oxford: Oxford University Press.

Lunbeck, E. (2006) 'Borderline histories: psychoanalysis inside out', *Science in Context*, 19 (1): 151–173.

Macfarlane, R. (2003) *Mountains of the Mind*. London: Granta.

Maddon, S. (2004) ''Anorexia nervosa' – still relevant in the twenty-first century: a review of William Gull's Anorexia Nervosa', *Clinical Child Psychology and Psychiatry*, 9 (1): 149–154.

Maier, W., Gansicke, M., Feyberger, H., Linz, M., Heun, R. and Lecrubler, Y. (2000) 'Generalised anxiety disorder (ICD-10) in primary care from a cross-cultural perspective: a valid diagnostic entity', *Acta Psychiatria Scandinavia*, 101 (1): 29–36.

Main, T. (1957) 'The ailment', *British Journal of Medical Psychology*, 30: 129–145.

Markham, D. (2003) 'Attitudes towards patients with a diagnosis of "borderline personality disorder"': social rejection and dangerousness', *Journal of Mental Health*, 12 (6): 595–612.

Mathews, A. and MacLeod, C. (2005) 'Cognitive vulnerability to emotional disorders', *Annual Review of Clinical Psychology*, 1: 167–195.

Matus, J. (2010) 'Psychological trauma Victorian style: from perpetrators and victims', *The Lancet*, 376 (9739): 410–411.

May, R. (1996) *The Meaning of Anxiety*, revised edition. London: Norton.

McDonald, M., Pietsch, T. and Wilson, J. (2010) 'Ontological insecurity: a guiding framework for borderline personality disorder', *Journal of Phenomenological Psychology*, 41 (1): 85–105.

McGuffin, P. and Katz, R. (1989) 'The genetics of depression and manic-depressive disorder', *British Journal of Psychiatry*, 155: 294–304.

McKay, M., Wood, J. and Brantley, J. (2007) *The Dialectical Behavior Therapy Skills Workbook: Practical DBT Exercises for Learning Mindfulness, Interpersonal Effectiveness, Emotion Regulation & Distress Tolerance*. Oakland, CA: New Harbinger.

McLeod, J. (2003) 'The humanistic paradigm', in R. Woolfe, W. Dryden and S. Strawbridge (eds), *The Sage Handbook of Counselling Psychology*, 2nd edition. London: Sage.

McPherson, S., Evans, C. and Richardson, P. (2009) 'The NICE depression guidelines and the recovery model: is there an evidence-base for IAPT?', *Journal of Mental Health*, 18 (5): 405–414.

Meares, R., Gerull, F., Stevenson, J. and Korner, A. (2011) 'Is self disturbance the core of borderline personality disorder? An outcome study of borderline personality factors', *Australian & New Zealand Journal of Psychiatry*, 45 (3): 214–222.

Meichenbaum, D. (1974) 'Self-instructional methods', in F. Kanfer and A. Goldstein (eds), *Helping People Change*. New York: Pergamon.

Mennin, D., Holaway, R., Fresco, D., Moore, M. and Heimberg, R. (2007) 'Delineating components of emotion and its dysregulation in anxiety and mood psychopathology', *Behavior Therapy*, 38: 284–302.

Mennin, D., Turk, C., Heimberg, R. and Carmin, C. (2004) 'Focusing on the regulation of emotion: a new direction for conceptualizing generalized anxiety disorder', in M. Reinecke and D. Clark (eds), *Cognitive Therapy Over the Lifespan: Evidence and Practice*. New York: Cambridge University Press. pp. 60–89.

Mercier, C. (2011 [1894]) *Lunatic Asylums: Their Organization and Management*. Milton Keynes: Lightning Source UK Ltd.

Messari, S. and Hallam, R. (2003) 'CBT for psychosis: a qualitative analysis of clients' experiences', *British Journal of Clinical Psychology*, 42 (2): 171–188.

Milton, M. (2012) *Diagnosis and Beyond: Counselling Psychology Contributions to Understanding Human Distress*. Ross-on-Wye: PCCS.

Mulder, R. (2008) 'An epidemic of depression or the medicalization of distress?', *Perspectives in Biology and Medicine*, 51 (2): 238–250.

National Institute for Health and Care Excellence (2004) *Guideline for Eating Disorders*, CG009, available at www.nice.org.uk/cg009niceguideline (last accessed 15 May 2013).

National Institute for Health and Care Excellence (2005) *Post-Traumatic Stress Disorder: The Management of PTSD in Adults and Children in Primary and Secondary Care*. London: Gaskell and the British Psychological Society.

National Institute for Health and Care Excellence (2006) *Bipolar Disorder: The Management of Bipolar Disorder in Adults, Children and Adolescents, in Primary and Secondary Care*, available at http://publications.nice.org.uk/bipolar-disorder-cg38/guidance#the-treatment-and-management-of-bipolar-disorder (last accessed 4 July 2012).

National Institute for Health and Care Excellence (2009a) *Borderline Personality Disorder: Treatment and Management*, CG78, available at www.nice.org.uk/CG78 (last accessed 17 May 2013).

National Institute for Health and Care Excellence (2009b) *Schizophrenia: Core Interventions in the Treatment and Management of Schizophrenia in Adults in Primary and Secondary Care*, CG82, available at www.nice.org.uk/CG82 (last accessed 17 May 2013).

National Institute for Health and Care Excellence (2009c) *The Treatment and Management of Depression in Adults*, CG90, available at www.nice.org.uk/CG90 (last accessed 17 May 2013).

National Institute for Health and Care Excellence (2011a) *Anxiety: Management of Anxiety (panic disorder with or without agoraphobia, and generalised anxiety disorder) in Adults in Primary and Community Care*, CG113, available from http://guidance.nice.org.uk/CG113 (last accessed 17 May 2013).

National Institute for Health and Care Excellence (2011b) *Psychosis with Co-existing Substance Misuse*, available at www.nice.org.uk/nicemedia/live/13414/53729/53729.pdf (last accessed 10 November 2012).

National Institute for Mental Health in England (2003) *Personality Disorder: No Longer a Diagnosis of Exclusion: Policy Implementation Guidance for the Development of Services for People with Personality Disorder*, Gateway Reference 1055. London: NIMH(E).

Neale, J. (1988) 'Defensive function of manic episodes', in T. Oltmanns and B. Maher (eds), *Delusional Beliefs*. New York: Wiley.

Nietzsche, F. (1990) *Beyond Good and Evil*. London: Penguin.

Nixon, G., Hagen, B. and Peters, T. (2010) 'Recovery from psychosis: a phenomenological inquiry', *International Journal of Mental Health Addiction*, 8: 620–635.

North, T., McCullagh, P. and Tran, Z. (1990) 'The effect of exercise on depression', *Exercise and Sport Sciences Reviews*, 8 (1): 379–416.

Oltmanns, T. and Maher, B. (1988) *Delusional Beliefs*. New York: Wiley.

Ozer, E., Best, S., Lipsey, T. and Weiss, D. (2003) 'Predictors of post-traumatic stress disorder and symptoms in adults: a meta-analysis', *Psychology Bulletin*, 129 (1): 52–73.

Paris, J. (2009) 'The bipolar spectrum: a critical perspective', *Harvard Review of Psychiatry*, 17 (3): 2006–2013.

Pearce, J. (2004) 'Richard Morton: origins of anorexia nervosa', *European Neurology*, 52: 191–192.

Pepys, S. (2003) *The Diaries of Samuel Pepys: A Selection*. London: Penguin.

Perceval, J. (1981 [1838]) 'A narrative of the treatment experienced by a gentleman during a state of mental derangement', in D. Peterson (ed.), *A Mad People's History of Madness*. Pittsburgh: University of Pittsburgh Press. pp. 92–107.

Perkins, R., Farmer, P. and Litchfield, P. (2009) *Realising Ambitions: Better Employment Support for People with a Mental Health Condition: A Review to Government*. London: Department for Work and Pensions.

Perry, J. (1993) 'Defences and their effects', in N. Miller , L. Luborsky, J. Barber and J. Docherty (eds), *Psychodynamic Treatment Research*. New York: Basic Books.

Perry, J. (2005) *The Far Side of Madness*. Englewood Cliffs, NJ: Prentice-Hall.

Peterson, D. (1981) *A Mad Peoples History of Madness*. Pittsburgh: University of Pittsburgh Press.

Pilgrim, D. (2007) 'The survival of psychiatric diagnosis', *Social Science and Medicine*, 65 (3): 536–547.

Pilgrim, D. and Bentall, R. (1999) 'The medicalisation of misery: a critical realist analysis of the concept of depression', *Journal of Mental Health* , 8 (3): 261–274.

Polanyi, M. (1967) *The Tacit Dimension*. Chicago: University of Chicago Press.

Porter, R. (2002) *Madness: A Brief History*. Oxford: Oxford University.

Post, R. (1992) 'Transduction of psychosocial stress into the neurobiology of recurrent affective disorder', *American Journal of Psychiatry*, 149: 999–1010.

Prochaska, J. and Velicer, W. (1997) 'The transtheoretical model of health behaviour change', *American Journal of Health Promotion*, 12 (1): 38–48.

Ram, R., Bromet, E., Eaton, W., Pato, C. and Schwartz, J. (1992) 'The natural course of schizophrenia: a review of first admission studies', *Schizophrenia Bulletin*, 18 (2): 185–207.

Ramana, R. and Bebbington, P. (1995) 'Social influences on bipolar affective disorders', *Social Psychiatry and Psychiatric Epidemiology*, 30 (4): 152–160.

Rapaport, D., Gill, M. and Shafer, R. (1946) *The Thematic Apperception Test in Diagnostic Psychological Testing 2*. Chicago, IL: Year Book Publishers.

Raque-Bogdan, T., Ericson, S., Jackson, J., Martin, H. and Bryan, N. (2011) 'Attachment and mental and physical health: self-compassion and mattering as mediators', *Journal of Counselling Psychology*, 58 (2): 272–278.

Reeves, A. (2007) 'Assessing suicide risk in counselling: training counsellors to integrate suicide risk assessment into the therapeutic discourse', *Therapy Today*, 18: 6.

Regal, S. (2010) 'Psychological debriefing – does it work?', *Counselling and Psychotherapy Journal*, 10 (2): 14–18.

Regier, D., Farmer, M., Rae, D., Locke, B., Keith, S., Judd, L. and Goodwin, F. (1990) 'Comorbidity of mental disorders with alcohol and other drug abuse: results from the epidemiologic catchment area (ECA) study', *Journal of the American Medical Association*, 264: 2511–2518.

Reich, T., Clayton, P. and Winokur, G. (1969) 'Family history studies, V: the genetics of mania', *The American Journal of Psychiatry*, 125 (10): 1358–1369.

Renwick, L., Jackson, D., Turner, N., Sutton, M., Foley, S., McWilliams, S., Kinsella, A. and O'Callaghan, E. (2009) 'Are symptoms associated with increased levels of perceived stress in first-episode psychosis?', *International Journal of Mental Health Nursing*, 18 (3): 186–194.

Richards, G. (2002) 'The psychology of psychology: a historically grounded sketch', *Theory and Psychology*, 12 (1): 7–36.

Roberts, G. (2011) 'Recovery in a nutshell: what does it mean and what are the implications for future practice and services?', *Recovery Devon*. Exeter: Devon Partnership Trust.

Roberts, G., Davenport, S., Holloway, F. and Tattan, T. (2006) *Enabling Recovery: The Principles and Practice of Rehabilitation Psychiatry*. Gaskell: Towbridge.

Robinson, P. (2009) *Severe and Enduring Eating Disorder (SEED): Management of Complex Presentations of Anorexia and Bulimia Nervosa*. Oxford: Wiley.

Roe, D., Chopra, M., Wagner, B., Katz, G. and Rudnick, A. (2004) 'The emerging self in conceptualising and treating mental illness', *Journal of Psychosocial Nursing and Mental Health Services*, 42: 32–40.

Roemer, L. and Orsillo, S. (2006) 'Expanding our conceptualization of and treatment for Generalized Anxiety Disorder: integrating mindfulness/acceptance-based approaches with existing cognitive-behavioral models', *Clinical Psychology: Science and Practice*, 9 (1): 54–68.

Roemer, L., Orsillo S. and Barlow, D. (2002) 'Generalized anxiety disorder', in D. Barlow (ed.), *Anxiety and its Disorders: The Nature and Treatment of Anxiety and Panic*. New York: Guilford. pp. 277–515.

Rogers, C. (1951) *Client-Centred Therapy*. Boston, MA: Houghton Mifflin.

Rogers, C. (1996) *A Way of Being*. New York: Houghton Mifflin.

Rogers, J. and Agius, M. (2012) 'Bipolar and unipolar depression', *Psychiatria Danubina*, 24 (1): 100–105.

Rosse, I. (1986 [1890]) 'Clinical evidences of borderland insanity', in M. Stone (ed.), *Essential Papers on Borderline Disorders: One Hundred Years at the Border*. New York: New York University Press. pp. 32–44.

Rosser, W., Reicher-Rossler, A., Angst, J., Murray, R., Gamma, A., Eich, D., Van Os. J. and Gross, V. (2007) 'Psychotic experiences in the general population: a twenty-year prospective community study', *Schizophrenia Research*, 92 (1): 1–14.

Rothschild, B. (2000) *The Body Remembers: The Psychophysiology of Trauma and Trauma Treatment*. New York: Norton.

Royal College of Psychiatrists and Royal College of Physicians (2010) *MARSIPAN: Management of Really Sick Patients with Anorexia Nervosa*. Report from the MARSIPAN group College, CR162. London: Royal College Royal College of Psychiatrists and Royal College of Physicians.

Royal College of Psychiatry (2012) *Bipolar Disorder*, available at www.rcpsych.ac.uk/mentalhealthinfo/problems/bipolardisorder/bipolardisorder.aspx (last accessed 4 June 2012).

Ruddy, R. and Milnes, D. (2005) 'Art therapy for schizophrenia or schizophrenia-like illnesses', *Cochrane Database of Systematic Reviews*, 4. Art. No.: CD003728. DOI: 10.1002/14651858.CD003728.pub2

Russell, G. (1979) 'Bulimia nervosa: an ominous variant of anorexia nervosa', *Psychological Medicine*, 9: 429–448.

Salokangas, R. and McGlashan, T. (2008) 'Early detection and intervention of psychosis: a review', *Nordic Journal of Psychiatry*, 62 (2): 92–105.

Sampson, M. (2006) 'The challenges community mental health teams face in their work with patients with personality disorder', in M. Sampson, R. McCubbin and P. Tyrer, *Personality Disorder and Community Mental Health Teams: A Practitioner's Guide*. Chichester: John Wiley.

Sandel, M. (2012) *What Money Can't Buy*. London: Allen Lane.

Scheel, K. (2000) 'The empirical cases of dialectical behaviour therapy: summary, critique, and implications', *Clinical Psychology: Science and Practice*, 7 (1): 68–86.

Schimmel, P. (1998) 'Medicine and the manic defence', *Australian and New Zealand Journal of Psychiatry*, 32: 329–397.

Schioldann, J. (2011) 'On periodical depressions and their pathogenesis by Carl Lange (1886)', *History of Psychiatry*, 22: 108–115.

Schmideberg, M. (1993 [1959]) 'Psychodiagnosis of Personality Structure 11: Borderline Personality Organization', *Journal of Personality Assessment*, 61 (2): 329–341.

Schreber, D. (2002 [1903]) *Memoirs of My Nervous Illness*. New York: New York Review of Books.

Schutters, S., van Megen, H., van Veen, J., Schruers, K. and Westenberg, H. (2011) 'Paroxetine augmentation in patients with generalised social anxiety disorder, non-responsive to mirtazapine or placebo', *Human Psychopharmacology: Clinical and Experimental*, 26 (1): 72–76.

Scull, A. (2009) *Hysteria: The Biography*. Oxford: Oxford University Press.

Segal, Z., Williams, J. and Teasdale, J. (2002) *Mindfulness-Based Cognitive Therapy for Depression: A New Approach to Preventing Relapse*. New York: Guilford.

Seligman, M. (1975) *Helplessness: On Depression Development and Death*. San Francisco, CA: Freeman.

Shapiro, F. (1995) *Eye Movement Desensitization and Reprocessing: Basic Principles, Protocols and Procedures*. New York: Guilford.

Shatan, C. (1972) 'Post-Vietnam syndrome', *New York Times*, 6 May, p. 35.

Shaw, I. and Taplin, S. (2007) 'Happiness and mental health policy', *Journal of Mental Health*, 16: 359–373.

Shephard, B. (2002) *A War of Nerves: Soldiers and Psychiatrists 1914–1994*. London: Pimlico.

Shifting Attitudes to Mental Illness (SHiFT), www.shift.org.uk/ (last accessed 7 August 2012).

Shorter, E. (1997) *A History of Psychiatry: From the Era of the Asylum to the Age of Prozac*. New York: Wiley.

Shorter, E. (2005) *A Historical Dictionary of Psychiatry*. New York: Oxford University Press.

Sibrava, N. and Borkovec, T. (2006) 'The cognitive avoidance theory of worry', in G. Davey and A. Wells (eds), *Worry and its Psychological Disorders: Theory, Assessment and Treatment*. Chichester: Wiley. pp. 239–258.

Skarderud, F. (2009) 'Bruch revisited and revised', *European Eating Disorders Review*, 17: 83–88.

Slade, M. (2009) *Personal Recovery and Mental Illness: A Guide for Mental Health Professionals*. Cambridge: Cambridge University Press.

Slade, P. (1982) 'Towards a functional analysis of anorexia nervosa and bulimia nervosa', *British Journal of Clinical Psychology*, 21: 167–179.

Slater, L. (1998) *Prozac Diary*. London: Penguin.

Smail, D. (1997) *Illusion and Reality: The Meaning of Anxiety*. London: Constable.

Smith, G., Gregory, K. and Higgs, A. (2007) *An Integrated Approach to Family Work for Psychosis*. London: Kingsley.

Soler, J. (2008) 'Stages of change in dialectical behaviour therapy for borderline personality disorder', *British Journal of Clinical Psychology*, 47 (4): 417–426.

Steinglass, J., Walsh, B. and Yaakov, S. (2006) 'Set shifting deficit in anorexia nervosa', *Journal of the International Neuropsychological Society*, 12: 431–435.

Stephen, S., Elliott, R. and Macleod, R. (2011) 'Person-centred therapy with a client experiencing social anxiety difficulties: a hermeneutic single case efficacy design', *Counselling & Psychotherapy Research*, 11 (1): 55–66.

Stern, A. (1938), 'Psychoanalytic psychotherapy in the borderline neuroses', *Psychoanalytic Quarterly*, 14: 190–198.

Stern, D. (2004) *The Present Moment in Psychotherapy and Everyday Life*. New York: Norton.

Stone, M. (1978) 'Toward early detection of manic-depressive illness in psychoanalytic patients', *American Journal of Psychotherapy*, 32 (3): 427–439.

Stone, M. (1985) 'Shellshock and the psychologists', in W. Bynum, R. Porter and M. Shepherd (eds), *The Anatomy of Madness*, 2. London: Routledge. pp. 242–271.

Strawbridge, S. (2002) 'Macdonaldization or fast-food therapy?', *Counselling Psychology Review*, 17 (4): 20–24.

Sullivan, E. (2010) *Secret Contagions: Sadness and the Self in Early Modern England*. Unpublished thesis, University College London.

Szasz, T. (1960) 'The myth of mental illness', *American Psychologist*, 15: 113–118.

Talbot, N., Houghtalen, R., Cyrulik, S., Betz, A., Barkun, M., Duberstein, P. and Wynne, L. (1998) 'Women's safety in recovery: group therapy for patients with a history of childhood sexual abuse', *Psychiatric Services*, 49: 213–217.

Tan, J., Stewart, A., Fitzpatrick, R. and Hope, T. (2010) 'Attitudes of patients with anorexia nervosa to compulsory treatment and coercion', *International Journal of Law and Psychiatry*, 33: 13–19.

Tarrier, N., Pilgrim, H., Sommerfield, C., Faragher, B., Reynolds, M., Graham, E. and Barrowclough, C. (1999) 'A randomised trial of cognitive therapy and imaginal exposure in the treatment of chronic posttraumatic stress disorder', *Journal of Consultant Clinical Psychology*, 67: 13–18.

Tarrier, N., Khan, S., Cater, J. and Picken, A. (2007) 'The subjective consequences of suffering a first episode psychosis: trauma and suicide behaviour', *Social Psychiatry and Psychiatric Epidemiology*, 42 (1): 29–35.

Tchanturia, K., Davies, H. and Campbell, I. (2007) 'Cognitive remediation therapy for patients with anorexia nervosa: preliminary findings', *Annual of General Psychiatry*, 6 (14).

Tedeschi, R. and Calhoun, L. (1995) *Trauma and Transformation: Growing in the Aftermath of Suffering*. Thousand Oaks, CA: Sage.

Thayer J., Friedman, B. and Borkovec, T. (1996) 'Autonomic characteristics of generalised anxiety disorder and worry', *Biological Psychiatry*, 39: 255–266.

Thomas, J., Vartanian, L. and Brownell, K. (2009) 'The relationship between eating disorders not otherwise specified (EDNOS) and officially recognising eating disorders: meta-analysis and implications for DSM', *Psychological Bulletin*, 135 (3): 407–433.

Thomas, P. (2007) *The Dialectics of Schizophrenia*. London: Free Association.

Tillich, P. (1961) 'Existentialism and psychotherapy', *Review of Existential Psychology and Psychiatry*, 1: 8–16.

Tone, A. (2005) 'Listening to the past: history, psychiatry and anxiety', *Canadian Journal of Psychiatry*, 50 (7): 373–380.

Torrey, E. (2006) *Surviving Schizophrenia: A Manual for Families, Patients, and Providers*. New York: HarperCollins.

Tuke, S. (2010 [1813]) *Description of the Retreat*. Massachusetts: Kessinger.

Turkington, D. and McKenna, P. (2003) 'Is cognitive behavioural therapy a worthwhile treatment for psychosis?', *The British Journal of Psychiatry*, 182: 477–479.

Tyrer, P. (2006) *Personality Disorder and Community Mental Health Teams: A Practitioner's Guide*. Chichester: Wiley.

Vandereycken, W. and van Deth, R. (1994) *From Fasting Saints to Anorexic Girls: The History of Self Starvation*. London: Athlone.

Vassilev, I. and Pilgrim, D. (2007) 'Risk, trust and the myth of mental health services', *Journal of Mental Health*, 16 (3): 347–357.

Vetere, A. (2012) 'Foreword', in M. Milton (ed.), *Diagnosis and Beyond: Counselling Psychology Contributions to Understanding Human Distress*. Ross-on-Wye: PCCS. pp. vii–ix.

Vincent, F. (2004) 'A qualitative analysis of asylum-seekers' experiences of trauma-focused psychological therapy for post-traumatic stress disorder', in V. Shearing, D. Lee and S. Clohessy (2011), 'How do clients experience reliving as part of trauma-focused cognitive behavioural therapy for posttraumatic stress disorder?', *Psychology and Psychotherapy: Theory, Research and Practice*, 84: 458–472.

Vygotsky, L.S. (1987) 'Thinking and speech', in R. Rieber and A. Carton (eds), *L.S. Vygotsky: Collected Works*. New York: Plenum.

Von Fuchtersleben, E. and Rvan-Lloyd, H. (2007 [1846]) *The Principles of Medical Psychology: Being the Outline of a Course of Lectures*. Massachusetts: Kessinger.

Von Peter, S. (2009) 'The concept of mental trauma and its transcultural application', *Anthropology and Medicine*, 16 (1): 13–25.

Waddell, M. (2002) *Inside Lives: Psychoanalysis and the Growth of the Personality*. London: Karnac.

War Office (2004 [1922]) *Report of the War Office Committee of Enquiry into 'Shell Shock'*, Imperial War Museum facsimile reproduction . Crawley: Xpress.

Weber, M. (1974) *The Protestant Ethic and the Spirit of Capitalism*. London: Unwin.

Wehowsky, A. (2000) 'Diagnosis as care – diagnosis as politics', *International Journal of Psychotherapy*, 5 (3): 241–255.

Wells, A. (1995) 'Meta-cognition and worry: a cognitive model of generalized anxiety disorder', *Behavioural and Cognitive Psychotherapy*, 23: 301–320.

Wild, J. (2009) 'Cognitive therapy for PTSD and permanent injury', in N. Grey (ed.) *A Casebook of Cognitive Therapy for Traumatic Stress Reactions*. London: Routledge. pp. 131–146.

Wilkinson, R. and Pickett, K. (2009) *The Spirit Level: Why More Equal Societies Almost Always Do Better*. London: Allen Lane.

Williams, G. (2003) *Internal Landscapes and Foreign Bodies*. London: Karnac.

Wilson, J., Friedman, M. and Lindy, J. (2001) *Treating Psychological Trauma and PTSD*. London: Guilford.

Winston, A. (2000) 'Recent developments in borderline personality disorder', *Advances in Psychiatric Treatment*, 6: 211–218.

World Health Organization (1992) *International Statistical Classification of Diseases and Related Health Problems* (10th revision). Geneva: World Health Organization.

World Health Organization (2005) *The ICD-10 Classification of Mental and Behavioural Disorders*. Geneva: World Health Organization.

Yalom, I. (1998) *The Yalom Reader*. New York: Basic Books.

Yoder, J. (1981) 'The existential mode and client anxiety', *Personnel & Guidance Journal*, 59 (5): 279.

Young, J. (1994) *Cognitive Therapy for Personality Disorders: A Schema-Focussed Approach*, revised edition. Sarasota, FL: Professional Resources Press.

Zanarini, M. (2009) 'Psychotherapy of borderline personality disorder', *Acta Psychiatrica Scandinavica*, 120 (5): 373–377.

Zanarini, M., Frankenburg, F., Hennen, J. and Silk, K. (2003) 'The longitudinal course of borderline psychopathology: 6-year prospective follow-up of the phenomenology of borderline personality disorder', *American Journal of Psychiatry*, 160: 274–283.

Zanarini, M., Frankenburg, F., Reich, D., Bradford, D. and Fitzmaurice, G. (2010) 'The 10-year course of psychosocial functioning among patients with borderline personality disorder and axis II comparison subjects', *Acta Psychiatrica Scandinavica*, 122 (2): 103–109.

Zayfert, C. and Black-Becker, C. (2007) *Cognitive-Behavioral Therapy for PTSD: A Case Formulation Approach*. New York: Guilford.

Zilboorg, G. (1941) 'Ambulatory schizophrenias', *Psychiatry*, 4: 149–155.

Zvolensky, M., John, P., Bernstein, A. and Leen-Feldner, E. (2007) 'A concurrent test of the anxiety sensitivity taxon: its relation to bodily vigilance and perceptions of control over anxiety-related events in a sample of young adults', *Journal of Cognitive Psychotherapy*, 21 (1): 72–90.

Index